THE DYNAMICS OF URBAN GOVERNMENT AND POLITICS

Jay S. Goodman

WHEATON COLLEGE

THE DYNAMICS OF URBAN GOVERNMENT AND POLITICS

SECOND EDITION

Macmillan Publishing Co., Inc.
NEW YORK

Collier Macmillan Publishers
LONDON

MACMILLAN PUBLISHING CO., INC.
866 Third Avenue, New York, New York 10022

COLLIER MACMILLAN CANADA, LTD.

Library of Congress Cataloging in Publication Data

Goodman, Jay S
   The dynamics of urban government and politics.

   Includes bibliographical references and index.
   1. Municipal government—United States. 2. Metropolitan government—United States. I. Title.
JS341.G58 1980   320   79-11431
ISBN 0-02-344830-X

Printing: 1 2 3 4 5 6 7 8   Year: 0 1 2 3 4 5 6

To Harold M. Goodman
*—with appreciation for introducing me
to the idea of cities*

PREFACE TO THE SECOND EDITION

This edition of *The Dynamics of Urban Government and Politics* benefits from the many helpful comments of professors and students who used the first edition. I am grateful for their suggestions and for their help in making the book a success.

Since the first edition some of the concerns of people with local life have changed. Everyone worries more about the cost of housing, the cost of living, and the cost of local government. The text continues its emphasis on the costs and benefits of local governments. Other concerns remain constant, with transportation, crime, schools. The patterns of local settlement, forms of government, and citizen participation continue in directions marked out in the first edition.

Faculty users of the second edition will find the book updated throughout. Students, I hope, will benefit from an extensive rewriting effort.

Student assistants Melanie Aska and Erika Rikoff aided greatly in the revision. Mrs. Nancy Shepardson typed the manuscript, which she has now worked on through numerous drafts and both editions. Clark Baxter works in the traditional mold of Macmillan editors—always constructively. I am responsible for any remaining mistakes of substance or form.

J. S. G.

PREFACE
TO THE FIRST
EDITION

The urban crisis has faded from the daily headlines, to be replaced by news of inflation and of a crisis of confidence in the morality of the federal government. With time we have realized that the urban crisis was part of a larger, complicated, ongoing political process. Years of substantial research have added to our understanding. We can grasp aspects of life in our great metropolitan areas much more clearly now than we could ten years ago, when many appeared to be going up in smoke. That may make this a good time for a new textbook about urban and suburban life. Without abandoning social concerns and the hope for better lives, we can analyze the world of local politics and life in an atmosphere of relative calm. I hope this book will add to our comprehension of the people, systems, forces, governments, policies, and histories that come together in our metropolitan civilization.

Every textbook draws heavily upon the work of other scholars in the field, and this one is no exception. I relied upon the work and ideas of those in political science, sociology, economics, and planning who are cited throughout the body of the text and the footnotes. In various earlier drafts, Michael P. Smith of Tulane University provided insight and probing suggestions, all of which were very helpful. My assistants at Wheaton College, Donna Garofano and Sharon Waterman, performed various research chores with enthusiasm. Mrs. Nancy Shepardson typed the manuscript through more drafts than either of us care to remember. When the project was still in its earliest stages,

Wheaton's Dean Walter E. Kenworthy offered very special support. Bertrand W. Lummus has been a tower of patience and good judgment at Macmillan. I am grateful to all of these people. I take, however, full responsibility for what follows, as is both customary and proper.

J. S. G.

CONTENTS

xi

113889

1
STUDYING URBAN LIFE AND URBAN POLITICS

THE SETTING

During the 1960s Americans talked about an "urban crisis." There were nightly television news features about that urban crisis and daily newspaper reports about it. What was it about? Its elements were racial conflicts in the core cities; the decay of the older central cities; and the conspicuous departure of middle-class white people to the suburbs.

The urban crisis faded from public consciousness during the 1970s, perhaps because there were no spectacular riots. Perhaps it was because of vastly accelerated federal programs, or because those within the cities most able to protest had moved away. In any case, the perspective of the 1980s is much different. There is no sense of crisis. We know now that long-term processes of technological, social, and economic change reflect how people live in local areas. We call these processes *urbanization*.

THE PLAN OF THE BOOK

This book stresses the position of local systems within national systems. We begin at the national center and work downward to the local level. The rest of this introductory chapter is an overview of urban governments and problems. Chapter 2 traces the path of urbanization into a metropolitan format. Chapter 3 discusses the relationships

1

of local communities with other units of government. Chapter 4 shows what powers local governments exercise in making public choices and producing public policies. Chapter 5 describes the forms of local government, how decisions are made, and what the consequences are.

Chapter 6 looks at some important theoretical considerations: who holds power in local communities and under what conditions? Chapter 7 continues the theoretical focus and reviews forms and models of metropolitan governance. In Chapter 8, the perspective is that of individuals and groups, rather than governments. People have attitudes and values that are relevant for local political life, and we will see what they are. Chapter 9 focuses on three important areas of local policy controversy: transportation, police, and schools. Chapter 10 surveys some different opinions about the future of urban and suburban America.

LOCAL COMMUNITIES IN THE AMERICAN POLITICAL CONTEXT

Local communities occupy a particular place in our political system. Understanding that place requires an awareness of certain special *limitations* on local governments. Because central cities and suburbs have governments, there is a tendency to assume that they are fundamentally the same kinds of entities as the state or federal governments. Local governments do have the same appearance. They can tax, relieving an individual of his money or property. They can arrest, try, and punish, relieving an individual of his personal freedom. The quality of individual lives can be improved or diminished by how local governments manage schools, parks, and neighborhoods. But the powers of all local governments are restricted. How these limitations operate is not widely understood.

There are four limitations: (1) local governments are the legal creations of the state governments; (2) local governments have been unable to persuade their citizens to stay within their boundaries; (3) the centralization of private economic power over the last 100 years has diminished local economic elites and made local governments vulnerable to external corporate decisions; and (4) the centralization of national government power in the federal government over the last 50 years has diminished the power of local political elites and made local governments dependent upon national political decisions. All of these limitations contribute to the vulnerability of local government to outside influences.

LOCAL GOVERNMENTS AS CREATURES OF THE STATES

In Chapter 3 you will see in a detailed way how local governments have come to have the special legal status of "creatures of the state." Localities have no independent sovereignty or protected existence as governments. They have what powers the state governments choose to give them and choose not to take away. The New York Assembly could abolish New York City as a governmental unit tomorrow if it chose to do so. The California legislature could rename Los Angeles "Spaceville."

These possibilities are unlikely, but the following are some realities that local governments must live with because of the legal superiority of state governments:

1. Major changes in city finances have to be approved through the political processes of state government.
2. State governments take for themselves the most desirable tax sources—those that are most automatic and flexible.
3. State governments set ceilings on local spending and borrowing.
4. State governments set conditions for the operation of city programs, especially where state monies are contributed.

The upshot of localities' inferior legal nature is that municipal governments are constantly enmeshed in state politics. Local elected and administrative officials are aware of their vulnerability. To protect their communities' interests, they pay close attention to state politics. They operate in part directly and in part through their communities' elected state representatives and state senators.

INABILITY OF LOCAL GOVERNMENTS TO MAKE THEIR CITIZENS STAY

A major problem for central cities and for older suburbs is that many citizens have moved on to places considered more desirable to live. And there is nothing the local governments can do directly to prevent such moves. Compare this vulnerability with the situation of the national government. Naturally, a national government wants businesses and citizens to stay voluntarily—but if they will not, there are still tools of coercion. A national government has means to keep its territory closed and its institutions and citizens in place.

A national government can command citizens to stay within its boundaries. It can use such devices as prohibition of emigration, internal passports, or even physical barriers. A national government can more easily prevent the exodus of economic enterprises. It can prohibit a departing company from doing further business within its borders, freeze assets, tax products, or penalize officers.

Local governments, in contrast, are relatively powerless to halt the departure of their citizens or businesses. In one five-year span, between 1970–1975, more than 200,000 middle-class whites moved out of Chicago. What could city hall do to prevent their leaving? Nothing. Similarly, what legal steps can New York City take when a large corporation decides to move its headquarters to Connecticut? None.

As a result, localities unfortunate enough to be undergoing a loss of popularity with their citizens or a decline in attractiveness to business are in a difficult predicament. If they could keep people and industries in place, perhaps there would be enough resources, human and financial, to bring about improvement. But those who leave do so *because* they do not want to bear additional burdens where they are, or because some other place has better schools or lower business taxes.[1]

VULNERABILITY OF LOCAL COMMUNITIES TO NATIONAL CORPORATE ECONOMIC DECISIONS

At one time, businesses were not only based in local communities, but the owners lived there.[2] In fact, in the America of 1860 to 1900, there was a considerable overlap between industrialists and holders of local political office. However, corporate power has increasingly throughout this century been consolidated at the national level. In 1941, for example, 1,000 of the largest manufacturing concerns controlled two thirds of all assets. Today two thirds of all assets are controlled by only 200 companies. We now live in an era in which capital moves to the least expensive production point on the globe and trade and natural resources are managed by international consortiums and blocs of nations. The United States has less economic autonomy than it did 25 years ago.

What do national and international corporate consolidation mean for local communities? Decisions of vital concern to communities are made by individuals far distant from the locality and for reasons having nothing to do with that locality's future.[3] What plants will be opened? What plants will be closed? Where will headquarters and marketing facilities be located? The corporate officers will decide on

[1] For an analysis of such considerations, see Mancur Olson, Jr., *The Logic of Collective Action* (New York: Schocken Books, 1968, 1971).

[2] See Robert A. Dahl, *Who Governs?* (New Haven: Yale University Press, 1961), Book I.

[3] For an elaboration of these concepts, see Roland L. Warren, *The Community in America* (Skokie, Ill.: Rand McNally, 1963).

the basis of criteria internal to the firm—the cost of that operation in comparison to every other community in the United States or maybe even the world. The economic life or death of a community may hang in the balance, but all local officials can do is plead their case and try to offer incentives to attract or retain the company. But in the end, the decision is made somewhere else.

Consider one seemingly mundane example: the suburban shopping center. Shopping centers, by their location, can determine the direction of future growth within a metropolitan area. At the beginning of vast suburban growth after World War II, these centers followed the population expansion. Today, the development of shopping centers is a sophisticated, national process, involving real estate and construction companies, banks, insurance companies, pension funds, and retail chains. These syndicates choose locales among competing sites and include residential real estate in their operations. The result is that they determine the future of suburban growth, rather than follow it.

DEPENDENCE OF LOCAL COMMUNITIES ON NATIONAL POLITICAL AND ADMINISTRATIVE DECISIONS

The period from the New Deal (1932) to the present has seen steady consolidation of political power in the federal government. Welfare, housing, environmental protection, racial policies, criminal justice, and energy policy were once domains left to state and local governments. They now are substantially national. Local autonomy is accordingly reduced. Washington also has a great impact through the federal budget and through fiscal policy on the national economy. Regional and local prosperity may hinge more on federal economic policy than on local efforts.

Again, consider a seemingly mundane example: housing. What could be more personal, more local, than the apartments and houses people live in? And what could be more within the control of local governments, which regulate housing through zoning ordinances, construction and safety standards, and property tax rates? About two thirds of all Americans own their own homes (often in conjunction with banks that loan them the money). In an area such as metropolitan Philadelphia, there are more than a million and a half housing structures. Yet, even housing patterns are largely a consequence of federal, not local, policy.

In practice, housing construction starts and home mortgage rates are highly dependent on the policies of federal administrative agencies. The most important factor in new home construction is the interest rate charged by local banks to developers. The rate, as well as the availability of funds, is determined by the Federal Reserve System in Washington, an independent agency with great powers to affect the national economy.

The federal impact on housing has been most pronounced in what the federal government has done for middle-income families. Two programs provided financing for the post-World War II population expansion into single-family homes in the suburbs: Federal Housing Administration (FHA) loans and Veterans Administration (VA) home loan mortgage insurance. During the 1950s and 1960s, when the suburbs were being formed, FHA insured between 16 and 34 per cent of all new home construction. This extensive financing activity gave the agency the leverage to establish the basic financing, construction, and social standards for the housing industry.

The FHA certainly did set standards. Until the mid-1950s, it would not insure racially integrated housing. Until the late 1960s, it would not insure central city housing, or multiple-dwelling rental housing. It liked the single-family, detached, suburban home, and the agency's preferences helped underwrite the pattern of settlement characteristic of every community in the country.

FHA today is different, and the point here is not to criticize, but to show the pervasive impact of federal policy on local life. Even within the housing area, the FHA and VA loan programs are not the only federal influence. The tax laws, for example, allow the deduction of mortgage interest and local property taxes from income, a very extensive indirect subsidy to homeowners. The federal government is also a builder and indirect operator of some 800,000 low-income housing units—the "projects." The location of these "projects" within a metropolitan area is a source of conflict.

The housing example could be multiplied many times. Washington affects localities not only by what it does. Choices made at the federal level about priorities exclude using those same scarce resources for local needs. A decision to build space platforms eliminates any chance that the same money will be funneled down to local hospitals or schools. Money for environmental construction, even when it does reach the local level, cannot be respent on parks. This line of reasoning indicates how urban policy cannot be studied apart from the totality of American politics.

A CONCEPTUAL FRAMEWORK: THE LOCAL GOVERNMENT NETWORK IN THE FEDERAL SYSTEM

It seems incredible, but there are 79,862 local governments in the United States. These local governments all have at least one legal power and, usually, many. They can tax; they deliver at least one service to some citizens. These local governments are quantitatively and qualitatively important parts of the American federal system, with national, state, and local levels.

Only about 21,000 of all the local governments are general-purpose governments. The remainder are either independent school districts or creatures known as "special districts." Independent school districts have some legal autonomy in the operation and financing of schools. Special districts are legal creations authorized to provide a service or set of services within the territories of an otherwise independent group of communities. Special districts may provide services as simple as a fire department for three rural communities. Or special districts may be as complicated as operating a train, bus, subway, and ferry boat mass transit system for an entire metropolitan area.

The number of local governments varies from metropolitan area to metropolitan area. Chicago has the largest number: 1,214 local governments in its metropolitan area. Table 1-1 shows the number of different local governments in the largest areas of the country. Taken collectively, these local governments are a large operation. They spend in excess of $82 billion each year, about 27 per cent of all money spent by governments in the country. From their own tax sources, they raise more than $53 billion each year, or 17 per cent of all the tax money collected. They have more than 6 million full-time employees, three times the civilian payroll of the federal government, and more than the federal government and all state governments combined.

Local governments deliver a wide variety of services to citizens. They pick up garbage, run schools, provide police protection, staff recreation programs, put out fires, maintain vital personal and property records. The nature of local government services places them closer to everyone's daily life than do most services provided by other levels of government.

Local governments are also targets of opportunity for persons seeking jobs or businesses seeking contracts. Government employment has been a channel of upward mobility for rising groups historically—immigrants in the nineteenth century, blacks and Hispanics today. And local government spending—for schools, for equipment, for police cruisers—is still of great interest to local businesses.

Local governments together are an interest network within each state political system. They band together in interest groups—Leagues of Cities—to press their common causes before the governor and the state legislature. At the national level, local governments are organized into the National League of Cities and the National Conference of Mayors to lobby on national policy affecting urban areas. Such national policy includes the size of the total federal commitment to

TABLE 1-1. Population and Number of Local Governments in America's 72 Largest Metropolitan Areas

Area	(in thousands) Population 1976°	Number of Local Governments
Akron, Ohio	670	102
Albany–Schenectady–Troy, N.Y.	797	54
Allentown–Bethlehem– Easton, Pa.–N.Y.	623	273
Anaheim–Santa Ana–Garden Grove, Calif.	1,756	108
Atlanta, Ga.	1,805	172
Baltimore, Md.	2,144	29
Birmingham, Ala.	800	113
Boston, Mass.	2,862	190
Buffalo, N.Y.	1,328	143
Chicago, Ill.	6,993	1,214
Cincinnati, Ohio–Ky.–Ind.	1,364	265
Cleveland, Ohio	1,967	211
Columbus, Ohio	1,072	196
Dallas–Fort Worth, Texas	2,611	368
Dayton, Ohio	837	162
Denver–Boulder, Colo.	1,438	329
Detroit, Mich.	4,406	349
Flint, Mich.	524	93
Fort Lauderdale–Hollywood, Fla.	847	52
Fresno, Calif.	464	200
Gary–Hammond–East Chicago, Ind.	644	140
Grand Rapids, Mich.	569	93
Greensboro–Winston Salem– High Point, N.C.	766	50
Hartford, Conn.	730	85
Honolulu, Hawaii	715	4
Houston, Texas	2,423	488
Indianapolis, Ind.	1,141	316
Jacksonville, Fla.	695	43
Jersey City, N.J.	573	39
Kansas City, Mo.–Kans.	1,281	280
Long Branch–Asbury Park, N.J.	494	139
Los Angeles–Long Beach, Calif.	6,997	232
Louisville, Ky.–Ind.	887	215
Memphis, Tenn.–Ark.	877	68
Miami, Fla.	1,450	33
Milwaukee, Wis.	1,415	154
Minneapolis–St. Paul, Minn.	2,048	406
Nashville, Tenn.	764	94
Newark, N.J.	1,993	268
New Brunswick–Perth Amboy– Sayreville, N.J.	593	76

TABLE 1-1. (Cont.)

Area	(in thousands) Population 1976*	Number of Local Governments
New Orleans, La.	1,137	25
New York, N.Y.	9,509	362
Norfolk–Virginia Beach– Portsmouth, Va.	782	9
Oklahoma City, Okla	762	133
Omaha, Neb.–Iowa	581	260
Orlando, Fla.	583	41
Patterson–Clifton–Passaic, N.J.	470	42
Philadelphia, Pa.–N.J.	4,803	864
Phoenix, Ariz.	1,224	115
Pittsburgh, Pa.	2,303	744
Portland, Ore.–Wash.	1,096	257
Providence–Warwick– Pawtucket, R.I.	905	67
Richmond, Va.	594	14
Riverside–San Bernardino– Ontario, Calif.	1,265	230
Rochester, N.Y.	978	244
Sacramento, Calif.	908	212
Salt Lake City, Utah	800	126
San Antonio, Texas	996	80
San Diego, Calif.	1,624	149
San Francisco–Oakland, Calif.	3,158	298
San Jose, Calif.	1,205	74
Seattle–Everett, Wash.	1,419	262
Springfield–Chicopee– Holyoke, Mass.	546	54
St. Louis, Mo.–Ill.	2,384	615
Syracuse, N.Y.	651	179
Tampa–St. Petersburg, Fla.	1,367	57
Toledo, Ohio–Mich.	780	198
Tulsa, Okla.	598	192
Washington, D.C.–Md.–Va.	3,037	92
Wilmington, Del.–N.J.–Md.	518	81
Youngstown–Warren, Ohio	544	106

* Population figures shown derived from 1977 Census Bureau data. The number of local governments is based on the 1977 *Census of Governments.*

urban and suburban programs and to specific programs such as revenue sharing and community development grants.

How much influence do local officials have as they interact with state and federal government on behalf of their community-oriented interests? Success depends in part upon the calculations that state and national leaders make about the popularity of urban and suburban needs as issues with the general electorate. Success also depends in part upon the calculations of state and national leaders about their own electoral needs in local constituencies and how much or how little local officials can help or hurt them. These linkages go under the mind-bending label of "intergovernmental relations." Beneath that label, the stakes are high. Local governments obtain about 30 per cent of their revenues from either their state or the federal government. In the other direction, local governments are often the administrative units of federal and state programs.

Intergovernmental relations also encompasses relations local governments have with each other in a metropolitan area. Sometimes local governments cooperate with each other. The firemen of one suburb will go to another to help put out a blaze. But sometimes local governments and their citizens are in conflict with each other. What happens then? We will look at the mechanisms that have developed for working out these problems and evaluate how well they work.

LIMITATIONS ON LOCAL POLITICAL ACTION

In a national federal system, local governments are limited in many ways. Complicated conditions must be met if local political forces are to get what they want, whether it is the freedom to run segregated school systems or federal funds to purify drinking water.

Consider some hypothetical possibilities. If national decision makers believe it is more important to use resources on foreign policy than on streets or sewers, then national funds will be used for nonlocal purposes. Those who man the positions of power in the White House, the Congress, and the huge federal bureaucracies will see to that. A change of emphasis could come only if national officeholders perceived local needs as paramount.

What could make national officeholders give high priority to urban programs? One hypothetical condition would be the existence of strong, centralized political parties, capable of mobilizing support and citizen activity at the local level. Yet, recent American political history points the other way. Parties have disintegrated, nonparty independent voters have increased, and local party organizations have vanished, replaced by mass media campaign specialists.

One way national resources might be diverted to local use would be if there were local constituencies so strong they would have to be heeded by national officeholders. Suppose people had the same loyalties to their local communities as they had to the nation, a kind of local nationalism? Then, through the electoral connection to elected national office, national elites would have to respond to local needs.

Evidence about the emotional attachments of citizens to their local communities is ambiguous. On the one hand, millions of Americans have moved from one local community to another, seeking better jobs, better housing, more status, or safer schools. Thus it appears that local attachments are weak, easily overridden by personal and family needs.

On the other hand, we know from a number of studies that local governments are not regarded negatively in the minds of the public.[4] Almost as many Americans believe that local government has as great an effect on daily life as the national government does (35 per cent, compared to 41 per cent). Almost as many Americans believe that on the whole the activities of local government tend to improve conditions in their areas as believe that federal activities bring such improvements (69 per cent to 74 per cent). More Americans believe they can understand local issues "very well" than believe they can so understand national and international issues (21 per cent to 7 per cent), and more also believe they can understand local issues "moderately well" (44 per cent to 38 per cent).

A survey done for the United States Senate had similar findings.[5] Slightly more people believed that local government had improved the quality of their lives than thought the national or state governments had done so. People believed they knew more about what was going on in their local government than they did at the federal or state levels. More citizens sought personal help from local government (24 per cent) than from state government (13 per cent), or the federal government (11 per cent). A 1977 poll showed 36 per cent of the public believed it got the most for its money from the federal government, 26 per cent thought it got the most from local government, and only 20 per cent rated state government as the best buy.[6] Local governments were most highly regarded by persons with college educations, managerial positions, and higher incomes.

Or, let us analyze in another way the concern Americans have for local governments. How much attention do people pay to each level of

[4] See the data in Thomas R. Dye, *Politics in States and Communities*, 1st ed. (Englewood Cliffs, N.J.: Prentice-Hall, 1969), p. 50, Table 2-6. Dye's data are drawn from an analysis by Robert A. Dahl in *Pluralist Democracy in the United States* (Skokie, Ill: Rand McNally, 1967), pp. 198–201, which in turn drew the raw data from unpublished parts of the survey done by Gabriel A. Almond and Sidney Verba for *The Civic Culture* (Boston: Little, Brown, 1963).

[5] See "Confidence and Concern: Citizens View of American Government: A Survey of Public Attitudes," Subcommittee on Intergovernmental Relations, Committee on Government Operations, U.S. Senate, 93rd Congress, 1st Session (Washington, D.C.: U.S. Government Printing Office, 1973).

[6] See Advisory Commission on Intergovernmental Relations, *Changing Public Attitudes on Government and Taxes* (Washington, D.C., 1977), pp. 4–5.

government? In one study local politics ranked next to national politics in the number of persons who said they paid the most attention to it—30 per cent.[7] Adding first and second choices, about 50 per cent seemed to give their closest attention to local politics. We do not know from this study how close the attention is. It could mean that citizens monitor local government behavior day to day. Or, it might mean nothing more than a careful scrutiny and a groan at the family property tax bill. The attention is probably something in-between.

Nor can we tell from this study what the particular characteristics of locally oriented publics might be. We do know that those who pay attention to state politics are different from those who pay attention to national politics. The state-politics-oriented public is likely to have resided longer in the same locale, to be more working-class than middle-class, and to have less education.

It seems reasonable to believe that the public for local government is the same as that for state government, but the diversity of suburbs is so great that few conclusions can be drawn. One conclusion is certain: we need to know more about which people are concerned with local affairs and under what circumstances. That knowledge would be the basis of any strategy to encourage loyal or nationalistic attitudes toward local government.

Despite the large number of Americans who change their residence every year—as many as one in seven—only a few of these moves are very extensive. Most are to some other location within the same metropolitan area. Thus, people may have strong ties to a metropolitan area, even when ties are not strong to particular individual localities. Studies have shown considerable attitudinal loyalties to metropolitan areas. Some differences among such areas are greater than those between dwellers of different communities within them.[8]

Whatever individual feelings about the local level of government are, local governments have some definite resources. There are still local elites—financial institutions, businesses, universities, hospitals, political leaders. Their concern remains the local area.[9] Most important, everyone's direct interest is affected by some aspect of local pub-

---

[7] See M. Kent Jennings and Harmon Zeigler, "The Salience of American State Politics," *American Political Science Review*, 64:2 (June 1970), 525.

[8] See Joseph Zikmund II, "Suburbs in State and National Politics," in *The Urbanization of the Suburbs*, ed. by Louis H. Masotti and Jeffrey K. Hadden (Beverly Hills: Sage Publications, 1973), and "A Comparison of Political Attitudes and Activity Patterns in Central Cities and Suburbs," *Public Opinion Quarterly*, Vol. 31, No. 1 (Spring 1967), pp. 69–75.

[9] For an interesting microlevel illustration of the concern and roles of local elites, see Thomas J. Anton's discussion of Lincolnwood, Illinois, in his "Three Models of Community Development in the United States," *Publius*, Vol. 1, No. 1 (1971), pp. 17–30.

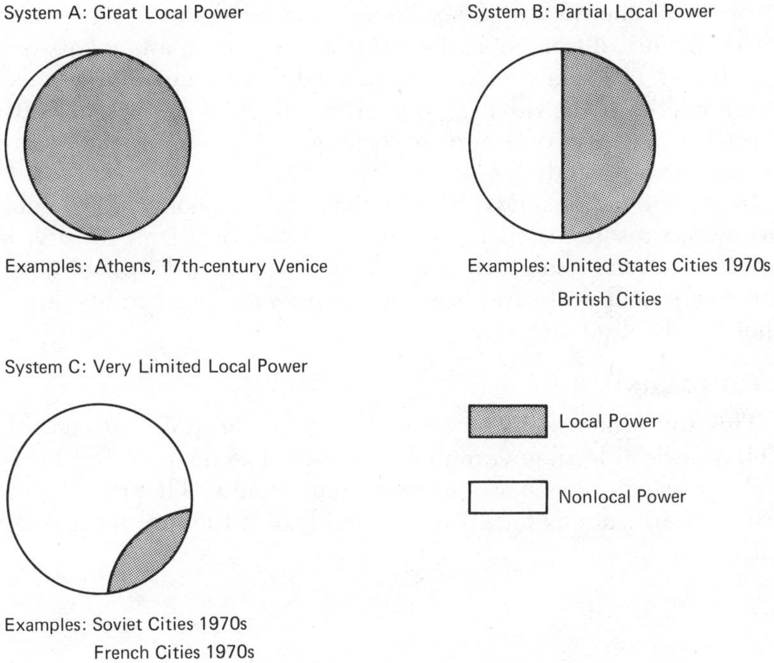

System A: Great Local Power

System B: Partial Local Power

Examples: Athens, 17th-century Venice

Examples: United States Cities 1970s

British Cities

System C: Very Limited Local Power

Local Power

Nonlocal Power

Examples: Soviet Cities 1970s

French Cities 1970s

FIGURE 1–1.   Three Hypothetical Political Systems.

lic policy. Schools, police, snow removal—basic services and their quality and cost affect almost everyone. This then is the basic American urban and suburban condition: local governments' place in the nation is not paramount, but they have a large residual following and tasks that are of great human concern.

To make this conclusion about the relative status of local government clearer, consider Figure 1-1, which shows diagrams of three hypothetical political systems. In System A, local governments are largely autonomous and they control a large portion of the resources in their area, the loyalties of their citizens, and the important programs of government. This is a system of virtual city-states, or cities operating in a territory in which the national government is weak and does nothing except manage defense. There are no contemporary local governments that match this system in the United States.

In System B, local governments are only partially autonomous. They control only a portion of the resources in their area, the loyalties of their citizens, and the important services of government. The American system fits pattern B. To what degree? Do American cities have 40 to 45 per cent of the total authority in a society, as the diagram indicates? Or should only 20 or 25 per cent be shaded? What are the relevant historical trends? Is the situation desirable, and what are the alternatives? The relative standing of local institutions will be treated throughout the text. Although our measuring devices are primitive, this relational aspect of American local governments has not received much systematic study.[10]

In System *C*, local governments have no autonomy. They control none of the resources in their areas, evoke no citizen loyalty, and administer services solely at the direction of higher levels of government. Such local units are, in essence, purely administrative arms of higher levels of government.

CONCLUSION

This introductory chapter has described the political context in which American local governments operate. The next chapter turns in detail to our emergence as a metropolitan society. That development has wide implications for every aspect of local life and local government.

---

[10] This concern is similar to what John Walton calls the *vertical axes* of community organization. Sociologists have been more aware of the relevance of the subsystem idea than most political scientists. See John Walton, "The Vertical Axis of Community Organization and the Structure of Power," *Social Science Quarterly*, Vol. 48 (December 1967), pp. 353–368.

2 METROPOLITAN AMERICA— WHAT IT IS, HOW IT GOT THAT WAY

This chapter traces the historical development of a metropolitan society. America today is a metropolitan nation, with its people clustered in centers of population called *Standard Metropolitan Statistical Areas* (SMSA's) by the Census Bureau. There are 264 such SMSA's, and they contain more than 72 per cent of the population within a bare 14 per cent of the national land area. Not only population, but material resources are concentrated in these metropolitan centers—four fifths of all savings and loan deposits; four fifths of all bank deposits; more than three fourths of the value added by manufacturing; three fourths of all personal income; and seven tenths of all assessed property values.

The development of a majority of our population within metropolitan areas reflects changes occurring over a long period of time. In 1790, the United States had only four communities containing more than 2,500 persons (the current definition of an *urban place*). Five per cent of the population was nonrural. It was not until 1920 that half the American population lived in urban areas.

The current figures camouflage some important aspects of American living patterns. Most Americans live in metropolitan areas, but they do not necessarily live in big cities. There are a lot of big cities, 27 with populations of more than 500,000. But, as Table 2-1 shows, within metropolitan areas not everyone chooses to live within the biggest cities. More Americans live in communities with less than 250,000 population than live in the biggest cities with populations of more than

15

TABLE 2-1. Number and Per Cent of the United States
Population Living in Urban Areas

Population of Area	Population Living in Area This Size	Per Cent of Total Population	Per Cent of Urban Population	
Less than 2,500	722,000	1.4	1.9	
2,500 to 5,000	8,041,000	4.0	5.4	
5,000 to 10,000	12,936,000	6.4	8.7	
10,000 to 25,000	21,414,000	10.5	14.2	62.7
25,000 to 50,000	17,820,000	8.8	11.9	
50,000 to 100,000	16,724,000	8.2	11.1	
100,000 to 250,000	14,285,000	7.0	9.5	
250,000 to 500,000	10,442,000	5.1	6.9	
500,000 to 1,000,000	12,967,000	6.4	8.7	
1,000,000+	18,472,000	9.2	12.5	
Unincorporated parts of urban areas	15,186,000	7.5	10.2	
	149,276,000	73.5	100.0	

SOURCE: *Statistical Abstract of the United States* (Washington, D.C.: Bureau of the Census, 1978), p. 23.

250,000. In fact, more than half of the urban population lives in communities with less than 100,000 people, and more than 60 per cent live in places with no more than 250,000. Americans have moved into large population centers, but they have located themselves within territorial and governmental units of relatively small size.

From the post-Civil War era until the early 1970s, urban areas and metropolitan areas showed the most rapid population growth. For the first time in a century, in the early 1970s, nonmetropolitan areas began growing more rapidly.[1] Small towns, rural areas, and communities well on the periphery of settled SMSA's became very attractive. At the same time, the older SMSA's of the East Coast and the Midwest lost population. Smaller SMSA's in the South and Southwest showed rapid growth. Cumulatively, the effects are deconcentration of people and national growth for our time in the Sunbelt.

This chapter presents a developmental model, using historical data, as background to answer the question, how did we become a metropolitan nation? An historical summary allows us to evaluate which forces have most shaped urban life at different times and, par-

[1] See Brian J. L. Berry, "The Counterurbanization Process: Urban America Since 1970," in *Urbanization and Counterurbanization*, B. J. L. Berry, ed. (Beverly Hills, Cal.: Sage Publications, 1976), p. 21.

ticularly, to rate the impact of political decisions in the formation of urban settlements. To bring us up to the present, we will look at four distinct time periods: (1) The Emergence of the Ocean-River Cities, 1789–1860; (2) The Era of Steam and Rail Technology, 1860–1910; (3) The Era of Mixed Rail/Automotive Technology, 1910–1945; and (4) The Automotive City, 1945 to the present.

When we get to the present, we analyze the population, racial, social, and economic characteristics of contemporary metropolitan areas. We will also see how central cities and suburbs are different and to what degree SMSA's are alike or different from each other.

THE EMERGENCE OF THE OCEAN/RIVER CITIES, 1789–1860

Population settlement in colonial and post-colonial America clustered around the water, the most convenient transportation route. The earliest cities are all ports—New York, Philadelphia, Baltimore, Newport, Newark, and New Orleans on the ocean, and Cincinnati and St. Louis on the Mississippi River. Inland, rivers became the centers for commerce or for early textile mills. Within the early cities, population grew around the warehouses and piers that were the centers of the maritime commerce. With limited surface transportation facilities, workers and bosses lived close together within walking distance (or a short horse ride) from the dock-based jobs.

At the beginning of the period, these settlements were tiny and a small part of the vast, empty agricultural new nation, an underpopulated developing country in today's terminology. In 1830, the urban population was 10 per cent of the country's total and not much different from what it was in 1790. But technology began to bring changes. In the 1830s, there were horse-drawn buses, and as the nationwide rail grid began to emerge in the 1840s, early commuter train lines were built.[2] People could live farther from work, and early suburbs were settled. By the Civil War, manufacturing began in New England mill towns and the various ports. Overall, however, it misleads to talk about urban or metropolitan development for this period. The vast unsettled North American continent contained some small settlements clustered on the water.

There is one significant remainder from these early water-bordering cities: the port areas were the "core cities" and still retain that economic function in many places. Central business districts of older cities are still likely to be very close to waterways.

---

[2] Charles N. Glaab and A. Theodore Brown, *A History of Urban America* (New York: Macmillan, 1967), p. 27.

THE ERA OF STEAM AND RAIL TECHNOLOGY, 1860–1910

The dynamic era of 1860 to 1910 saw industrialization, migration, unions, work specialization, and corporate centralization. Glaab and Brown state that "between 1860 and 1910, the modern American city emerged."[3] Population grew from 31 million to 91 million, and the urban percentage grew from 20 per cent to 45 per cent of the country. All cities that today are of even moderate size were founded by the end of this era. As the city population expanded from 6 to 44 million people, migrants flooded into the cities from the farms and also from abroad.

People went to the cities from farms because of the rapid mechanization of agriculture that reduced the need for human hands. The mechanical reaper increased productivity five times and corporate-owned farms developed. White, native-born Americans moved first into smaller cities and then to growing great central cities. The writer Hamlin Garland chronicled this painful rite of passage in *Son of the Middle Border*.[4]

At the same time, another great population surge came to the cities from Europe. More than 5 million people immigrated in the decade of the 1880s, and although the depression of the 1890s slowed the flow, 8 million more people arrived between 1900 and 1910. In 1910, close to 20 per cent, more than 9.5 million of all people living in American cities were foreign-born. The major city streets heard a virtual Babel of different languages, and cities developed separate ethnic neighborhoods. Foreign immigrants were absorbed politically by "machine" government, which eased the entry into American politics in exchange for votes.

The economic equality that characterized American life before the Civil War vanished in this period. When the Frenchman Alexis de Tocqueville visited the United States in the 1830s and wrote his classic *Democracy in America*, he had noted with amazement the relative economic and social equality of Americans.[5] But after the Civil War, that equality began to vanish as industrial capitalism took hold. Nowhere were disparities between rich, poor, and the middle class more visible than in the teeming cities. The new rich organized the great capitalist enterprises in oil, steel, railroads, meat packing, and finance. Merchant princes built department stores to serve them. Their wealth, in an era without a federal income tax and with minimal taxa-

---

[3] Ibid., p. 107.
[4] (New York: Grosset & Dunlap, 1928).
[5] Reprinted by Vintage Books (New York: 1954).

tion from state or local governments, set them apart from farm and overseas immigrants. Those at the top of the economic ladder underwrote new cultural enterprises in the cities with their wealth: museums, orchestras, parks.

At the lower end of the economic spectrum, life was grim. Oscar Handlin describes the psychological traumas of immigrant life in his famous book *The Uprooted*.[6] Jacob Riis described the physical conditions of the worst slums of New York City in a book called *How the Other Half Lives.* Following is his description of the sweltering summers in the teeming lower East Side of Manhattan, packed with immigrant Irish, Italians, Jews, and Chinese:

> With the first hot night in June police despatches (sic), that record the killing of men and women by rolling off roofs and windowsills while asleep, announce that the time of greatest suffering among the poor is at hand. It is in hot weather, when life indoors is well-nigh unbearable with cooking, sleeping and working, all crowded into the small rooms together, that the tenement expands, reckless of all restraint. Then a strange and picturesque life moves upon the flat roofs. In the day and early evening mothers air their babies there, the boys fly their kites from the house-tops undismayed by police regulations, and the young men and girls court and pass the growler. In the stifling July nights, when the big barracks are like fiery furnaces, their very walls giving out absorbed heat, men and women lie in restless sweltering rows, panting for air and sleep. Then every truck in the street, every crowded fire escape, becomes a bedroom, infinitely preferable to any the house affords. A cooling shower on such a night is hailed as a heaven-sent blessing in a hundred thousand homes.[7]

Wide differences in wealth resulted in widely different life-styles and patterns of settlement. The poor clustered in tenements around the heavy industries, within close distance of their jobs. The rich had town houses and also estates or farms on the outskirts of the city. The middle class, unable to afford the expensive accommodations of the rich, moved to the cheap land on the fringes of the city. By the 1860s, the horse-drawn street railway, dirty, cramped, and slow, but used in most large cities, reached the limits of its capacities. In New York, the five main systems carried 35 million passengers a year; Boston's Metropolitan Railroad Corporation carried 6.5 million.

[6] (Cambridge, Mass.: Harvard University Press, 1951).
[7] Reprinted by Sagamore Press (New York: 1952).

In the 1870s, innovative urban technologies arrived—the elevated train (the "El) and the electrical street trolley. The elevated system placed steam trains on tracks built above the streets and supported by large pillars. The elevateds started in New York City in 1870 and came to Kansas City and Brooklyn in the 1880s. Chicago, which still maintains miles of "El" got them in the 1890s. During the 1890s, San Francisco built its cable car system. The cable cars are towed along city streets by a continuous underground cable; various difficulties prevented its adoption elsewhere.

Frank Julian Sprague was the engineer who liberated the crowded urban populations by inventing the electrified street railway, the trolley. With trolleys, a central electrical power source passed current to car through an overhead wire. Fast, clean transportation resulted. By 1895, the horse-drawn trains were almost gone, made obsolete by 850 new electrical trolley systems in different cities, with 10,000 operating miles. Sprague also figured out how to electrify the urban railways of the elevateds and how to eliminate the technical bottlenecks to building similar systems underground. Consequently, the major urban subway systems still in existence began between 1895 and 1910, most notably in New York and Boston.

Other engineering innovations affected city development during this period. Steel suspension bridges allowed linking outlying areas to the center city as well as the expansion of commerce. By 1910, 365 bridges, each more than 500 feet long, were constructed. The city-building reflected the raw industrial power of a growing country, and the vast urban construction created its own boom in jobs, financing, and franchises.

The 1860–1910 period may have been the heyday of the central city. The period also marks the beginning of American suburbanization on a major scale. The trolley system made possible extending the boundaries of settlement. Ambitious developers, following the trolley lines, built apartments and houses on what had previously been empty land on the city outskirts.

Table 2-2 illustrates the process of people moving outward from the central city, as, for example, from Boston. As early as 1840–1850, small towns surrounding Boston were growing faster than the main city. Boston increased its growth by the then available expedient of legally annexing Dorchester, Brighton, Charlestown, and West Roxbury. But after 1880, the growth of all the rings of smaller communities around Boston was much greater. With each succeeding period, the format repeats: the fastest rate of growth moves progressively outward. Technology, wealth, and expanded opportunities to live and to work sent people outward from the core city.

TABLE 2-2. Intercensal Growth Rates in Boston and
Surrounding Rings, 1790–1960

Decade	Boston	First Ring	Second Ring	Third Ring	Fourth Ring
1790–1800	36.1*	27.0	10.3	9.9	10.5
1800–1810	35.5	7.4	13.4	21.8	8.8
1810–1820	28.2	17.3	17.9	6.6	6.5
1820–1830	41.8	34.9	17.9	9.5	7.3
1830–1840	52.1	35.8	25.3	19.7	14.4
1840–1850	46.6	81.3	42.0	38.1	31.4
1850–1860	29.9	67.6	32.4	27.7	18.2
1860–1870	40.9	44.7	23.8	19.9	11.3
1870–1880	44.8†	33.1	24.3	29.3	18.4
1880–1890	23.6	41.3	46.6	26.0	17.5
1890–1900	25.1	42.6	36.8	20.1	16.2
1900–1910	19.6	21.8	26.9	23.6	17.2
1910–1920	11.6	22.5	31.6	9.5	16.7
1920–1930	4.4	22.6	39.4	12.9	20.1
1930–1940	−1.3	0.8	7.1	3.3	7.8
1940–1950	4.0	8.4	14.6	11.1	19.0
1950–1960	−13.0	0.6	20.4	22.8	55.9

SOURCE: Leo F. Schnore and Peter R. Knights, "Residence and Social Structure: Boston in the Ante-Bellum Period," in Stephan Thernstrom and Richard Sennett (eds.), *Nineteenth Century Cities* (New Haven: Yale University Press, 1969), p. 250. Reprinted by permission.

* The highest value for each decade is italicized.

† Boston annexed Dorchester in 1870, and three towns in 1874; these towns, together with their 1870 populations, were:

Brighton (1874)	4,967
Charlestown (1874)	28,323
West Roxbury (1874)	8,683

Assume that these three areas did not grow between 1870 and 1880. Subtracting their *1870* total population (41, 973) from the recorded *1880* Boston total (362,839), and computing the Boston growth between 1870 and 1880 in the area unaffected by annexation yields an adjusted growth rate over the decade of 28.1%.

Sam Bass Warner, Jr., describes the magnitude of the urban transformation of this era in *Streetcar Suburbs: The Process of Growth in Boston, 1870–1900.*[8] The suburbs began and the middle class developed. The middle class lived in separated enclaves, available to all who could increasingly afford the price and could reach the new areas by streetcar or subway. The decentralization of present-day cities, the

[8] (Cambridge, Mass.: Harvard University Press, 1962), p. 160.

fragmentation of metropolitan government and life, begin here. Warner writes:

> Two qualities mark off the Boston of 1900 from all preceding eras: its great size and its new suburban arrangement. In 1850 the metropolitan region of Boston encompassed a radius of but two or three miles, a population of two hundred thousand; in 1900 the region extended over a ten-mile radius and contained a population of more than a million. A change in structure accompanied this change in scale. Once a dense merchant city clustered about an ocean port, Boston became a sprawling industrial metropolis. In 1850 it was a fairly small and unified area; by 1900 it had split into two functional parts: an industrial, commercial and communications center packed tight against the port, and an enormous outer suburban ring of residence and industrial and commercial subcenters. . . .[9]

Other cities underwent the same process. Leo F. Schnore studied 99 cities of more than 100,000 in size, and 23 began to decentralize by 1910.[10] Philadelphia underwent greater suburban growth between 1860 and 1910 than between 1900 and 1950. Jobs moved outward along with the people. Industrial employment grew faster outside the central cities than within them. In 12 of the 13 largest industrialized metropolitan areas between 1900 and 1910, job growth was 97.7 per cent in the suburbs and 40.8 per cent inside the central cities.[11]

THE ERA OF MIXED RAIL/AUTOMOTIVE TECHNOLOGY, 1910–1945

From 1910 to 1945 was a transitional era for metropolitan development. The country went through two depressions, 1919–1922 and 1930–1940. Both imposed severe economic hardships on individuals and also slowed development of available technologies, especially between 1930–1940. Television, for example, was available by 1929 but not marketed until after World War II.

The 1919–1945 era brought wide-ranging changes in American society. Corporate centralization continued. The federal government role in the private economy expanded greatly. The era marked the end of unfettered free enterprise and the beginning of vast federal activity in the economy. The federal government assumed pre-eminence in

[9] Ibid., p. 153.
[10] "The Timing of Metropolitan Decentralization," in *The Urban Scene* (New York: Free Press, 1965), pp. 98–113.
[11] Glaab and Brown, op. cit., p. 277.

comparison to state and local governments, which were swamped by the demands of the Great Depression. Until the 1930s, state and local spending equaled or exceeded that of Washington. Using distribution of resources as the criterion, a relative equality of governments existed in the country. By the end of World War II, that financial parity had forever vanished.

During this period, America became the leading world power in international politics. At the beginning, the country was already an industrial giant and a military power of great potential because of the techniques developed during the Civil War. But most American global power operated only regionally, through interventions in Central and South America, the Caribbean, and the Philippines. The United States was a developing, industrializing regional actor. Foreign investment continued to play a major part in American economic development, as European nations with heavy investments here ran large trade surpluses in their favor.

World War I changed the world role of the United States. America was physically intact and a creditor to Europe. The country opted not to exercise its military power or much of its diplomatic leverage, but involved itself intimately in European postwar finances in an effort to recoup the World War I war loans. World War II brought American power and involvement to full fruition. The only physically undamaged nation among the larger powers, the United States became the world's major military force.

Meanwhile, America's larger corporations also centralized their power in the economic sector. National companies continued to absorb smaller companies, and the number of firms in steel, autos, and oil declined. Giant financial holding companies bought out local transportation franchises operating buses or trolleys and also local utility companies operating gas, water, and electric services. The new management located in New York or Chicago.

All these changes occurred in response to forces beyond the control of local officials or businessmen. The federal government grew because of the Great Depression and the world wars. The national corporations grew because of accumulated capital and the drive for profits and efficiency through larger markets.

The urban population continued to move out from central cities into surrounding suburbs, although the rate of movement was radically slowed by the Depression in the 1930s. The 1910 census brought the first full-fledged statistical analysis of the new suburban phenomenon. The Census Bureau identified 25 areas called *metropolitan districts.* These began with the New York district, with more than six million people (including Newark) and more than 600,000 acres, and ended with Portland, Oregon, which then had less than a quarter million people within 44,000 acres. The distinguishing characteristic of metropolitan districts appeared to be economic integration. The Census Bureau's view seemed to be that the expanding areas absorbed previously old and independent towns. The census recognized the interdependence of connected communities on the San Francisco Bay, of the Minneapolis-St. Paul twin cities, and of the many entities around Boston, Philadelphia, and Pittsburgh.

During this era, the automobile also became a shaper of urban development. Automobiles, made individually by skilled mechanics, appeared in the United States and Europe in the 1890s as toys of the rich and mechanically minded. Only 8,000 were registered in 1900, but by 1910 registrations reached 450,000. Major innovations opened a whole new market for cars, especially the use of standardized parts on a moving assembly line to build Henry Ford's Model T. By 1915 the number of cars registered reached 2.5 million. Another production and sales spurt after World War I brought the number to nine million in 1920, then to 26 million in 1930 and, despite the Depression, to 32 million by 1940.

The automobile is a special transportation form. It allows point-to-point movement at the driver's convenience, advantages present with horses but not with trains or trolleys. The auto is dependable, fast, and with the original Model T's, cheap. For the expanding middle class, the automobile brought the land sites around the city within reasonable commuting time and costs. Commuters no longer needed to live near mass transit stops. With the car came trucks, revolutionizing plant and freight requirements almost as much as cars changed residential patterns. Industries no longer needed to be next to railroad sidings.

At first, highways were primitive and followed railroad lines. Construction improved after passage of the first Federal Highway Act in 1916. During the 1920s and 1930s, highway engineers developed the cloverleaf traffic interchange, grade separation, dual separated roads, and synchronized stoplights. In older cities auto traffic caused congestion, because it traveled on the already established routes, built for horses, walking, or rail, in central business districts.

In cities that were just developing, however, the auto permitted an entirely new pattern of settlement. Los Angeles, for example, grew enormously, but without a well-defined center. The new city expanded along the roads and along the outlines of an early interurban electric railway system. During the 1920s, Los Angeles suburbs exploded: Beverly Hills, 2,485 per cent population growth; Glendale,

365 per cent; Inglewood, 492 per cent; and Huntington Park, 444 per cent.[12]

New incorporations bloomed around older cities. Many of the fast-growing suburbs became homogenous communities on racial or religious bases, some by the deliberate effort of developers and promoters. Some developers attempted wholly planned communities, especially where the towns could be connected to rapid-transit lines extending outside the central city or to new highways. One of the most famous of these developments was Shaker Heights, outside Cleveland, where expensive houses on curving and eliptical roads were built to the strict construction and aesthetic requirements of the Van Sweringen brothers. Shaker Heights' population increased from 1,700 in 1919 to 15,550 in 1929; today, it is a wealthy and famous suburb. Another such community was University City, outside St. Louis, where planned subdivisions, parks, and green spaces were part of an ingenious promotional design.

Downtown central business districts prospered. Land values increased and, simultaneously, new technologies made possible more intensive use of downtown real estate. The invention of the elevator liberated builders to create skyscrapers, the first of which was New York's Woolworth Tower, built in 1913. The 1920s brought a central city skyscraper boom in Manhattan, Chicago, Cleveland, and Pittsburgh. During this era of optimistic construction, 377 skyscrapers of more than 20 stories went up—a record not to be matched in urban areas again until the 1950s (when the building was in the newer cities of the Southwest and West). The jewel of the period is the Empire State Building in New York, completed in 1931, 102 stories high, and not fully rented, because of the Depression glut of office space, until well after World War II.

The automobile brought prosperity and rapid growth to cities involved in its production. Detroit, center of the new factories; Akron, tire construction; Cleveland, oil refining; and Toledo and Dayton, parts and electrical systems—all shot ahead during this era.

Other events of great significance for the metropolitan patterns of the future took place between 1910 and 1945. A set of political decisions changed the patterns of urban growth by halting European immigration. Anti-immigrant sentiment had a long history in the country, beginning with the Know-Nothing party of the 1850s and 1860s. Prejudice against the Irish during their widespread immigration in the 1870s and 1880s was open and widespread. But around 1890 the bulk

[12] Ibid., p. 281.

of immigration from Northern Europe and Ireland ceased. The new immigrants flooded in from Eastern and Southern Europe—an influx of non-English-speaking Catholics and Jews from Italy, Eastern Europe, and Russia. Native American Protestants reacted by seeking to halt the immigration, which still included 800,000 persons a year as late as 1921.

Heavy lobbying ensued in the Congress, and the Immigration Restriction Act passed in 1924, supported by delegations from the West, the South, and the rural parts of the Northeast. The act set limits on the total number of immigrants permitted and also on the number of persons who could come from each originating country. The country limitations favored the North European, Anglo-Saxon, Protestant regions. The overt goal was to restrict further arrival of the newer immigrants. In addition, the act excluded the Japanese, who had settled in large numbers on the West Coast, entirely as future immigrants. The legislative act contained blatant religious, ethnic, and racial discrimination. The Immigration Act of 1965 finally removed the odious restrictions of the 1924 act. In the meantime, however, the immigration flow dropped from 706,000 in 1924 to 300,000 per year for the rest of the 1920s to even less thereafter.

The 1924 Immigration Restriction Act ended the great era of European immigration as a main force in settling America's cities. The tightly knit ethnic communities in the cities could not expect to maintain their identity into the future through further immigration. Unity hereafter could only come from other sources: efforts to combat continuing prejudice while climbing the difficult American economic and social ladder; the mobilization of the old symbols by politicians seeking a block ethnic vote by giving "recognition" to ethnic group members; or by a conscious effort to remain separate, to maintain the "old country" culture. The Little Italys, Little Warsaws, and other ethnic enclaves were on their own, and in the schools and at work, pressure on the children to assimilate, to Americanize, was intense.

Growth continued in the cities, but now from different sources. Internal migration from rural America provided the bulk, with the high birth rate providing the balance. Migration from the farms to the cities, as always, included whites, but now for the first time, between 1910 and 1945, blacks came to the urban areas at a higher rate. Southern crop failures plus the job opportunities of World War I and the new auto industry provided the driving economic impetus. In 1910, almost 90 per cent of all black people lived in the South, mostly in the rural areas. By 1930, 20 per cent lived in the largest cities.

The black migrants from the South did not meet a friendly reception in the North. Racial relations in the North, despite the general absence of legal segregation, had always been difficult. Residential segregation prevailed and, in a tense atmosphere, white attitudes reflected the worst antiblack stereotypes of the popular culture, as reflected in the 1915 movie *Birth of a Nation* or in the segregated armed forces of World War I.

After World War I, in the competition for jobs amidst economic recession, whites attacked blacks in a number of direct clashes. A major riot occurred in 1918, in East St. Louis, Illinois, a grim industrial suburb across the Mississippi River from St. Louis. An aluminum plant there hired blacks as strikebreakers, and, after a series of incidents, the black neighborhoods were invaded by rioting whites as local police watched. One description relates:

> streetcars were stopped, and Negroes, without regard to age or sex, were pulled off and stoned, clubbed and kicked, and mob leaders calmly shot and killed Negroes who were lying in blood in the street. As the victims were placed in an ambulance, the crowds cheered and applauded. Other rioters set fire to Negro homes, and by midnight the Negro section was in flames and Negroes were fleeing the city. There were 48 dead, hundreds injured, and more than 300 buildings destroyed.[13]

In Chicago, the "Black Metropolis" was second in size only to New York's Harlem.[14] Chicago's black population grew rapidly during World War I, and in 1919 a major riot broke out. Twenty-five people died in four days of fighting. In the end, the northern cities absorbed 600,000 black migrants during the 1920s, 170,000 in New York City alone. Major black political movements began during this era, including the Garvey black nationalism. Black poets, writers, and musicians flourished in Harlem. The mass movements and racial consciousness of the 1960s had their intellectual origins and genesis during this 1910–1945 era.

Two other developments of this era require brief mention. First, organized crime emerged in most major cities. Urban gangs existed in the United States as early as the 1850s. Their members always came from the lowest socioeconomic group, usually the last immigrants off the boat—first the Irish, then the Jews, then the Italians. Gangs operated at a neighborhood level, with extortion, theft, prostitution, and minor gambling. National prohibition, coming in 1919, made these

[13] National Advisory Commission on Civil Disorders, *Report* (New York: 1968), p. 218.

[14] See St. Clair Drake and Horace R. Cayton, *Black Metropolis*, originally published in 1945, reprinted by Harper Torchbooks (New York: 1962).

gangs into big time, big money businesses, as they imported or produced and then distributed and sold beer and liquor on the flourishing black markets. Money from liquor led them into related enterprises: bars, restaurants, real estate, garbage collection, large-scale betting.

The gangs needed legal protection and, to get it, they developed corrupt connections with local police and public officials. Al Capone's gang dominated Chicago headlines, liquor, prostitution, and politics for the decade of the 1920s. But non-Italian organized criminals reigned in New York, Cleveland, and St. Louis. The skills and capital these urban criminal syndicates developed in the 1920s formed the basis for their more national activities after World War II. Urban needs and slum-toughened entrepreneurs provided the initial impetus.

Second, during this era, local officials first became conscious of the need to work with each other in national politics for common ends. After the Civil War, it was apparent that the burgeoning cities had much in common: industrial vitality, growing slums, social problems, the enmity of the countryside, and a bad popular image ("the sinful city"). Still, cities competed with each other for industry and prominence, as "boosterism" became the local civic style. The Depression changed the pattern of every city for itself.

During the 1930s, cities began to cooperate in national politics, primarily to encourage the federal government to take a new and large role in funding recovery through urban programs. Fifty mayors met in Washington on February 17, 1933 and organized the United States Conference of Mayors (USCM). They then appealed for aid from the new Roosevelt Administration. These pleas apparently had some indirect impact on the passage of the Industrial Recovery Act, which provided for $3.3 billion in public works projects.

Various forms of federal relief played an enormous role in the cities throughout the 1930s. The Works Progress Administration (WPA) built airports, zoos, parks, libraries, and provided artwork for public buildings and live theatre and music for urban audiences. The Conference of Mayors went on to participate in the first federal housing program, put into operation in March 1938. Urban public housing, aimed at slum clearance, became a reality. This new federal connection, the first direct governmental relationship between Washington and the cities,[15] was launched in this era of desperation and disaster.

THE AUTOMOTIVE CITY, 1945 TO TODAY

Almost everything that has happened in metropolitan America since the end of World War II seems to have roots in the earlier pe-

---

[15] See Blake McKelvey, *The Emergence of Metropolitan America, 1915–1966* (New Brunswick, N.J.: Rutgers University Press, 1968), pp. 83–98.

riods. Consider some of the more important trends. The automobile is the dominant variable in residential settlement patterns. Private car registrations increased from 27 million in 1940 to more than 90 million today. In 1950, about 59 per cent of all families owned one car, and 7 per cent owned two or more cars; today, almost 85 per cent of all families own one car, and more than 30 per cent own two cars. Trucks on the road increased from five million in 1940 to roughly 20 million today.

To service this massive increase in private transportation vehicles, the country underwent a massive road-building program in the 1950s and 1960s. More than 900,000 miles of highway construction received federal funds. These highways include the interstate systems as well as hundreds of thousands of miles of federally aided urban connecting roads, urban roads, and the inner and outer "ring" highways that surround major cities. The inner and outer ring roads make possible fast commuting and also industrial and commercial development outside the central city. The process converted millions of acres of surrounding farmland to suburban uses.

Mass transit usership declined drastically, reflecting the impact of the car in another way. Between 1950 and 1970, SMSA population increased by 50 million people, but the number of people using mass transit systems dropped from 24 billion rides in 1945 to less than 8 billion in 1969. The energy crisis that first forced itself on the American consciousness in 1973 has not reversed the trend. New mass transit systems, federally funded, are gradually coming on line in some cities, including in Washington, D.C., and San Francisco. These systems may eventually lure riders back, especially as gasoline becomes more expensive and in shorter supply. But energy problems cannot quickly change the basic alterations made by the car. The investment in spread-out suburban housing, shopping centers, and industrial plants is too great and too widely distributed to be changed rapidly.

Other technological changes after World War II also affected American culture and urban life. Most had the effect of building a national culture and reducing the impact of local elites and the hold of local citizen loyalties. Television grew from a minor form of electronic wizardry to a mass instrument in 96 per cent of all SMSA homes. National networks and national programming dominated the medium from the beginning. In addition, new techniques in long-playing records and tapes created a nationalized mass music audience, once again dominated by national companies.

CORPORATE CHANGES

Trends toward private economic concentrations, begun after the Civil War, continue. In 1940, 1,000 of the largest corporations controlled two thirds of all corporate assets. By 1970, the concentration was even greater. Only 200 companies control two thirds of all buildings, jobs, patents, equipment, financing, and technology that comprise such private assets. Two other economic developments further weaken the economic power of local elites and centralize economic control in national firms. One development is the rise of the conglomerate, the firm that operates companies in many different fields at once, providing centralized management and control. Conglomerates developed by buying up numerous smaller, often locally controlled companies, thus moving major economic decisions from the local to a national level.

A second development is the rise of the multinational company. Multinationals have many countries of origin, and French, English, German, Dutch, Swedish, and Japanese multinational firms operate within the United States. American-owned multinationals are our main concern, however, and these companies have large-scale overseas operations—in investments, production, marketing, and sales. When multinationals invest overseas, they choose, by so using their resources, not to invest the same funds in American facilities and jobs. When they search the world for the lowest wage rates, the companies frequently move plants and assembly facilities that previously were located in the continental United States. There is no direct way to tie overseas American activity by multinationals to net losses of jobs and capital investments in metropolitan areas. But certainly job losses in the least-skilled fields are substantial. The new multinational corporate form marks still another step in the centralization of decision making. All local communities now compete for investment against all the cities of the world.

THE FEDERAL GOVERNMENT EXPANSION

After World War II, the nation became the pre-eminent global power, diverting talent, loyalties, and funds from domestic affairs and local needs. The major aspects of the United States as a world superpower have receded slightly from view today. Until the early 1970s, the country maintained more than 300 overseas military bases and treaty obligations to dozens of nations on three continents. Defense was 10 per cent of the gross national product and half the federal budget (compared to 5.6 per cent and a fourth in 1978). A million nonmilitary Americans lived abroad, and the armed forces maintained an average of three million troops in uniform (compared to 2 million now). The nation was engaged in shooting wars in Asia from 1950 to 1953 and from 1961 to 1974. National security monopolized the time of a succession of presidents.

The ideological conflict of our world dispute with the Soviet Union and the Peoples Republic of China must have had a nationalizing impact upon public opinion and citizen loyalties. As the federal government spent more on public information to mobilize opinion than the combined news budgets of all the television networks and newspapers in the country, interest in local problems and local loyalties had to decline.

The American preoccupation with foreign affairs brought prosperity to some urban areas that specialized in defense and scientific production. Los Angeles and Long Island with aerospace, Seattle with airplanes, Boston with electronic systems, St. Louis with fighter planes all prospered. However, studies indicated that the high defense spending of the 1945–1970 era deferred spending on domestic programs.[16] Some of that money surely would have gone toward urban programs.

While American globalism was at its peak, federal domestic programs began to expand, building upon the categorical grant format. Some new programs provided for urban development. In 1949 a major housing act was passed, providing for urban renewal. Numerous other programs followed, especially during the 1960s: model cities, urban mass transit, aid to urban elementary and secondary education, and food distribution. Each categorical program involved a federal agency to review the applications, decide on them, disburse the funds, and review the work, extending a federal presence deep into day-to-day urban affairs. These federal-local interactions on program approval and administration wear the label of intergovernmental relations. After 1972, another approach to funneling federal funds to cities came into use. Direct revenue transfers, called revenue sharing, supplemented the categorical grant programs. In Chapter 3 we will explore how categorical grants and revenue sharing work.

METROPOLITAN AMERICA: A CONTEMPORARY DEMOGRAPHIC PORTRAIT

Figure 2-1 shows the most dramatic population change in our era: the rapid growth of suburbs. In 1940 in metropolitan areas, 60 per cent of the people lived in the central cities and 40 per cent lived in the surrounding suburban communities. By 1975, the numbers were exactly reversed. Sixty per cent lived in the suburbs, 40 per cent in the old cities, and the suburban growth rate was four to five times that of

---

[16] See Bruce M. Russett, *What Price Vigilance?* (New Haven: Yale University Press, 1970).

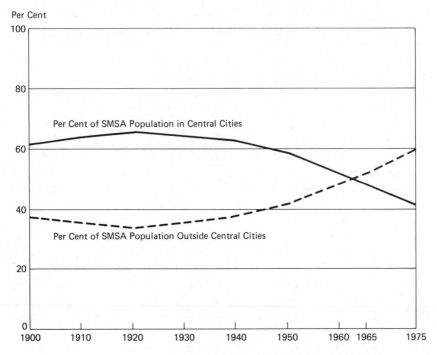

FIGURE 2–1.   Proportion of SMSA Population Living in Central Cities and in Suburbs, 1900–1975. SOURCE: Advisory Commission on Intergovernmental Relations, *Fiscal Balance in the American Federal System*, Vol. 2 (Washington, D.C.: U.S. Government Printing Office, 1967), p. 30.

the cities. Table 2-3 gives some idea of growth rates: outside central cities, 45 per cent from 1950–1960; 26 per cent, 1960–1970; 20 per cent, 1970–1974. In contrast, the growth rates of central cities were 1 per cent, 1950–1960; 6 per cent, 1960–1970; a loss of almost 5 per cent, 1970–1974.

Cumulatively, the decrease in central city populations is taking place in the larger SMSA's, rather than in the medium-sized and smaller ones. The central cities lost 4.6 million population to suburbs in net migration between 1970–1974, all of this loss being whites. The average income of families who move out of cities is chronically higher than that of those who move into cities or of those who stay behind.

At the same time that the suburbs have expanded vastly, the composition of the central city populations has changed. Black migration to the large industrial cities began first in earnest around World War I. At

33

TABLE 2-3. Change in Population of Metropolitan and Nonmetropolitan Areas, 1950–1960, 1960–1970, 1970–1974 (thousands)

	1950	1960	1970	Per cent Change, 1950–1960	Per cent Change, 1960–1970	1970	1974	Per cent Change, 1970–1974
United States, total	151,326	179,323	203,300	+18.50	+13.37	199,819	207,949	+10.17
All Metropolitan Areas								
Total	94,579	119,595	139,419	+26.45	+16.58	137,058	142,043	+9.09
In central cities	53,696	59,947	63,797	+11.64	+6.42	62,876	61,650	−4.87
Outside central cities	40,883	59,648	75,622	+45.90	+26.78	74,182	80,394	+20.93
Metropolitan areas of 1 million or more in 1970	54,524	69,070	80,657	+26.68	+16.78	79,498	81,059	+4.91
In central cities	32,272	34,010	34,824	+5.39	+2.39	34,332	33,012	−9.61
Outside central cities	22,252	35,060	45,833	+57.56	+30.73	45,166	48,047	+15.95
Metropolitan areas of less than 1 million in 1970	40,055	50,525	58,762	+26.14	+16.30	57,570	60,985	+14.83
In central cities	21,424	25,937	28,973	+21.07	+11.71	28,554	28,638	+0.74
Outside central cities	18,631	24,588	29,789	+31.97	+21.15	29,016	32,347	+28.70

SOURCE: Committee for Economic Development, *An Approach to Federal Urban Policy* (New York, 1977), p. 40, based upon U.S. Department of Commerce data.

the end of World War II, the migration increased again, in response to new political and economic forces. The mechanization of farms in the South made the subsistence living of the black sharecropper, tenant, or wage-earning field hand difficult. In the decade 1945–1955, the political freedom and equality of the North loomed relatively large in comparison. More jobs were available in the North. And, if there were no jobs, the welfare benefits were much more liberal.

The end product is one of the great internal migrations of all time in any country. In 1940, 77 per cent of all American black people lived in the South. By 1975, almost 60 per cent lived in metropolitan area central cities. Close to 4 million black persons migrated to a different section of the country and from a rural to an urban existence, a transition equal to the arrival of the white immigrants from Europe in the nineteenth and twentieth centuries. Figure 2-2 shows how these trends operated and how, at the same time, whites migrated out to the suburbs. Despite population pressure and federal open housing legislation, the racial integration of the suburbs had not occurred. Between 1960 and 1974, the proportion of the total suburban population that

FIGURE 2–2.   Population Changes in Metropolitan Areas, by Race: 1950–1975. SOURCE: Department of Commerce, Bureau of the Census, *1977 Statistical Yearbook.*

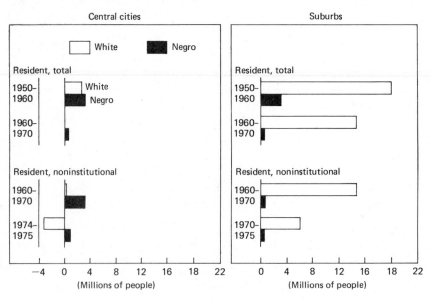

was black remained unchanged at 5 per cent, although there was an increase in absolute numbers.[17]

Earlier migrants to America's cities had received hostile welcomes. The Irish of the Civil War era encountered heavy discrimination. They were stereotyped as hopeless, violent drunks, capable only of manual labor, and prone to desert their families and form street gangs. The Irish led the 1863 New York City draft riots against blacks, and they exploded for reasons still germane to understanding the frustrations of new city dwellers:

> All the frustrations and prejudices the Irish had suffered were brought to a boiling point. . . . At pitiful wages, they had slaved on the railroads and canals, had been herded into the most menial jobs as carters and stevedores. . . . Their crumbling frame tenements . . . were the worst slums in the city.[18]

Other groups had similar troubles winning acceptance. Italian immigrants were stereotyped as stupid, clannish, often criminal, and fit only to labor with pick and shovel. Jews were viewed as strange, untrustworthy, and greedy, and they too faced widespread discrimination.

All of these unpleasant experiences were repeated for the black migrants. A hostile stereotype portrayed blacks as lazy, shiftless, anxious to live on welfare, and prone to high illegitimacy and family breakdown. Discrimination extended into housing, schools, legal and civil rights, and employment. A rule from the 1940s to today is that black unemployment will be double the white rate, and that ghetto unemployment for black teen-agers will reach 30 to 40 per cent.

Black urban frustrations came to a boil in the mid-1960s. Summer riots began in black ghettos in 1963 in Manhattan, extended to Watts in Los Angeles in 1965, and reached a peak in 1967. In the 1967 peak year, there were 164 civil disorders in cities of all regions of the country. The worst were in Newark, Detroit, and Cincinnati. In Detroit, 43 people died and property destruction reached $45 million.[19]

The late black civil rights leader Dr. Martin Luther King called riots "the language of the unheard."[20] The President's Commission on Civil Disorders interviewed more than 1,200 riot area residents and

---

[17] U.S. Bureau of the Census, *Special Report: Social and Economic Characteristics of the Metropolitan and Nonmetropolitan Population, 1970 and 1974* (1977), p. 4.

[18] *National Advisory Commission on Civil Disorders*, op. cit., p. 212.

[19] Ibid., Chapters 1 and 2.

[20] *Where Do We Go From Here: Chaos or Community* (New York: Harper & Row, 1967), p. 112.

found a long set of grievances, with police practices, first; unemployment, second; and poor housing, third. Although many of the conditions have not improved, the riots stopped as inexplicably as they began. Why did they occur during the 1960s when government at the federal level was most sympathetic to black urban aspirations? Why do they not recur when for many people conditions are still very poor? Social science does not know the answers to these questions about urban dynamics.

Blacks are not the only minorities in the cities. There are now almost 11 million Spanish-speaking persons living in the United States, more than 80 per cent of whom live in metropolitan areas. Although 40 per cent of all Hispanics live in suburbs and not in central cities, most of the suburbanites are in the Southwest, where suburbs are often poorer areas. The large Spanish-speaking minorities meet the same problems of discrimination as blacks and great difficulty in obtaining political recognition.

THE ECONOMIC PICTURE

When people move, jobs move. The move outward from the central cities contained a strong economic motivation, as factories sought cheaper land and advantageous property tax rates. As early as the 1920s, real estate developers completely incorporated suburban municipalities and designed "industrial parks." Trucks liberated commerce from the fixed grid of rivers and railroad, and the airplane allowed further freedom to choose commercial locations. When people moved for residential purposes and industry moved for economic reasons, retail trade became profitable in suburban locations. Shopping centers proliferated over the suburban landscape.

Between 1960 and 1970, 60 per cent of all new construction took place in the suburbs. In the largest SMSA's, despite some downtown skyscraper building booms and federal urban renewal, 90 per cent of all new construction was in the suburbs. Table 2-4 shows how retail trade declined in the central cities between 1958 and 1972. Even in cities such as Kansas City, Atlanta, Houston, and San Diego, where there was growth in the older city, the growth rate of retail sales in the suburbs was greater. And for the older cities, Newark, Providence, Cleveland, there was an absolute loss of retail trade downtown and huge surges in the suburbs.

The bottom line in economic development is jobs. Table 2-4 indicates how employment in central cities has chronically declined. The "net shift" figures on the far right camouflage some of what has taken place. The big losses are in manufacturing and in retail and wholesale trade. Increases in services and especially in local government em-

TABLE 2-4. Changes in Employment in Selected Central Cities, by Major Employment Sector, 1958 to 1972 (in thousands)

| City | Major Employment Sector | | | | | Total Job Losses | Total Job Gains | Net Employment Shift | Total Employment 1972 | Net Shift as Per Cent of 1958 Employment |
	Manufacturing	Retail Trade	Wholesale Trade	Selected Services	Local Government					
Baltimore	-20.5	-16.1	-2.1	5.6	13.0	-38.7	18.6	-20.1	260.4	-7.7
Boston	-27.2	-14.6	-9.1	19.9	4.0	-50.9	23.9	-27.0	244.3	-11.1
Buffalo	-17.6	-10.3	-4.9	4.1	3.2	-32.8	7.3	-25.5	149.7	-17.0
Chicago	-104.3	-32.0	-31.1	32.9	7.8	-167.4	40.7	-126.7	1,053.5	-12.0
Cincinnati	-8.1	-6.9	-1.0	31.3	5.4	-16.0	36.7	20.7	160.9	12.9
Cleveland	-43.6	-20.5	-10.5	5.9	-1.0	-75.6	5.9	-69.7	319.0	-21.8
Detroit	-24.0	-31.1	-12.1	0.6	0.6	-67.8	1.2	-66.6	421.5	-15.8
Jersey City	-9.6	-0.7	-0.6	1.5	-1.8	-12.7	1.5	-11.2	62.7	-17.9
Kansas City	4.2	00.4	-3.1	12.7	0.9	-3.5	17.8	14.3	140.1	10.2
Los Angeles	-7.3	22.7	-1.7	57.5	8.2	-9.0	88.4	79.4	625.3	12.7
Louisville	4.5	-1.5	0.6	4.0	0.4	-1.5	9.5	8.0	110.6	7.2
Milwaukee	-17.0	-5.6	-6.5	8.1	5.0	-29.1	13.1	-16.0	219.9	-7.3
Minneapolis	-0.5	-4.6	-4.8	9.2	0.4	-9.9	9.6	-0.3	143.3	-0.2
Newark	-13.3	-12.1	-5.6	1.2	1.8	-49.0	3.0	-46.0	151.6	-30.3
New Orleans	-0.5	-3.9	-2.4	10.2	1.9	-6.8	12.1	5.3	115.5	4.6
New York	-138.5	-31.4	-42.1	72.9	126.7	-212.0	199.6	-12.4	2,164.8	-0.6
Oakland	-7.9	-4.5	-0.9	5.6	0.8	-13.3	6.4	-6.9	83.1	-8.3
Philadelphia	-84.0	-16.4	-13.8	16.3	6.0	-114.2	22.3	-91.9	541.4	-17.0
Pittsburgh	-2.3	-12.1	-9.7	6.0	-0.4	-24.5	6.0	-18.5	166.8	-11.1
Providence	-9.9	-5.8	-1.1	1.7	-0.4	-17.2	1.7	-15.5	80.6	-19.2
Rochester	-3.6	-4.0	-0.6	3.0	2.4	-8.2	5.4	-2.8	143.5	-2.0
St. Louis	-38.6	-22.6	-11.1	5.1	1.1	-72.3	6.2	-66.1	273.3	-24.2
St. Paul	9.4	-1.6	-0.8	5.5	-1.7	-4.1	14.9	10.8	83.8	12.4
San Francisco	-11.9	0.7	-11.6	21.5	5.4	-23.5	27.6	4.1	197.4	2.1
Washington, D.C.	-1.4	-9.1	-4.7	20.4	25.2	-15.2	45.6	30.4	158.6	19.2

SOURCE: Committee for Economic Development, *An Approach to Federal Urban Policy* (New York, 1977), p. 38, from U.S. Department of Commerce data.

FIGURE 2–3. Clayton, Missouri: A Suburb That Has Many High-Rise Office Buildings. SOURCE: Courtesy of the Clayton, Missouri, Chamber of Commerce.

ployment have picked up some losses. Without local government in its role as employer, the economic plight of central cities would be even worse than it is.

The present economic arrangements create vested stakes in their own continuance. Most studies predict increased suburbanization of economic activity.[21] But the costs of doing business in central cities are now declining relative to what are growing costs in suburbs. One researcher finds evidence that central cities finally possess advantages over suburbs and actually stand on the brink of a resurgence.[22] By the beginning of the 1980s central city job creation showed signs of a

[21] See John D. Kasarda, "The Changing Occupational Structure of the American Metropolis: Apropos the Urban Problem," in *The Changing Face of the Suburbs*, ed. by Barry Schwartz (Chicago: University of Chicago Press, 1976), p. 131.

[22] T. D. Allman, "The Urban Crisis Leaves Town," *Harper's*, 257 (December 1978) pp. 41–56.

come-back, narrowing the gap between central city job growth and suburban job growth. In Chapter 10, we will consider these processes of urban economic development again and whether, in a value sense, public policy should aim to influence what happens.

CENTRAL CITIES AND SUBURBS: A SUMMARY OF THEIR DIFFERENCES

The prior sections of this chapter outlined historical trends leading to central city decline and suburban growth and detailed population and economic changes. Summary data based upon the census shows the following economic differences: suburbs have a higher percentage of white-collar workers, higher median income, more families with incomes of more than $25,000, and fewer persons under the poverty level.

As for social difference, suburbs show higher educational attainment, more physical mobility in living arrangements, fewer minorities, and a higher fertility rate in the suburbs. On the other hand, in median school year completed, families with children under six years old, and women in the labor force, differences between central cities and suburbs are slight.

These broad patterns of central city/suburban economic and social differences are not found uniformly in all SMSA's in the United States. The differences are greatest in the oldest and largest SMSA's with the most suburbs. The differences are least in the newer, smaller SMSA's in the South and Southwest. The northeastern patterns are actually reversed. The central cities are more affluent and the suburbs contain more poverty in the rapidly growing Sunbelt region.[23]

A BROAD-GAUGE ANALYSIS OF CENTRAL CITY AND SUBURBAN CHARACTERISTICS BY TYPE OF METROPOLITAN AREAS

The lack of universal application of generalizations about central cities and suburbs bedevils social scientists, planners, and policy makers. The Advisory Commission on Intergovernmental Relations, a federal agency that publishes frequent studies on metropolitan problems, has attempted to determine what is true for all metropolitan areas and what is true for only some of them.[24] The results of this effort comprise Table 2-5.

---

[23] For a collection of analyses of distinctive qualities of communities in the Southwest, see *The Rise of the Sunbelt Cities*, David C. Perry and Alfred J. Watkins, eds. (Beverly Hills, Cal.: Sage Publications, 1977).

[24] *Metropolitan Social and Economic Disparities: Implications for Intergovernmental Relations in Central Cities and Suburbs* (Washington: 1965).

TABLE 2-5. Similarities and Differences in Central City and Suburban Social and Economic Characteristics

Central City % Greater	Central City/ Suburb the Same	Suburb % Higher
1. In SMSAs in general, all regions and sizes:		
Elderly		Young children
Unrelated individuals	Age 10–44	
Broken families		Migrants
Clerical & sales workers	Nonwhite craftsmen	Families with children
Household & service workers		Craftsmen
Working wives		Upper-middle rentals
Unemployed		
Nonwhite movers		
Nonwhites		Commuters
		Highest nonwhite
		Housing values (except South)
2. In addition, in large SMSAs in all regions:		
Nonwhite clerical & sales		Upper-middle nonwhite housing values
Low-income unsound rentals		Highest rents
3. And in the North as well as large SMSAs:		
Nonwhites		Managers
Young nonwhite children		Highest housing values
Middle-age people		
Movers		
Undereducated		
Operatives		
Low rents		
4. But in the large and Northeast SMSAs:		
		College graduates
		Professional & technical workers
		Income over $8,000
5. In the North without respect to size:		
Nonwhites under age 10	Working mothers	Nonwhite professional & technical workers
Nonwhite families with children		
Nonwhite undereducated		
School dropouts		Nonwhite managers
Laborers		
Nonwhite operatives		
6. And in the Northeast, without respect to size:		
Operatives	Nonwhite middle income	Middle-aged and elderly
Nonwhite low income	Unsound owner-occupied housing	Blacks
Nonwhite unemployment		Nonwhite Unrelated individuals

TABLE 2-5. (Cont.)

Central City % Greater	Central City/ Suburb the Same	Suburb % Higher
		Nonwhite college graduates Upper-middle housing values Highest nonwhite rents

7. *But in the South and West, without respect to size:*

Central City % Greater	Central City/ Suburb the Same	Suburb % Higher
Middle-age & elderly nonwhites	Nonwhite professional & technical	Young nonwhite children
College graduates	Nonwhite managers	
Professional & technical	Nonwhite operatives Nonwhite unemployment	Nonwhite families with children
Managers		
Income over $8000	Upper-middle housing values	
Nonwhite middle income		Undereducated
Nonwhite middle housing values	Lower-middle rents	School dropouts
		Nonwhite low income
		Middle income
		Working mothers
		Unsound owner-occupied housing
		Lowest nonwhite rents

8. *In small SMSAs all regions:*

Central City % Greater	Central City/ Suburb the Same	Suburb % Higher
College graduates	Movers	Undereducated operatives
Professional & technical workers	Nonwhite clerical & sales	Middle-income unsound rentals
Managers		
Household & service workers	Unemployed	
Income over $8000	Highest rents	
Highest housing values		
Upper-middle nonwhite housing values		

9. *SMSAs with dispersed population in all regions and sizes also have:*

Central City % Greater	Central City/ Suburb the Same	Suburb % Higher
Upper-middle nonwhite rentals		Age 30–44

10. *In dispersed as well as large SMSAs:*
Low income

11. *In dispersed SMSAs as well as large and Northern:*

Central City % Greater	Central City/ Suburb the Same	Suburb % Higher
Nonwhite		Managers

12. *In dispersed SMSAs, as well as large and northeastern:*

Central City % Greater	Central City/ Suburb the Same	Suburb % Higher
		Nonwhite college graduates Professional & technical Nonwhite income over $8000

TABLE 2-5. (Cont.)

Central City % Greater	Central City/ Suburb the Same	Suburb % Higher

13. *In SMSAs which are dispersed as well as small or in the South and West:*

	Laborers	Middle-income operatives

14. *But in SMSAs with population concentrated in the central city, all regions and sizes:*

		Unsound owner-occupied housing
		Lowest housing value
		Commuters

15. *In SMSAs with a high percentage of nonwhites, irrespective of region, size, or population dispersal:*

Central City % Greater	Suburb % Higher
Nonwhite age 30–44	Families with children
Nonwhite movers	
Broken families with children	Craftsmen
Household & service workers	Migrants
Unemployed	

16. *And in SMSAs with a high percentage of nonwhites as well as large SMSAs all regions:*

Central City % Greater	Suburb % Higher
Low income	Highest rents

17. *In SMSAs with a high percentage of nonwhite as well as large and northeastern:*

Central City % Greater	Suburb % Higher
Nonwhite low-middle rents	Upper-middle income

18. *In SMSAs with a high percentage of nonwhite as well as in the Northeast, all sizes:*

Central City/ Suburb the Same	Suburb % Higher
Clerical & sales workers	Upper-middle housing values

19. *In SMSAs with a high percentage of nonwhite and concentrated population, all sizes and regions:*

Suburb % Higher
Commuters

20. *In small concentrated SMSAs with a low percentage of nonwhite:*

Central City/ Suburb the Same
Low income

SOURCE: Advisory Commission in Intergovernmental Relations, *Metropolitan Social and Economic Disparities: Implications for Intergovernmental Relations in Central Cities and Suburbs* (Washington, D.C.: U.S. Government Printing Office, 1965), pp. 200–206.

The commission considered all the SMSA's together and also divided them into types on the basis of region, size, the dispersal of the population, or racial composition. Within each type, the commission indicates how 15 variables are arranged. On some, the percentage of a particular variable is greater in the central city. For other variables, the percentage is greater in the suburbs. And in still other situations, the central cities and suburbs are similar. The 15 variables are as follows:

Race
Age
Movers
Migrants
Families with children under 18
Unrelated individuals
Education
Occupation
Married women in the labor force
Family income
Unemployment
Housing condition (owner- and renter-occupied)
Value of owner-occupied housing
Gross rent of renter-occupied housing
Commuters

The 20 numbered propositions in Table 2-5 constitute a successively modified and refined listing of characteristics by types of metropolitan areas. The list begins with the broadest generalizations possible for all metropolitan areas. Then it narrows and is successively modified to cover specific situations and differences.

Scanning Table 2-5 indicates that the most significant propositions in terms of differentiating between central cities and suburbs are Numbers 1 through 8. What is especially interesting, as Numbers 7 and 8 show, is that the patterns of the large SMSA's and the northeastern SMSA's are reversed in the newer cities of the South and West, and also to some degree in the smaller SMSA's. In these latter instances, the cities have the younger, more affluent, and white populations, and the suburbs contain greater poverty and more nonwhite people. Thus, although we can talk about broad patterns of development, we also have to look at regional culture, at the effects of more recent settlement, and at purely local characteristics.

Finally, small-scale changes do not show up in these broad data. For example, national media report that in some older cities, upper-middle-class families are buying up slum houses and restoring them to former elegance as their own dwellings. This process, labeled "gentrification," occurs in a small number of cities in media centers—New York, Baltimore, Boston, Washington, D.C. There are no data on the numbers involved, or whether "gentrification" will become a nationwide phenomena, suddenly bringing affluent persons back to the old cities and pushing the poor out.

SUMMARY AND CONCLUSIONS

This chapter has discussed a diverse range of materials, and a summary of the main points may be helpful. From the historical section of the chapter, we conclude about metropolitan development:

1. Changes are continuous, because of new technologies that eventually have enormous impact. From the introduction of the automobile to the triumph of the automotive city was a 50-year process. At the same time, the change in the population and social structure of cities takes on, with the perspective of time, a remorseless aspect that suggests the future will not only resemble the immediate past, but any alterations of patterns already set will be very hard to achieve.
2. Factors *other than* local political choices seem to set the pattern of the most important trends. The forces of technology, war, internal migration, a changing national economy in expansion and depression, a nation with an enlarging world role, and a centralizing private and public national sector are *not* within the decision-making realm of local politics or local elites.
3. Where local politics seem to have an effect is in the development that comes from boosterism and helps particular cities forge ahead, and also in the virtually nationwide acceptance going back to the post-Civil War era that allows suburbs to develop autonomously.

From the detailed social and economic profile of contemporary metropolitan America, we conclude:

1. In terms of population settlement patterns, suburbanization is the most stunning and significant feature of the present scene.
2. Racial patterns of settlement are sharply differentiated. The largest internal migration in American history of black people from southern farms to northern cities has left the larger central cities increasingly black as whites moved to suburbs. The suburbs have so far largely maintained white racial autonomy.
3. In terms of the wealth of the citizens, the central cities have more poor people and the suburbs have more affluent people living in them, although there are variations. In the southern and southwestern SMSA's, this pattern does not hold.
4. It is possible to draw many distinctions among types of SMSA's in terms of the characteristics of their central cities

and suburbs, as Table 2-5 shows. The basic distinction appears to be between the northern, northeastern, and larger SMSA's and the southern, western, and smaller SMSA's. In the first set of metropolitan areas, the image of poorer, central cities with more aged and black persons and suburbs with more affluent whites is a correct one. In the latter set of metropolitan areas, the first image is reversed and we find more whites and more affluence in the central cities and more poverty and more nonwhites in the suburbs.

In Chapter 3, we turn to more political concerns and examine how power is distributed among national, state, and local levels of government.

3
LOCAL COMMUNITIES
AS POLITICAL SUBSYSTEMS

All governments in the world are subsystems. There is an international political system, and even powerful national governments are subsystems within that global network. Further, national governments must cope with an essentially international economic system. However, national governments in the more industrially advanced sector of the world, Communist and non-Communist alike, possess sufficient autonomy over their internal life that we could analyze them as systems in themselves. Such is not the case for American local governments. They must be seen as subsystems within larger units.

What we are talking about is commonly called federalism or intergovernmental relations. We consider two sets of such linkages in this chapter: state-local relations and federal-local relations. In Chapter 7, we analyze the relationships among municipalities within metropolitan areas.

LOCAL COMMUNITIES AS SUBSYSTEMS IN THE STATES

A good way to begin analyzing intergovernmental politics is to examine local communities as subsystems within state political systems. The constitutional-legal status of local communities is inferior to that of the federal and state government. The Constitution of the United States rests on a grant of power from the people, and federal supremacy is established in Article VI, Section II, and accepted judicial interpretation. Still, the Constitution was created out of a loose (and politically unsuccessful) confederation of semisovereign state governments. As a result, the states retain a variety of constitutional guarantees. The most basic guarantees are territorial integrity and their own governmental systems. Further, whatever the federal government is not able to do by acting within its granted authority is reserved to the states. In addition, in the absence of federal action the states can act in many domestic policy realms *until* the federal government develops an interest.

In contrast, local governments start from a markedly different position. They are, in constitutional-legal terms, municipal corporations. They owe their existence to charters issued them by state governments. This constitutional status dates from Roman colonial practice.[1] Lockard notes that:

> To manage its empire Rome made the cities that it took under its control municipal corporations and allowed them certain powers of local self-management. The fall of Rome almost extinguished urban life, and with it the legalistic niceties that had characterized Roman municipal law.[2]

In British practice, from which American practice is derived directly, until the fifteenth century, localities had whatever powers they could buy, bargain for, or get away with in their dealings with the crown. By the fifteenth century, there were charters that made municipalities recognizable corporations, with precisely designated procedures and powers granted by a central authority. The practice carried over into the American colonies. Some early charters were for "close" corporations. The governments of such cities were run as privately held commercial corporations under the complete control of a self-perpetuating group of owner-individuals. There were no public rights of participation in city affairs. New York began with such a charter, and Philadelphia operated under one from 1701 to 1706. Gradually, however, charters were democratized to permit citizen election of officials.

After the Revolution, various changes occurred in American municipal governments and, most noticeably, the separation of powers so that mayors emerged as rivals in authority with the previously all-powerful city councils. But the legal format remained unchanged. The cities were legal creations of what were by then the state governments

---

[1] See Duane Lockard, *The Politics of State and Local Government* (New York: Macmillan, 1969), p. 106.

[2] Ibid., p. 106.

(formerly the colonial governments). The state legislatures controlled the details of the city charters and held a close rein over what cities could or could not do. Rural-dominated, they were, for example, unwilling to make broad grants of authority to the cities in advance of particular needs. Richard C. Wade discovered that in Cincinnati the charter had to be changed in major ways five times between 1815 and 1827, with the consent of the legislature necessary each time.[3]

Today's situation derives directly from these historical antecedents. Cities are all municipal corporations whose boundaries, powers and functions, structure of government, methods of taxation and expenditure, and systems of choosing officials and employees are set forth in charters granted to them by state governments. Yet, we can imagine a situation in which localities would be independent once the original charter was issued. Suppose the charter was a broad grant of authority in generalized language. Could the municipality then do largely whatever it wanted?

Such, however, is not the case in common American practice. The fundamental legal rule in judicial interpretation of municipal charters is that whatever is not expressly granted is therefore, by its absence from the detailed grant, assumed to be prohibited. This narrow and restrictive interpretation developed by the end of the nineteenth century, partly in response to generalized distrust of cities and partly as a result of the abuses and corruption of the urban machines of the day. The classic statement of this limitation of municipal autonomy was delivered by an Iowa state judge, John F. Dillon, and is known as "Dillon's Rule":

> It is a general and undisputed proposition of law that a municipal corporation possesses and can exercise the following powers, and no others: first, those granted in express words; second, those necessarily or fairly implied in or incident to the powers expressly granted; third, those essential to the accomplishment of the declared objects and purposes of the corporation—not simply convenient, but indispensable. Any fair, reasonable, substantial doubt concerning the existence of power is resolved by courts *against a corporation, and the power is denied.*[4]

The consequences of Dillon's Rule are quite striking. In a classic text, Edward C. Banfield and James Q. Wilson observed, "This means

[3] *The Urban Frontier: The Rise of Western Cities, 1790–1830* (Cambridge, Mass.: Harvard University Press, 1959).

[4] *Commentaries on the Laws of Municipal Corporations,* 5th ed. (Boston, 1911), p. 448. Italics added.

that a city cannot operate a peanut stand at the city zoo without first getting the state legislature to pass an enabling law, unless, per chance, the city's charter or some previously enacted law unmistakably covers the sale of peanuts."[5] One visible result is that every city charter is lengthy and detailed. Everything the city is allowed to do or might want to do must be listed explicitly. New York City's charter, for example, is several hundred pages in length.

TYPES OF CHARTERS

There are three types of charters: the special act charter, the general act charter, and the home rule charter.

The Special Act Charter. The special act charter gives the state legislature the greatest amount of potential control. Under this system, each city gets its charter by name and requires specific legislative approval for any change in its governmental structure or programs. Special act charters bring the legislature deeply into the details of local affairs, as, for example, when the Massachusetts legislature decreed that "Fall River be authorized to appropriate money for the puchase of uniforms for the park police and watershed guards of said city."[6] At an early point in its history, the California legislature enjoyed requiring localities to erect municipal buildings at specific costs at specific sites, becoming, through the process, the local contracting and planning authority. At the end of the nineteenth century, an era of corruption in American life, in many states, the state legislators accepted bribes to allow streetcar franchisers to operate in particular cities (often different claimants from those who had bribed the city councilmen). At the peak of manipulating local government through special act charters, state legislatures spent an extraordinary proportion of their time on local matters. As many as half or two thirds of the bills passed in a session would be local special legislation.[7]

The General Act Charter. As part of the municipal reform movement that began in the United States in the 1880s, described in detail in Chapter Five, a reaction set in against special act charters. Some states constitutionally prohibited them outright, and others developed alternatives for chartering municipalities. One alternative was the general act charter. Under this system, cities are classified according to size, and the state legislature sets regulations for all cities falling into a particular size classification. A common set of

---

[5] *City Politics* (New York: Vintage Books, 1963), p. 65.
[6] Ibid., p. 66.
[7] Lockard, op. cit., p. 117.

classifications of cities under general act charters is less than 10,000 people; from 10,000 to 25,000 people; from 25,000 to 50,000; and on up the size scale. There are limitations on the insulation that general act charters can provide municipalities. Because the problems of cities of the same size are different—for example, sea ports may have different needs than resort communities—municipalities still go to the legislature for special authorizations.

More important, general act charters do not restrain state legislative activity where there is an interest in exercising such power. What about when a general act applies to only one case, where a state has only one city of a certain size? Then what appears to be a general law is really a special act that gives the legislature authority over individual cities. For example, Philadelphia, Pittsburgh, and Indianapolis are single-city classifications in their states.

Another system, a variation of general act charters, allows communities to choose from several optional charter plans. The state legislature sets general regulations for different structures of local government. Then, communities can pick whether they prefer a strong mayor–weak council or weak mayor–strong council, commission, or city manager structure. There are general rules that apply to all communities opting for each of the alternative plans. In Massachusetts, there are 5 alternative plans, and in New Jersey, 14.

The Home Rule Charter. The major thrust to enhance the position of local communities *vis-à-vis* state power has been to win what are called home rule charters. Home rule charters allow municipalities to adopt forms of government and to provide services as they choose, without reference to state government, on all local as opposed to state questions.

The philosophical intent of home rule theory is to turn Dillon's Rule on its head. Under home rule, a city is permitted to do anything that the legislature has not specifically *prohibited* it from doing. Home rule charters have a checkered history. An initial problem is how is home rule to be granted? Do municipalities have the right under state constitutions to obtain home rule charters upon asking and upon meeting standard conditions? Or is the granting of home rule charter done by special act of the legislature, city by city? In the latter case, what the legislature gives, it can always take away.

Problems also arise from the ambiguity of charter language. Litigation results from such phrases (common to home rule charters) as "all laws and ordinances relating to municipal concerns" (Michigan), "all powers of local self-government" (Ohio), and "in respect to municipal affairs" (California). Duane Lockard, noting that home rule charters involve an effort to distinguish between the general powers of the state and municipal concerns, pinpoints the problems.

> What does a court do when it faces a dispute about local control of traffic on a state highway which runs through the middle of a city? Is that a local matter because the street is in the city, or a state matter because it concerns a state highway? Are the working hours and conditions of local employees entirely a matter of "municipal affairs" or does the state's power over labor and public employment supersede the powers of the city?[8]

About half the states provide for home rule in their constitutions and another dozen allow home rule charters by statutory enactment of the legislature. In all, almost two thirds of cities with more than 200,000 population have some variety of home rule charter. In practice, home rule charters rarely fulfill the hopes of those who sought them. Legislatures carve out pieces of what was thought to be a municipal decision-making domain simply by declaring a particular subject a statewide concern. That declaration supersedes a municipal ordinance, even when a locality previously operated unimpeded. Wherever there is any doubt, the issue is resolved in the state courts. And the courts have continued to apply Dillon's Rule against municipalities, by and large, despite home rule charters.

As a result, city attorneys, advising the mayor, the manager, or the city council, take a conservative position and advise that any new departure be cleared with the state legislature. Otherwise, there could be taxpayer lawsuits claiming an action was illegal. Even if the lawsuits fail, the desired action can be delayed for a long time. Knowing that state courts may be on their side encourages individual taxpayers and groups who have lost a policy conflict to litigate whenever the city government does not have state legislative authorization. This means that local governments must work through state politics to achieve their goals.

LOCAL GOVERNMENTS IN STATE POLITICS

What types of situations require local governments to obtain approval from state governments? The following are typical examples:

1. A city borrows money up to the limit allowed by its charter (expressed as a percentage of assessed valuation). Each new bond issue then requires specific authorization, a special act of legislature, signed by the governor.

[8] Ibid., p. 122.

2. The city wants a new source of revenue not mentioned in its charter, such as a commuter tax (a payroll tax to be paid by all who work in the community, whether they live there or not). To be sure that the action of the city council in passing such an ordinance is not ruled unconstitutional under the state constitution (and surely some outraged suburbanite would institute such a lawsuit), the city must go to the state legislature for a special act, signed by the governor.

3. A city wants to allocate its police force patrols differently, using more men during the high crime, nighttime hours and fewer in the mornings. The policeman's union maintains such action is not specifically authorized in the charter and threatens a court suit. The municipal government goes to the state legislature for a special act, signed by the governor.

4. A suburb wants to change its building code to permit a new form of construction in a new subdivision. Other owners and developers in the community fear that the new construction will hurt their investments and maintain that such changes are not specifically authorized in the charter. The city manager goes to the statehouse for a special act.

5. A suburb wants to change the structure of its government, altering the arrangement of various boards, especially those dealing with zoning, parks, and health. Yet, the arrangements for these boards—number and qualifications of members, terms of office, methods of selection, legal definition of duties and powers—are part of the original charter. Once again, off to the statehouse for the authorization.

These examples could be multiplied tenfold. Yet they deal with only one case: when a locality wants to be sure it can legally enact a program of its own. There is another case that sends localities to the statehouse with equal regularity. Because state aid provides (through various sorts of transfer payments) almost 20 per cent of municipal budgets, localities are vitally interested in what happens on *state* programs. To protect those interests, they must be involved in state politics.

What state programs require the political attention of municipal governments? The following are a few examples:

1. The legislature is considering altering the "foundation" program, the formula under which it determines what percentage of local education costs it will pay; it is also considering what, if any, conditions (structure of schools, curriculum, perfor-

mance, or pupil attendance) it should set or alter in the foundation program. Depending on its decision, big city, suburban, or rural school districts gain, or lose, disproportionately.

2. The governor is thinking about changing the state higher education system, specifically by building extensions of the prestigious and expensive state university in three urban centers. The existing main campus—in a rural region of the state—feels threatened and lobbies against the change.

3. As administrator of the federal highway program and selector of the routes, the state government is planning an urban connector highway through residential sections of a large city; the road will also affect suburbs in its path by heightening development and reducing commuter time. Both opposition and support develop locally.

4. Many rules of the federal welfare program are set at the state level, including the size of payments. The state government is considering reducing payments to aid to dependent children, a major source of income for the urban ghetto poor.

5. The state has a Department of Community Affairs, a state-level version of the federal Department of Housing and Urban Affairs (HUD). The main responsibilities of the Department of Community Affairs are housing and community organization. There is a drive by rural and suburban legislators to cut its budget as an economy move.

CITY LOBBYING

In seeking special acts from the state legislature authorizing some activity, localities follow several techniques. The first move is to contact members of the state legislature whose districts lie within the locality and ask for their support. On most routine local matters that come before the state legislature a kind of legislative courtesy known as "logrolling" prevails. That means, bluntly, that each state representative and senator understands that if someone supports local legislation she sponsors, she will, in turn, support the other person's bills. Thus, if the legislators from a community are willing to back a bill, it passes until it has wider implications or in some way engages the concern of more powerful state politicians—legislative party leaders, committee chairmen, or the governor.

Turning to the home community's state legislators as a first course has an obvious consequence: these individuals become a powerful part of the local political structure. They expect to be consulted about the content of bills and about other local matters, including city patronage. The process works in the other direction as well. State politicians, including the governor and other party leaders, utilize home-based legislators to carry out *their* concerns, from the shape of a city's tax program to jobs. The largest cities sometimes maintain lobbyists full time. The lobbyist is a liaison with state officials as well as with the local delegation.

The largest cities watch state politics on a continuing basis, because they have had the most difficult time in the state area. Controlled until the 1960s by rural majorities, state legislatures are often hostile to the largest central cities. Today, the rural majorities are gone, but replaced by large suburban delegations of equally suspicious mien. Reflecting these underlying cleavages are party splits, because the largest cities are almost always Democratic, but the governorships are often held by Republicans. To further complicate matters, often intense personal rivalries exist between well-known governors and equally prominent urban mayors. In this milieu, all the largest cities know how determined state officials can limit autonomy (and what can be done to a large city can also be done to a smaller suburb). As just one example, the Missouri legislature decades ago gave the power to appoint the powerful police commissioner of the city of St. Louis to the governor of Missouri.

Municipalities have political resources in any struggle against state officials, including the public appeal to local pride against state "dictation." State politicians must run for office in local communities at some point. These are powerful incentives for state officials, especially at the legislative level, to bargain and cooperate with local leaders. Nonetheless, the basic legal position of the individual municipality is weak. Much time for every city and suburb go toward the yearly or biennial state legislative session.

WORKING IN COALITIONS

On issues that affect many localities, banding together in formal and informal confederations for a big city program or a suburban program is a smart way to do political business. The advantage is strength in numbers. The disadvantage is that, unless there is an absolute identity of interests, the price of harmony is a lowest common denominator position acceptable to all in the group. The usual means is a statewide association of chief municipal officers (mayors and managers), or municipal finance officers (budget directors), or school superintendents, or police chiefs. Organization of functional area allows for specialized lobbying. Sometimes big city mayors organize separately (in states such as New York where there are the "Big Eight" cities); rural and suburban interests often operate through associations of county officials in the state.

What issues are important? First, certain structural questions are always of concern. These include ease or severity of incorporation provisions (under which new suburbs can be formed) as well as the terms of granting and interpreting local charters. Policy in these areas, once set, remains set for relatively long periods of time. Second, some issues are of annual concern because they involve continuing questions of state aid or state rules on federal programs affecting local residents. The category includes public school policy, highway and road policy, and welfare rules. Third, both general and particular questions of municipal finance come before the state legislature. Such issues include authorization for total bonding authority (the dollar amount of debt municipalities can incur), for specific borrowing projects, as well as for new forms of local taxes or changes in local tax rates. Finally, regulatory problems with local application periodically come before state authorities. In this category are problems ranging from granting cable television licenses to setting closing hours in bars and nightclubs to determining whether merchants can stay open on Sundays.

Municipalities exist within state boundaries, but also within the national system. An analysis of this subsystem arrangement follows.

CITIES IN THE FEDERAL SYSTEM: THE BEGINNING OF A RELATIONSHIP

In American political thinking, federalism meant two tiers of government: the national government and the state governments. The cities had no standing in federal constitutional law. In federal practice there was no relationship between the national government and city governments. Local governments were supposed to be self-supporting, maintaining their services from local revenues. When problems were beyond their ability to cope, they were expected to work with their state governments. To the degree that municipalities wanted to communicate with the federal government, they were expected to do so through the state governments.

The Depression of the 1930s changed that pattern. Roscoe C. Martin has noted that "the year 1932 constitutes a sort of geologic fault line in the development of the federal system."[9] As late as 1932, federal grants-in-aid, money for city programs that went directly to cities, to-

[9] *The Cities and the Federal System* (New York: Atherton Press, 1965), p. 111. See also Robert H. Connery and Richard H. Leach, *The Federal Government and Metropolitan Areas* (Cambridge, Mass.: Harvard University Press, 1960).

taled no more than $10 million. And that $10 million went almost exclusively to the District of Columbia, then administered almost entirely by the federal government. From that point onward, the cities played a continually increasing and open role in the practice of federalism, becoming, in essence, the third tier of the federal system. Over the 31 years from 1932 to 1963, direct federal payments to local governments rose from $10 million to $941 million. Federal aid to state governments was rising during the same period, but the federal-city growth rate in aid was much more rapid. Over this period, direct federal payments to localities multiplied 94 times, three times as much as the growth in federal-state payments, and seven times as fast as the growth in state aid to localities.

What was the political process that brought about so striking a departure? Suzanne Farkas observes that

> by 1932 . . . it was clear that the financial structure of the country was close to disintegration and that municipal governments were near paralysis—as little able to support themselves as were individuals and even economic giants throughout the nation. The tradition of city "self-reliance" began to fade immediately following President Roosevelt's commitment to use the spending and regulatory power of the federal government for national recovery. Like the economic interest blocs of prior decades, the cities depended for their rescue on a general federal bail-out.[10]

The Emergence of Urban Interest Representation

Faced with the Depression, the cities needed a federal bail-out. But how to get that bail-out? The standard procedure is to organize into interest groups that will lobby for your cause in the Capitol. And that is exactly what happened. There was, by 1932, already one broad-based group that had city governments as its members, the National League of Cities (then called the American Municipal Association). The NLC, however, organized on a state-by-state basis and focused on state governments. The mayors of the biggest cities with the largest political clout (in terms of voters and congressional representation) were members of the NLC only indirectly, through the state organizations. Thus, not surprisingly, in this hour of urban need, with the federal treasury the only likely donor around, a new system of urban-oriented groups emerged.

The new group was the United States Conference of Mayors

---

[10] *Urban Lobbying* (New York: New York University Press, 1971).

(USCM), which was formed in 1933. It grew out of an earlier conference, held one year before, at the call of Mayor Frank Murphy of
Detroit, who convened the mayors of the 50 largest cities to draft a
program for the federal government to share the cost of unemployment
relief with the cities. In 1933 the mayors came together again. This
time their problem was fiscal crisis brought on by the almost total
collapse of municipal credit. The mayors decided to organize themselves into a permanent lobby, with the rationale that

> a permanent organization offers the only opportunity for a con-
> tinuous inquiry into municipal questions in order that the needs
> of municipal government will be properly presented before (the)
> public and before Congress and the President.[11]

The USCM became the first city lobby. It also became a quasi-
official mechanism for encouraging cooperation and communication
among the cities as well as between city governments and federal
officials. After the formation of the USCM, the NLC began to direct
more of its attention toward Washington, and the two organizations
worked together on many programs, primarily, in the early years,
emergency relief and public works measures. The USCM represented
the largest cities, and the NLC included almost all cities, large and
small alike. USCM and NLC were different from other urban-oriented
organizations already in existence or soon to come into being, because
their concern was generalized. They wanted, more than "any other
program or set of programs. . . . : MORE MONEY. . . ."[12]

In addition, in the first third of this century, specialized urban
interests organized the National Municipal League, the International
City Managers Association, the American Association of Public Welfare Officials, the American Society of Municipal Engineers, and the
Municipal Finance Officers Association. The National Municipal
League concentrated largely on the reform of the structures of urban
governments. The other organizations tended, naturally, to be most
concerned with their particular functional area of operations—
municipal construction, welfare programs, and finance. Two other
functional groups, which were to work closely with the mayors, came
into existence. One was the National Housing Conference (NHC), established in 1931, with the goal of lobbying for public housing. Its
membership consisted of all those with a stake in public housing, as
well as those construction elements with an interest in building it.

[11] Ibid., p. 36.
[12] Ibid., p. 47.

Another organization was the National Association of Housing and Redevelopment Officials (NAHRO), a voluntary association of public officials involved in some way in the field of state and local housing. This group brings together bureaucrats from all three levels of government with a common interest in housing.

The Goals of the Urban Interest Network

Circumstances forced municipalities to turn to Washington. Organization was the medium to establish a claim on the federal purse. What were the goals as this relationship emerged? Naturally, the specific programs that were sought varied. But from the beginning, through the USCM, basic goals were set forth, most of which are germane to the urban perspective on federal policy today. At a philosophical level, the urban groups had to establish urban welfare as a genuine national policy concern. The orientation of the federal government was—and largely still is—toward functionally organized groups: labor, business, the elderly, the defense industry. Or it is oriented toward functional fields: defense, energy, health, welfare, the economy. The city interests were trying to persuade government to consider a new configuration, to force the federal government to see localities as distinct structures, more than legal subdivisions of the state governments, with their own special claims and needs.

The USCM then, as now, had a framework of goals: to obtain direct federal grants rather than loans; to have a larger rather than smaller federal contribution to all federal-city matching programs; to nationalize under federal responsibility problems such as relief and welfare; and to leave cities maximum autonomy to operate within any federal aid programs. The aim was to make cities the third partner in federalism. Based upon their experiences at the state level, municipalities sought as much home rule as they could get in their dealings with Washington. Of course, if they could not win money *plus* autonomy, they would still take the federal money.

Working Toward the Urban Goals: A Federal Urban Policy System

Any interest, including cities, could organize, formulate goals, and still fail. There must be other links in the chain before favorable policies emerge from the political system. Thus, political scientists talk about policy systems—all of the people, groups, and officials in and out of government who, together, define issues and make decisions in a particular area. A policy system includes key individuals in the bureaucracy, authorization and appropriations committees in the Congress, staff people in the White House and, sometimes, the President himself, and organized clientele and interest groups.

For the urban interest, a policy system was put together at the federal level slowly and over a long period of time, beginning in the 1930s. One aspect was the slow creation of a network of officials within the federal government, including establishing new agencies and departments. Another aspect was the development of specific programs.

The policy network evolved as the urban interest groups present at the start—USCM, NLC, NHC, and NAHRO—worked on specific programs. Their first success was a $1 million allocation to local governments as part of the National Industrial Recovery Act of 1933, almost 30 per cent of the total allocated for public works. At the same time, the urban interest groups used the mayors as lobbyists with the President, the Congress, and the Secretary of the Interior. They decided upon the use of federal highway funds within municipal limits—a new departure. In a fashion that was to become the norm, after the legislation was passed, the USCM was officially invited to share in formulating the administrative rules and regulations for the office of Federal Emergency Administration of Public Works. It also was designated liaison between the Public Works Administration and the cities, between the government and its own membership.

The early program concerns of the urban interest groups focused on recovery: public works and emergency relief. As the 1930s progressed, the focus shifted to another area that was to become *the* urban policy domain for decades: housing. Urban interests began with a concern for publicly built and operated low-income housing in particular, a goal that saw its first legislative success in the landmark Housing Act of 1937. As World War II ended and the exodus to the suburbs began, the focus shifted to removing urban "blight" and "renewing" the central cities, especially their business districts. The result was the Housing Act of 1949, which included an urban renewal program. In the mid-1960s, the urban network greatly expanded. A cabinet department of Housing and Urban Development (HUD) was created by combining housing and other agencies previously scattered within the federal government. Power in politics requires the appropriate symbolism and structures. The creation of HUD in 1965 marked the institutional parity of the urban interest network with such functional powers in American life as labor (the Labor Department), business (the Commerce Department), and the military (the Defense Department), all of whom had their departments to serve and represent them at the highest level.

In the legislative arena, the focus was broadened beyond housing. With the creation of the short-lived Office of Economic Opportunity

(OEO) in 1964, the "war on poverty" had a big-city urban orientation in its community action programs. The Demonstration Cities Act of 1966 created another short-lived program, "model cities," to consider the totality of city problems—housing, social structure, jobs, and health—in an integrated effort in selected communities. Under Republican leadership, a different type of program was instituted in the 1970s, a system of block grants called revenue sharing. Under revenue sharing, the cities are given a flat amount of money to use as they please. This approach was continued in the Community Development Act of 1974, renewed in 1978, which combines a series of former programs into lump sum grants, with local discretion as to use within some categories.

THE FEDERAL EXECUTIVE BRANCH

The contemporary urban policy network is made up of elements of the federal executive branch, the Congress, the interest group environment, other urban groups, and nonurban groups.

The President.   The president's leadership role in urban affairs hinges on party affiliation. Democratic presidents are historically heavily dependent on the big-city vote and are more responsive to big-city perspectives. Republican presidents have been sensitive to suburban and small-town interests. Democratic presidents have favored extension of the direct federal role in urban areas and have sponsored a variety of specific programs. Republican presidents have favored decentralizing programs, such as revenue sharing, which gives monies to localities to use as they like. Whatever the emphasis, however, all presidents since Franklin D. Roosevelt (1932–1945) have had an urban program.

The Vice President.   In recent presidencies the vice president has been given a coordination role with local communities. The vice presidents' impact has been slight, and there are those who say the job has been given them just to give them something to do. Nonetheless, the Office of the Vice President is seen by local officials as a place to call for a sympathetic hearing for their problems.

The Department of Housing and Urban Development (HUD). Created in 1965 with the strong support of urban interest groups (and thus a symbol in some ways of their collective national power), HUD is the repository of the major urban programs dealing with housing, including public housing, the Housing and Home Finance Agency (which provides Federal Housing Authority loans), and other operations, including urban research.

Other Cabinet Departments. Other federal cabinet departments administer programs with an important impact on local life. Health, Education, and Welfare (HEW), for example, administers the welfare program through the state governments, as well as school assistance. The Department of Transportation (DOT) is responsible for mass transit for urban areas, which includes experimental programs, construction, equipment funds, and small operating subsidies to local systems. The Department of Labor enforces federal labor standards, collects employment data, and administers many manpower programs. The Treasury Department administers the revenue sharing system and monitors whether localities spend the money they receive in accordance with federal guidelines.

Other Executive Offices. Legal Services provides free legal help to the poor in urban areas around the country and is the largest single employer of lawyers in the nation. The president's Office of Management and Budget (OMB) reviews requests for funds on behalf of the chief executive, integrates urban programs into the executive budget, and has its own specialized staff to negotiate with federal agencies and urban groups.

Commissions and Task Forces. Commissions and task forces under the executive branch serve as research centers, sounding boards, and program evaluation units for urban issues. The most important is the Advisory Commission on Intergovernmental Relations (ACIR). Formed in 1959, the commission's membership includes members of the Congress, state officials, local officials, and often a few scholars in the field plus professional staff. An important sounding board for ideas, the commission over the years has published studies on local and intergovernmental tax and fiscal problems, population settlement and development, governmental organization, and regionalism. The commission has had a noteworthy concern for metropolitan cooperation.

In addition, special task forces and commissions have studied aspects of urban problems (going back to President Eisenhower's Special Commission on Housing in 1953). Important temporary units include the President's Commission on Civil Disorders, 1967 (the Kerner Commission); the National Commission on Urban Problems, 1968 (the Douglas Commission); and the President's Commission on Urban Housing of 1968 (the Kaiser Commission). In national politics, appointing a commission is a quick and easy way to respond to problems without committing resources or making hard choices. It is revealing that much of the federal response to urban problems took this form. On the other hand, the published studies may become a source of important programs years later. The studies provide a base of information from which those in the urban policy network can form shared values and promote their ideas.

THE CONGRESS

The House and Senate Banking and Currency Committees. The House and Senate Banking and Currency Committees, especially the Housing Subcommittee in the House, play a crucial role in all new legislation and in the yearly "oversight" review of existing programs. They have been sympathetic to urban problems because their members either come from urban constituencies or are concerned with making a favorable reputation with urban interests. These committees have experienced professional staffs with recognized expertise and a network of personal ties in the policy network.

The House and Senate Appropriations Committees. Both houses of Congress have an overlapping committee structure. Subject-matter committees consider new legislation and review existing programs. In addition, on a year-to-year basis, the exact dollar amounts that will go to any new or ongoing programs are set by the House and Senate Appropriations Committees. These especially powerful bodies do their work in subcommittees organized around particular specialties. In each body a number of such appropriations subcommittees control urban appropriations. With much urban legislation already in effect, lobbying attention from urban groups now focuses on these subcommittees.

The House Ways and Means and the Senate Finance Committees. New legislation that alters the tax or revenue structure of the federal government must win approval from the House Ways and Means and the Senate Finance Committees. The formulas for eligibility and levels are set by these committees on a continuing basis. Any tax reform, federal offset of local property taxes, or federalization of welfare financing must go through these very powerful committees.

The House and Senate Committees on Government Operations. The House and Senate Committees on Government Operations belong to the urban network because of their Subcommittees on Intergovernmental Relations. Each subcommittee, with its professional staff, serves as a congressional counterpart to the Advisory Commission, holding hearings and developing information on a multitude of topics.

The House and Senate Budget Committees. These committees set overall ceilings on appropriations. Increasingly, their recommendations influence total spending, in every general area including urban policies.

THE INTEREST GROUP ENVIRONMENT

Groups at the Core of the Urban Policy System.[13] The interest groups at the core of the federal urban policy system are those mentioned earlier: the United States Conference of Mayors, the National League of Cities, the National Housing Conference (NHC), the Urban Coalition (new merged), the National Association of Home Builders, and the National Association of Housing and Redevelopment Officials (NAHRO). These organizations coordinate and cooperate with each other. The United States Conference of Mayors and the National League of Cities have largely merged their staffs and also created a third organization, National League of Cities-United States Conference of Mayors, Inc. (NLC-USCM, Inc.) This last operation contracts with federal agencies, according to William P. Browne and Robert H. Salisbury, "to assist them in the development and implementation of government programs."[14] Thus, NLC-USCM, Inc., not only advises member cities of the parent organizations but also services the very federal agencies among which the parent groups lobby for programs. In the wondrous world of intertwined government and interest groups in the United States, these interconnections are not untypical.

OTHER URBAN GROUPS

Besides those groups at the core of the urban policy network, there are other groups concerned with urban policies in general or special functional areas in particular. Table 3-1 lists more than 40 groups, most of them outside the core units and having a wide variety of concerns. Some of these, such as the National Governors Conference or the American Association of State Highway Officials, often oppose the policy goals of the core groups. What ties them into the network is the

---

[13] For the most detailed analysis of the behavior of interest groups comprised of city officials, see Donald H. Haider, *When Governments Come to Washington: Governors, Mayors, and Intergovernmental Lobbying* (New York: The Free Press, 1974).

[14] "Organized Spokesmen for Cities: Urban Interest Groups," in *People and Politics in Urban Society,* ed. by Harlan Hahn (Beverly Hills, Calif.: Sage Publications, 1972), p. 266.

TABLE 3-1.   An Inventory of Urban Interest Groups

Associations of Units of Government: American Association of Port Authorities, Council of State Governments, National Association of Counties, National Governors Conference, National League of Cities, National School Boards Association, National Service to Regional Councils, U.S. Conference of Mayors.

Professional Based Associations: Airport Operators Council International, American Association of School Administrators, American Association of State Highway Officials, American Institute of Planners, American Public Power Association, American Public Welfare Association, American Public Works Association, American Society of Planning Officials, American Society for Public Administration, American Transit Association, American Water Works Association, Inc., Building Officials and Code Administrators International, Inc., Institute of Traffic Engineers, International Association of Auditorium Managers, Inc., International Association of Assessing Officials, International Association of Chiefs of Police, Inc., International Association of Fire Chiefs, International Bridge, Tunnel, and Turnpike Association, Inc., International City Management Association, International Institute of Municipal Clerks, Municipal Finance Offices Association, National Association for Community Development, National Association of Housing and Redevelopment Officials, National Association of State Mental Health Program Directors, National Association of Tax Administrators, National Institute of Governmental Purchasing, Inc., National Institute of Municipal Law Officers, National Recreation and Park Association, Public Personnel Association, Water Pollution Control Federation.

Independent Associations: National Municipal League, Public Administration Service, Urban America, Urban Coalition, Urban Institute.

The table from "Organized Spokesmen for Cities: Urban Interest Groups," by William P. Browne and Robert H. Salisbury in Harlan Hahn (ed.), *Urban Affairs Annual Reviews*, Vol. 6 (1972), p. 258, is reprinted by permission of the publisher, Sage Publications, Inc. (Beverly Hills/London).

positions they take on urban policy concerns as they try to achieve their own goals.

NONURBAN GROUPS

Many other groups pursue federal policies and thus become part of the policy network. Many are liberal groups supporting positions of the urban groups at the core of the network: the AFL-CIO, Americans for Democratic Action, the NAACP, and the Urban League. Other interest groups consistently oppose the core groups. These include the Mortgage Bankers of America, the United States Savings and Loan League, the National Association of Mutual Savings Banks, the National Association of Manufacturers, the United States Chamber of Commerce, and the National Association of Real Estate Boards.

FEDERAL POLICY IN URBAN AREAS: A PROGRAMMATIC OVERVIEW

Not all participants in the urban interest network agree. But if we consider as a reference point the goals of the United States Conference of Mayors—big-city, liberal Democrats—we can analyze the urban impact on federal policy. The main questions are these: How successful has it been in obtaining money? In achieving recognition for urban areas as a special and legitimate domain? In obtaining local autonomy over various aspects of federal programs? In obtaining programs that reflect the administrative provisions urban interests favor? First, we will look at federal urban policy overall in terms of scope and expenditures. Then we will analyze four important federal programs.

THE SCOPE OF FEDERAL URBAN POLICY: DOLLARS

If dollars are the measure, local interests have scored great success in tapping the federal treasury. Localities obtained 14 times as much money from Washington in 1975 as in 1956. Revenues as transfer payments from Washington increased much faster than the increase in local funds from their own tax sources. As a consequence, local governments spend much more than they raise locally and, thus, are more active governments than their own tax bases alone would permit them to be. Local governments raise about 17 per cent of all the governmental revenues in the United States but spend about 34 per cent of all that is spent.

Federal monies reach localities in several different ways: (1) federal outlays on federal programs spent in local areas—such as defense installations and contracts, or interstate highway construction; (2) federal monies that go to state governments but ultimately find their way to local residents—such as public assistance (welfare) or higher education funds; and (3) monies that go directly to local governments from Washington.

As one indicator of the magnitude of federal involvement, total aid to state and local governments grew from $10 billion in 1965 to over $80 billion in 1978. By 1978, this aid was 17 per cent of all federal spending and 28 per cent of all state and local revenue.[15] For some individual cities, the federal government delivered almost as much in aid as they raised themselves. For Buffalo, Cleveland, and Detroit, federal aid represented 70 per cent of the amount they raised on their own (or a matching of 70 cents from Washington for each dollar raised

---

[15] See Robert D. Reischauer, "The Economy, the Federal Budget, and the Prospects for Urban Aid," in *The Fiscal Outlook for Cities: Implications of a National Urban Policy*, ed. by Roy Bahl (Syracuse, N.Y.: Syracuse University Press, 1978), pp. 93–110.

locally). For Phoenix, St. Louis, Newark, and Philadelphia, over 50 cents of federal monies came in for each dollar raised through local taxes.[16]

Monies going directly to localities came wrapped in some 15 major program areas: revenue sharing, community development, the Comprehensive Employment and Training Act (CETA) Bloc Grants, wastewater treatment construction, emergency public works, categorical CETA grants, Urban Mass Transportation Administration grants, programs consolidated into the new bloc grants, job training and employment assistance, federal aid to impacted schools, Community Services Administration funding, airport development assistance, emergency school assistance, economic development assistance, and rural water and waste disposal grants.

These 15 program areas deliver funds in one of two basic formats. *Categorical* programs are project grants. A local government proposes to the federal government, a specific project within the program's eligibility rules, receives approval, and then proceeds under federal supervision. Traditional public housing, urban renewal, public works, and water and sewage construction programs were categorical. *Categorical* programs favor the largest cities because they have the professional staffs to work out the projects and shepherd them through the complicated paper work required.

Formula programs dispense monies automatically upon the basis of some criteria set by the Congress. The criteria may be total population, low-income population, amount of deteriorated housing, or number of children in elementary school. Until the early 1970s, categorical programs were most popular with the Congress. They allowed precise identification of the uses of the funds and extensive federal controls thereafter. But the two major urban programs of the 1970s are revenue sharing and community development grants, both formula programs.

Formula programs shift the struggle over distribution to the floors of the Congress, because how the formula is drawn determines who gets what (not which locality is most adroit at federal paper work). The formula programs of revenue sharing and community development grants have been more advantageous to suburbs and smaller communities than were the categorical programs.

Let us now look at two examples of each form of program. The two categorical programs are low-rent public housing and urban renewal. The two formula programs are revenue sharing and community development grants. This examination gives a flavor of how the federal

[16] See T. D. Allman, "The Urban Crisis Leaves Town," *Harper's*, 257 (December 1978), p. 47.

government and local communities interact. It also allows tracing federal program development from the earliest federal-city efforts to the most recent.

Two Categorical Programs Low-Rent Public Housing and Urban Renewal

Low-Rent Public Housing. One of the first major federal urban programs was low-rent public housing. Confronted with a severe housing crisis during the Depression of the 1930s, the Roosevelt New Deal Administration took a two-pronged approach: it underwrote mortgage loans for individuals, and it created government-owned housing, a program known as public housing. The first such operations were under the Public Works Administration (PWA), a creation of the National Industrial Recovery Act of 1933. The PWA bought land, cleared old dwellings, and built public housing, some 21,000 apartment units in 50 low-rent projects in 37 cities between 1933 and 1935. The construction was halted, however, by court decisions decreeing that the federal government could not use its power of eminent domain to force the sale of land that it would then sell or lease to private citizens. The decisions blocked the development of a completely federally operated housing program and led to the alternative that remains the standard procedure.

That alternative emerged in the landmark Wagner–Steagall Low Rent Housing Bill, passed in 1937, which established the United States Housing Authority. This act set up the direct federal-local administrative link and also stated the philosophical underpinning of the program, namely:

> to provide financial assistance to the States and political subdivisions thereof for the elimination of unsafe and unsanitary housing conditions, for the eradication of slums, for the provision of decent, safe, and sanitary dwellings for families of low income, and for the reduction of unemployment and the stimulation of business activity. . . .[17]

Under this act, Local Housing Authorities (LHA's) were to obtain the land, construct, and operate the low-rent housing under grants and contractual arrangements, including eligibility rules for occupancy, negotiated with the federal government. These LHA's required

[17] Cited in Michael Aiken and Robert R. Alford, "Community Structure and Innovation: The Case of Public Housing," *The American Political Science Review*, 64:3 (September 1970), p. 846.

specific authorizing legislation from state government. State authorization—hotly contested in many states—provided the necessary legal authority to obtain land through the power of eminent domain.

Under the 1937 act, the federal government provided the LHA's with 60-year loans covering up to 90 per cent of the development costs and also provided a subsidy that covered the difference between the actual economic costs of operating the units and the "social rent," the amount the lowest-income group could actually afford to pay. The connection between Washington and the LHA's were, even at that early stage, quite complicated. As Harold Wolman notes:

> Despite the fact that the projects had to be initiated, approved, and operated by local authorities, the federal requirements to be fulfilled were quite rigorous. They included specifications for the physical structure of the project . . . and income limitations on inhabitants (both maximum and minimum) as well as required local contributions (10 per cent of the cost of building and 20 per cent of the annual federal subsidy). In addition, there was a requirement that for each unit of public housing erected, a slum dwelling unit had to be torn down.[18]

Some 168,000 units were constructed under the 1937 Act, which was superseded by the Housing Act of 1949. That act had the ambitious goal of constructing 810,000 units of low-rent public housing in six years. The goal was never met. Through the end of 1970, only 789,000 units were under management. The pace of construction was always slow, partly because of the procedures that had to be followed. For example, the following steps had to accompany every project:

1. The LHA applies to the federal authority for a program reservation.
2. The federal government approves the program reservation application.
3. The LHA executes a preliminary loan contract for surveys and planning (which requires approval of the local city council).
4. The LHA and HUD sign an annual contributions contract (after the LHA and the city council have signed a cooperative agreement giving the housing tax exempt status and after the community has a workable program for the eradication of slums).

[18] *Politics of Federal Housing* (New York: Dodd, Mead, 1971), p. 30.

5. Site acquisition.
6. Advertising, opening, and awarding construction contracts.
7. Construction starts.
8. Construction ends.
9. The facilities enter the management phase; qualifications for occupancy are set, rents fixed, units rented, project income computed, and net deficit (to be covered by the federal government) is established.

One of the more interesting policy questions of American society is what happened to the concept of public housing? In the 1930s those liberal reformers who pushed public housing had great hopes. Public housing was expected, first of all, to provide decent, low-cost housing for poor people. Second, it was expected to eliminate slum housing and to improve the aesthetics of the cities. Third, it was genuinely believed that the better housing would reduce the social disorder of slums. These goals were heartily endorsed by the big-city mayors, in whose communities low-rent housing primarily has been built.

Objections to public housing were not clearly focused during debate on the 1937 act, but opposition was well organized by the time of the 1949 act.[19] The main group opposition came from the private housing sector: banks, savings associations, real estate boards, and the construction industry. Opponents argued that public housing was socialism, maintained that the poor were subsidized at the expense of homeowners, and that such housing would compete unfairly with private enterprise.

With the passage of the 1949 act, the battle shifted to the local level, where state authorization had to be obtained for LHA's, where city council approval was needed for specific project applications, and where, often, public housing questions were put to the voters in local referenda. At this point another negative factor entered into opposition campaigns. Low-rent public housing was exclusively for poor people. As the income of any tenant family rose above the low-income ceiling set for eligibility, that family was forced to move. In other words, the most stable and successful families are forced out as ineligible. The argument was made that placing a public housing project in any neighborhood would concentrate the poor, with all of their social problems, in that area. Local resistance was, on this basis, easy to organize. Complicating the issue was race. Because of their lower incomes com-

---

[19] For the best accounts of public housing controversies and issues, see Leonard Freedman, *Public Housing: The Politics of Poverty* (New York: Holt, Rinehart and Winston, 1969).

pared to whites and the difficulty they had obtaining housing on the private market, black people were anxious to enter public housing. More and more public housing in the larger northern cities became heavily, if not all, black, and public housing became identified as a black program.

The first wave of resistance to public housing in the late 1940s and early 1950s was based on the novelty of the public-supported program and was led, essentially, by the private sector of economic enterprises associated with housing. In the mid-1950s and into the 1960s, the resistance broadened to include racial factors. Between 1949 and 1965 there were about 250 local referenda, and about 60 per cent resulted in votes against public housing, including in such cities as Los Angeles, Seattle, Portland, and Akron.[20]

Further, in the 1960s, groups that had always supported public housing began to have second thoughts. The white liberals who had seen public housing as a cure for social ills took another look at the huge projects in many cities and found that such installations merely concentrated the very problems they hoped would be cured.[21] Black organizations began to see high-density public housing as perpetrating racial segregation, because sites for such projects were almost always selected where there was least neighborhood resistance, that is, in areas that were already heavily black.

The result was that support for public housing in its original form was almost nonexistent by the mid-1960s. After that, the program took a variety of new turns. Large-scale projects of high density were rarely undertaken any more, as the emphasis shifted to rehabilitating existing structures of various kinds. The LHA processes were to be speeded up by a system known as "turnkey," under which the laborious negotiations were short-circuited by having housing first built by private developers, then turned over in finished form to the local agency. More than half of the new housing was reserved for the elderly poor because such projects had wide-scale political and social support, were popular with older persons, and seemed to work out much better in terms of low disorder and low neighborhood resistance than had other conventional projects. A substantial effort was made through a special form of FHA loans to shift the focus of housing for the poor into home ownership rather than renting. Black groups sought to have new public housing built in small units at scattered sites throughout the entire metropolitan area. This concept, in turn, generated resistance in the

[20] Ibid., pp. 54–55.
[21] For an interesting set of remedies from such a perspective, see Oscar Newman, *Defensible Space: Crime Prevention Through Urban Design* (New York: Macmillan, 1972).

suburbs, where housing for poor people, especially of racial minorities, is not viewed with much enthusiasm.

In summary, low-rent public housing in urban areas has had a checkered history. Local Housing Authorities, under conventional, turnkey, and elderly programs, are now the proprietors of more than 1 million units of such housing. For poor people, this housing, whatever its shortcomings, has almost always been preferable to the local private housing market. For local governments, these programs have provided a response to low-income citizens, a way of meeting public needs. At the same time, the low-rent public housing generates group opposition in the private housing sector and public opposition at the neighborhood level. One of the first of the federal-urban programs, it continues in operation but without the support that once raised so many expectations.

Urban Renewal. Under Title I of the 1949 Housing Act, the federal government, through local government, would underwrite broad-scale clearance of whole slum areas and replacement with residential and commercial structures. The program lasted in separate form until 1974, when it became one element under the community development bloc grant system. One novel element was that the local redevelopment agency could sell the cleared land to private developers who would then build in accordance with a plan the agency approved. The idea combined the public power of eminent domain for the taking of land with the private enterprise system. Conservatives bitterly criticized this extension of governmental authority over private property.[22] Nonetheless, the Supreme Court held urban renewal constitutional, provided that the reuse of the land by the private developer was deemed in the public interest by properly constituted authority.[23]

Urban renewal projects got off to a very slow start. Ten years after the program enactment there were only 390 projects in the execution phase and, of these, there was ongoing disposition of cleared land in only 86. Only 25 projects were listed as completed. By the end of 1971, however, the program was much further along. There were then more than 2,000 projects in 964 localities (including all but three states), of which 622 projects in 388 localities were completed. Another 1,230 projects were in various active phases in 724 localities. The total amount of federal money spent or authorized on urban renewal exceeds $10 billion.

[22] See Martin Anderson, *The Federal Bulldozer: A Critical Analysis of Urban Renewal, 1949–1962* (Boston: MIT Press, 1964).

[23] *Berman v. Parker*, 348 U.S. 26 (1954).

Urban renewal was originally for the largest cities. The largest cities, and some older medium-sized cities, such as New Haven, Connecticut, had the need, the technical know-how, and the political leadership to obtain the federal funds and launch renewal projects.[24] At the end, however, the distribution of projects cut across cities of all sizes. Almost 65 per cent of the projects and 40 per cent of the total funds were allocated to cities of 100,000 population or less.

Urban renewal projects ran the gamut from less than one acre to more than 2,500 acres, from displacing few people or businesses to requiring tens of thousands of citizens and hundreds of businesses to move, and from less than $50,000 to more than $100 million. A major renewal project in a large city could easily take 10 years from the time the proposal was approved to the time the last building put in place by the developer became operative.

Thus, the program gained acceptability over time, and the expertise needed to conduct a project filtered down to smaller communities and to the older, more urbanized suburbs bordering on central cities. In addition, redevelopment for substantially nonresidential uses was made acceptable wherever the locality deemed it necessary for the proper development of the community. The goals of renewing the commercial sections of cities (especially the central business districts) and expanding the urban tax base won equal recognition with residential housing. Such a broadened emphasis made the program more attractive, and provisions for rehabilitation of existing housing appealed to smaller cities.

Criticisms of Urban Renewal. Urban renewal has had serious critics.[25] There were three main grounds of attacks. First, at a philosophical level, Martin Anderson argued that the program extended government power too far, that private property should not be taken by legal authority for different private development.[26] A second criticism came from liberals such as Herbert J. Gans.[27] The liberals' thrust was that urban renewal displaced poor persons from the always tight supply of cheap housing in order to serve the needs of middle- and upper-class persons and of private business. Gans cited the devastat-

---

[24] For a seminal study of urban renewal in general and New Haven in particular, see Raymond E. Wolfinger, *The Politics of Progress* (Englewood Cliffs, N.J.: Prentice Hall, 1974).

[25] For a thoughtful critique from a social science perspective, see Scott Greer, *Urban Renewal and American Cities* (Indianapolis: Bobbs-Merrill, 1965).

[26] Anderson, op. cit.

[27] "The Failure of Urban Renewal: A Critique and Some Proposals," *Commentary* (April 1965), pp. 29–37.

ing effect renewal of Boston's West End had on the very stable Italian ethnic community there. Others have called urban renewal "Negro removal," because at least two thirds of the more than one million persons forced to relocate have been black. For many small businesses, the neighborhood clienteles can never be regained. For individuals and families, where there is a sense of community, those relationships may be hard to re-establish. Still a third critique was that urban renewal did not make sense from an economic perspective. The argument was that new middle- and high-rent private housing would have been built anyway.

Defenses of Urban Renewal. Defenders of the program agreed with some criticisms: that development was slow, that the program represented a new extension of federal power, that many people were forced to resettle. But they maintain that this must be seen in the light of what was attempted. Raymond F. Wolfinger argued that "urban renewal is a common and important example of comprehensive, coordinated, innovative policy directed toward solving major city problems."[28] The legal authority of urban renewal, as the courts have viewed it, is seen as a logical extension of existing powers. The delays are seen as natural in a program so very complicated and ambitious. The displacement of low-income persons is seen as serious but mitigated by other considerations. Thus, one of five Americans moves each year, and this natural high mobility is higher in slum areas. Despite the heavy loss in low-income housing brought about by urban renewal, this loss does not begin to approach the net overall loss in population of most central cities. The exodus to the suburbs should have actually increased the number of housing units available to low-income persons in central cities, as housing filters down from middle-class to poorer users.

Wolfinger notes some of the practical and political difficulties inherent in the program.[29] For any mayor, the program had visible liabilities long before it had visible assets: the dislocated people, the displacing of merchants, the rerouting of traffic, the dust. In addition, even central city businessmen, who are supposed to have the most to gain, may be reluctant to cooperate. Renewal involves uncertainty. Those with interests in the suburbs, retailers, for example, will see

[28] Wolfinger, op. cit., p. 133. See also the rejoinders to Herbert J. Gans by George M. Raymond and Malcolm D. Ruikin in *Commentary* (July 1965), 72–80. For an extensive collection of articles, see *Urban Renewal: People, Politics and Planning*, ed. by Jewel Bellush and Murray Haushnecht (Garden City, N.Y.: Doubleday, Anchor Books, 1967).

[29] Ibid.

renewal as competitive. Many developers are national operators, with nonlocal bases of expertise and capital, and local interests may resent them. Politicians on city councils may fear hostile reactions from their constituents, or the displacement of their constituencies. There will have to be negotiations of considerable difficulty. And, they reason, the gains for all of this will be at least one election in the future and more likely some 10 years way. The wonders are that political leaders had the enthusiasm, especially at the beginning, to undertake these projects and that so many projects came to successful fruition.

TWO FORMULA PROGRAMS: REVENUE SHARING AND COMMUNITY DEVELOPMENT GRANTS

Revenue Sharing. Odd coalitions sometimes come together to produce national programs. Such is the case with general revenue sharing, passed as the State and Local Fiscal Assistance Act of 1972 and renewed in 1976. The act distributes a fixed amount of federal funds, $25.6 billion over three and three quarter years after 1976. Some 37,000 state and local units receive the funds.

No application is required to receive the monies, which are distributed automatically by the Treasury Department, according to a complex formula. State governments get one third of the total monies, and the local units, the remaining two thirds. The funds may be used for any legal purpose, as long as there is no discrimination in the distribution chosen. The funds may even be used to match the money required under other federal grants. The formula for distribution for local governments takes into account population, general tax effort, and relative income. Although some aspects of the formula benefit the poorest central cities, other restrictions limit the amount any one single central city can receive. The result is that revenue sharing seems to give some advantage to the most populous and poorest cities, but not much.[30] These results reflect the compromises built into passage of the program. It contains something for every community, from the largest to the smallest. This reflects the politics behind the original passage of the act.[31]

The original sponsors of the revenue sharing concept had different uses for the monies in mind. For some communities, the idea was to

[30] See Richard P. Nathan and Charles F. Adams, *Revenue Sharing: The Second Round* (Washington, D.C.: The Brookings Institution, 1977) p. 106; and Kent Eklund and Oliver P. Williams, "The Political Ingenuity of the Revenue Sharing Act," in *Revenue Sharing*, David A. Caputo and Richard L. Cole, eds. (Lexington, Mass.: Lexington Books, 1976) p. 84.

[31] See Richard P. Nathan, Allen D. Manuel, and Susannah E. Calkins, *Monitoring Revenue Sharing* (Washington, D.C.: The Brookings Institution, 1975) p. 333.

TABLE 3-2.　How Local Communities Are Using Revenue Sharing Funds

	Mean Percentages	
Net Fiscal Effect	*Local*	*State*
New spending	57.5	35.7
New capital	46.0	21.6
Expanded operations	10.8	11.6
Increased pay and benefits	0.8	0.0
Unallocated	0.0	2.5
Substitutions	42.5	64.3
Restoration of federal aid	0.3	3.0
Tax reduction	3.5	13.2
Tax stabilization	13.8	0.0
Program maintenance	12.6	15.3
Avoidance of borrowing	9.5	3.3
Increased fund balance	2.7	4.5
Other	0.1	0.0
Unallocated	0.0	25.0
Total	100.0	100.0

SOURCE: Richard P. Nathan, Allen D. Manuel, and Susannah E. Calkins, *Monitoring Revenue Sharing* (Washington, D.C.: The Brookings Institution, 1975), p. 193. Copyright by the Brookings Institution. Reprinted by permission.

use the funds for new social programs; for others, to defer a rise in costs by paying for existing services; for still others, to buy amenities. The results are mixed, but Table 3-2 shows that a large portion of the funds go to substitute for city revenues that otherwise would have been used for some necessary purpose. Substitution works to stabilize a tax rate that otherwise would have to be raised, to maintain a program at existing levels that otherwise might have to be cut, and to provide funds that otherwise would have had to be borrowed.

On the other hand, for local government units, 57.5 per cent of the funds went for new spending that was not for social programs. It went primarily for new capital projects,[32] in transportation, environmental protection, recreation, and public safety. That means spending on busses, subway cars, sewers, treatment plants, park facilities, and police equipment. Analyzed somewhat differently, taking into account all uses, new and substitutions, the major local programs funded under general revenue sharing were public safety, education, public transportation, general government, environmental protection, health services, and recreation.

[32] Ibid., pp. 200–202.

Revenue sharing has become important to local budgets. The funds represent from 5.3 to 7.9 per cent of all local revenues, depending upon the type of the community and how it fits into the formula. The program has something, literally, for everyone, with no requirements or strings attached. Originally conceived by Republican congressmen in 1958 under the general title "bloc grants," general revenue sharing won Democratic endorsement in the mid-1960s and has been supported by presidents and legislators of both parties ever since.

All the elements of the urban interest network—the National Conference of Mayors, the National Association of Cities, the National Governors Conference, and the National Conference of State Legislative Leaders—support revenue sharing. Thus, although money commitments have remained constant in the face of general inflation, the program continues to be renewed. Michael D. Reagan has appropriately asked, "What is the source of this extraordinary sex appeal?"[33] For Republicans, the answer seems part ideological and part political. The program is congruent with the party's philosophical commitment to decentralization and to increasing the stature of state governments especially. In addition, revenue sharing benefits *all* local governments, the prosperous and the impoverished. Thus, of all the federal programs, revenue sharing is most likely to benefit the Republican suburban constituencies.

For Democrats, the program promises *new* monies to urban areas at a time when increasing either the number or the funding of categorical grant programs is difficult. Thus, although many Democrats, especially those in the Congress, are skeptical, the program has won party support. For mayors, support has been reluctant but, because the long-term permanent goal is more funds, whatever the method, revenue sharing has been seen as better than no funds.

Community Development Grants.   The Community Development Act of 1974 responded to criticisms of categorical federal programs by consolidating 11 such programs into one lump sum grant to local governments. The recipient locality then decides to which of the covered uses to allocate the funds.

The 11 original program elements of community development are public facility loans, advance planning grants, open-space land program, water and sewer facility grants, neighborhood center grants, land acquisition for future facilities, urban renewal, housing code enforcement monies, neighborhood development grants, model cities grants, and loans to low-income homeowners to rehabilitate property.

[33] *The New Federalism* (New York: Oxford University Press, 1972), p. 92.

Two new program elements were added when the act was renewed in 1977. These are loan guarantees for the locality by the Secretary of HUD, and Urban Development Action Grants, discretionary with the secretary, for projects the provide special opportunities to attract private investment.

As with revenue sharing, the allocation formula for the community development grants focuses conflict at the congressional level. Putting certain variables into the formula guarantees more funds for older cities with the worst housing; other formulas provide more funds to growing cities in the South and Southwest. The original 1974 act promised cities that their share of community development funds would not be less than their share of all the former categorical programs, even though automatic application of the formulas would always produce such reductions. Eventually this provision was phased out.

Cities may now choose between two formulas to determine their block grant. One takes into account population, poverty (counted twice), and housing overcrowding; the other considers age of housing (two and a half times), poverty (one and one half times), and growth lag compared to the average population growth rate of all metropolitan cities. The effect is to give some weight to locations of urban decline but to ensure that some funds go to all communities, whatever their social or economic condition. By law, 80 per cent of all funds go to SMSA's, and the rest to nonmetropolitan areas.

Although the funds are allocated by formula and usage is permissive among any of the consolidated, formerly separate programs, each city must still submit an application for its funds. The applications set out a summary of housing and community development needs and explain how the choices the community makes will improve conditions for low- and moderate-income persons.

Because of the flexibility for local choice deliberately built into the program, it is not surprising that different localities have had different preferences. One study showed that most of the funds went to neighborhood conservation and prevention of urban blight, in the form of housing rehabilitation and related improvements.[34] Preliminary studies also show that the program benefits the low- and moderate-income groups intended to be the recipients. Fifty-five per cent of all program benefits went to these groups.[35] Community development

[34] See Richard P. Nathan and others, *Block Grants for Community Development* (Washington, D.C.: U.S. Department of Housing and Urban Development, 1977).

[35] See Sarah F. Liebschutz, "Community Development Bloc Grants: Who Benefits," paper delivered at the 1977 annual meeting of the American Political Science Association, Washington, 1977.

grants are now an annual appropriation of $2.8 billion, about 3 per cent of total federal aid to state and local governments.

LOCAL COMMUNITIES AS SUBSYSTEMS: SOME CONCLUSIONS

Various conclusions emerge from this treatment of local communities as political subsystems. With state governments, the subordinate legal position of localities guarantees a complicated web of relationships. Municipalities must influence state politics to achieve routine governmental ends. They must work for influence as individual communities on problems peculiar to themselves and in coalition with other localities on common issues.

The relationship with the federal government is a newer role, dating from the 1930s and flowing from the need for money. To obtain federal funds there developed a network of urban interest groups, whose perspective is epitomized by the United States Conference of Mayors. The fight for federal funds has been successful. At the same time, one cost has been a dilution of local governmental autonomy. The focus of attention is on Washington, the source of program sustenance, and on relationships with bureaucratic counterparts in federal agencies and in the Congress for the newer formula programs. Thus federal programs have mixed consequences for local governments.

4 LOCAL GOVERNMENTS AS PUBLIC POLICY PRODUCERS

Local governments are not trivial structures. By the very hard criterion of money raised and spent, local governments are powerful policy instruments. They raise more than $97 billion a year from their own tax sources, about 17 per cent of all taxes raised in the United States. Because they receive money from the federal and state governments, local governments spend substantially more than they collect on their own, about $161 billion a year. That amounts to 34 per cent of all the government money spent in the United States.

There are other gross indicators of the scope of local governments. They have incurred outstanding debt—usually for capital expenditures such as roads and schools—of more than $93 billion, a total almost one fifth as large as the more publicized federal debt and more than twice as large as the combined debt of all the state governments. Local governments have more than 7 million full-time employees, of whom about 70 per cent work in cities with more than 50,000 population. For these larger cities, there are almost 200 employees for every 10,000 citizens. By comparison, there are only 2.5 million full-time federal government civilian employees, and that number is steadily declining.

79

LOCAL GOVERNMENT ACTIVITIES IN A POLICY FRAMEWORK

One way to show the scope of local government activities is to place them in a framework of policy analysis. Figure 4-1 lists six elements of any public policy: (1) mobilizing resources, (2) choosing priorities, (3) distributing benefits, (4) imposing costs, (5) manipulating controls, and (6) reaction and adaptation. These are universal elements, processes that occur in every policy from the first establishment of a police force to building a new city golf course.[1]

1. Mobilizing Resources. On every policy, especially at the stage of initiation, resources in favor of the policy—support in the form of ideas, numbers, campaign contributions, commitments from private and political leaders—have to be mobilized.

2. Choosing Priorities. Once a policy is adopted, priorities have to be set. Economic and political resources are always scarce. There has to be some way to make choices. You will see later in this chapter how various rules of choice making are developed and followed in the municipal budget process.

3. Distributing Benefits. Every policy distributes benefits, symbolic or tangible. Local governments distribute statuses (awards and appointments to civic committees) as well as cash in the form of jobs and contracts. These choices allocate among alternatives. For example, using revenue sharing funds for sewer treatment plants means those same funds cannot be used for summer camps for ghetto children or to hire additional garbage collectors.

FIGURE 4-1.

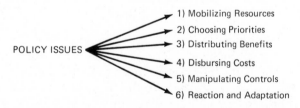

POLICY ISSUES
1) Mobilizing Resources
2) Choosing Priorities
3) Distributing Benefits
4) Disbursing Costs
5) Manipulating Controls
6) Reaction and Adaptation

The other side of the coin is that all local public policy costs. All governments seek to provide specific benefits but to disburse costs widely through the general public by broad-based taxes and putting

[1] See Joyce M. and William C. Mitchell, *Political Analysis and Public Policy* (Skokie, Ill.: Rand McNally, 1969).

the money into a general treasury. Thus, whoever benefits will know precisely what he or she is getting, but those who pay will have only a vague notion about for what the money is used. Taxes are not transferred directly or earmarked for specific uses, but go into a general fund. Making costs difficult to assess mutes resentment and conflict.

4. Imposing Costs.   Local governments have difficulty imposing costs because the higher levels of government capture the best tax sources. Personal income taxes, for example, can be withheld by employers. Personal income taxes also have elasticity, meaning that they go up automatically without further governmental action when incomes increase. Yet, national and state governments pre-empt personal, as well as corporate, income taxes. Some cities have local income taxes, called city earnings taxes, but these provide a very small portion of total local revenue. The bulk of local revenue comes from property taxes that possess special disadvantageous qualities. The worst quality is that it is impossible to camouflage the impact.

5. Manipulating Controls.   Every policy carries some form of control, either the carrot or the stick, to induce compliance. Governments maintain a legal monopoly on armed force and can always resort to legal violence to obtain compliance. Local governments have extensive control forces, courts, and jails. All local governments prefer voluntary compliance to force, but behind local policy lies the potential of coercion.

6. Reaction and Adaptation.   Reaction and adaptation refer to the process of adjusting to a policy once it is set in motion. With time, the controversial becomes routine. Day-to-day dealing with an issue is performed by middle-level government employees who apply standardized rules of procedure, as opposed to top officials who respond to political pressures. For example, in the late nineteenth century, franchises to provide municipal services were hotly contested by private companies, especially in transit and waterworks. The controversies over who would get what rights and the corruption frequently accompanying these struggles were massive.[2] Today, these systems are municipally owned and operated throughout almost all of the country, and the operations are routine civil service functions. It is hard to believe today, but at one time the concept of public schools engendered bitter local controversies. More recently, urban renewal pro-

---

[2] For realistic fictional accounts of some of these struggles, see the novels by Theodore Dreiser, *The Financier* and *The Titan*.

grams were hot local issues. Familiarity breeds acceptance. Not only government but people touched by a program learn to live with it. One reason everyone adapts is that once a program is going, bureaucrats work out all the details between their administrative agency and the affected clienteles.[3]

A TYPOLOGY OF LOCAL PUBLIC POLICIES

We characterize local policies by level of mobilization, how benefits and costs are distributed, and how visible adaptation and reaction are in the political system. Political scientists identify four categories of public policy: (1) distributive; (2) regulative; (3) self-regulative; and (4) redistributive.[4] Table 4-1 illustrates each type of policy, along with the local political institution that plays the main role in each.

Distributive Policies. Distributive policies are not policies in the sense of a set of overall priorities being imposed by the municipal government, nor are they a political response to a widely agreed-upon set of goals. They are *ad hoc* responses to demands as claimants on the municipal treasury manage to mobilize political support. Most urban policies of the nineteenth century could be labeled as distributive. The streets, sewers, bridges, public buildings, parks, and schools were built for citizens but provided contracts and jobs for politically loyal contractors and voters. City councils sold public transportation and utility franchises.

The distributing of city jobs during the eras of immigration was a main function of city politics. Justice, too, was often distributed case by case or sold outright, when liquor laws, prostitution, or even police jobs were involved. Much of urban politics in the 1980s remains distributive, dispensing various benefits to groups and individuals. Patronage is still important in municipal politics, especially in the larger cities. Although residents of exclusive suburbs may consider themselves above claiming jobs, they often ask for exemptions and variances from zoning boards (or at least the developers who build the suburbs and the suburban shopping centers do). With distributive pol-

[3] For the best account of how this process works, see Murray Edelman, *The Symbolic Uses of Politics* (Champaign-Urbana: University of Illinois Press, 1964).

[4] For a seminal article on distribution, regulation, and redistribution, see Theodore J. Lowi, "American Business, Public Policy, Case Studies, and Political Theory," *World Politics,* **16**:4 (July 1964), 677–715. Robert H. Salisbury added the self-regulative category in "The Analysis of Public Policy: A Search for Theory and Roles," in Austin Ranney (ed.), *Political Science and Public Policy* (Chicago: Markham, 1968), pp. 151–178.

TABLE 4-1. Local Public Policies: Some Illustrations of the
Four Types with the Political Institutions Involved

DISTRIBUTIVE POLICIES
Mayor and City Council
   Road construction contracts
   New schools
   New street lights
Mayor or City Manager
   Appointment of city department
      heads
   Appointment of local judges
City Council
   Approve zoning variances
   Approve property tax abatements
   Place constituents in city jobs
Local Courts
   Appointing lawyers in probate
      cases
   Damage awards in torts cases
   Decisions in housing cases
Local Regulatory Agencies
   Construction permits
   Restaurant licenses
   Liquor licenses
   Taxi licenses
   Nightclub licenses
REGULATIVE POLICIES
The Mayor
   Strictness or permissiveness of
   local vice law enforcement
   Housing code proposal

City Council
   Any licensing legislation
      (hairdressers, barbers, cabs, auto
      repair shops, restaurants, bars).
   Housing construction and
      minimum standards code
Local Regulatory Agencies
   Zoning policy
SELF-REGULATIVE POLICIES
City Council
   No housing code
   No licensing regulations
   No local vice laws
REDISTRIBUTIVE POLICIES
Mayor or Manager and City Council
   Local contribution to welfare
   Public housing program
   School busing
   Local income tax
   Local property tax
City Council
   Reapportioning council districts
Local Charter Commission
   Rewrites local charter to change
      structure of local government

icies, each beneficiary is isolated from other beneficiaries. Support in the city council is obtained by logrolling. Councilmen all vote for everyone else's pet project. The losers are vague entities such as the public, unorganized and unaware of their losses. They never, therefore, mobilize to confront the winners. As units of gain and loss are small, distributive policies have low visibility and produce minimal public conflict.

As long as the resource pie or the total local economy grows, distributive policies lead to stable local politics. Thus, during the era of rapid growth of the core cities between 1850 and 1920, the distributive style typified the urban "machines," and whatever one thinks of this mode of politics, it got the job done. Wherever there is current growth or sufficient resources, distributive policies are the dominant mode.

Regulative Policies.   Regulative policies apply general rules to whole categories of firms, industries, groups, or individuals. The point is to limit, channel, and regulate the behavior of sectors of the local community. Someone can clearly be identified as the winner and loser. Because a general rule of policy making has to be established, the scope of local government is enlarged. Because much regulatory activity is preempted by the federal and state governments, local regulation exists only in a few distinct fields:

1. Setting minimum standards for construction and for the maintenance of rental housing.
2. Licensing various types of commercial enterprises in which there is an accepted public interest because of health, safety, or moral standards.
3. Setting zoning regulations which, through specifying what types of commercial or residential construction can go in what areas of the community, vastly influence land use patterns.

Regulation establishes the right of local government to intervene in the behavior of firms or individuals that might have previously operated subject only to the restraints of the free market economy. Even when local regulatory agencies are relatively inactive, there exists a potential threat. That is why various local interests, from real estate firms to restaurant operators to owners of taxicab firms, try to influence appointments to the regulatory agencies and hire politically well-connected local lawyers to represent them before such agencies. For a nightclub operator or a suburban developer, local regulatory boards shape economic opportunities and basic livelihoods.

Self-regulative Policies.   The goal of self-regulation is to avoid intervention by the government. Groups that manage to win the power to regulate themselves have demonstrated real power. Thus, groups as diverse as craft unions, plumbers, hairdressers, college professors, and doctors all seek control over their own activities. At the local level, self-regulation may take the form of allowing real estate and construction interests to determine housing standards by having no local ordinance setting forth such standards. Or hotel and restaurant operators may have a trade association that sets the standards on health for public places in the community. Local medical societies (often organized at the county level) determine who may practice in local hospitals, often including local public hospitals.

Redistributive Policies. A final kind of public policy is the redistributive policy. Redistributive policies require broad mobilization and have, at least in a psychological sense, the most visible distribution of benefits and imposition of costs. Redistributive policies force people, groups, elites, and political leaders to choose among alternative goals, to pick priorities. Broad categories of winners and losers are involved, often whole social classes, racial elements, or ethnic groups. Such policy may pit the middle class versus the poor, or the haves versus the have-nots. Impact distinguishes redistributive policy. Some sought-after value in life—money, office, power, recognition, status, cultural pre-eminence—is taken from one segment of the community and passed on to a different local claimant.

Redistributive policies involve great tension. Reaction and adaptation may take a long time, because winners are insecure in their gains and losers constantly try to reverse the verdict. There is little doubt about who won and who lost. The possibilities for direct confrontations are high, especially if the redistribution takes place in an era when the local economic pie is fixed or contracting. For example, heavier property taxes come visibly from one group's pocket and, because city services generally benefit the lowest-income groups disproportionately, are handed over directly to someone else. The redistribution tension is heightened in central cities, where winners and losers live close together in adjacent or even the same neighborhoods.

A number of local policies are redistributive. Welfare, because it consists of direct money payments to local citizens, is clearly redistributive, and it is often an intense local issue. Welfare is a national program, but local communities may contribute, and many, such as New York City, make very substantial payments to the individuals. Local communities must also decide whether to sponsor public housing. Although the money comes from the federal government, the selection of a *site* is a decision of the local housing authority. If that housing is placed in middle-class neighborhoods, it redistributes desirable neighborhood values. Lower-middle-class and middle-class persons have cultural and life-style values different from those of lower-class poor persons. Placing hundreds or even thousands of poor persons in middle-class neighborhoods in city-sponsored housing is almost always viewed with intense distaste.

Another redistributive local policy is busing school children from one area to some other area in the city to achieve a balanced racial mix in the public schools. Many white parents perceive this policy as one of imposing hardships, either in the classroom or through the process of transport, on their children in order to benefit black children. Schools are seen as major factors in the life chances of children. Schools formally and informally transmit different cultural values and are very important to parents. Although neighborhoods are often racially, ethnically, or economically homogeneous, busing children out exposes them to different and threatening ways of life. Thus, what some call an educational issue is seen by others as a highly charged redistributive political issue.

Or, as another illustration of a redistributive local policy, consider the city or town charter. In central cities and in suburbs there are frequent charter commissions, brought into being by those who want to restructure local government. The frequency of the charter revision process indicates that the structure is among the stakes of local politics. People and groups believe one of two major alternative systems—mayor-council or council-manager government—is to their advantage or disadvantage and act accordingly. Proposed changes within a system, to add independent boards and commissions or to delete them, to give more or less independence to a school board, offer redistributive advantages within government and to different groups in the community.

PATTERNS OF LOCAL GOVERNMENT POLICIES

There are different ways to illustrate the main policy directions of local governments. Policies of government that involve spending money are not the only important activities, or even necessarily, from the perspective of people involved, the most important. But expenditure data do at least give an outline of dollar priorities in the aggregate. And, in a general way, dollar costs can be taken as an indicator of which items, among those that cost money, local governments consider most important.

Table 4-2 summarizes the distribution of municipal government general expenditures for 1976. Functions are listed in declining order of their importance. Five activities—education, police protection, sewerage, public welfare, and highways—account for over half, 51.5 per cent, of all expenditures. Table 4-2 also indicates what local governments do: they spend money to educate children, police their communities, build and maintain local roads, protect against fires, carry away sewerage, distribute funds to the poor (public welfare), operate public hospitals, provide and maintain parks and recreation programs, provide other sanitation functions (such as disposing of solid wastes and trash), make contributions to housing and urban renewal plans, pay the interest on their debts, and pay the administrative costs of staying in operation. The category in Table 4-2 labeled "All other functions" includes such items as libraries, zoos, airports, and neighborhood youth programs.

T A B L E 4-2. Distribution of Local Government Spending

Activities	Per Cent of Funds Spent
Total general expenditure	100.0
Education	14.0
Police protection	11.3
Sewerage and other sanitation	10.1
Public welfare	8.3
Highways	7.8
Hospitals and public health	6.3
Fire protection	6.0
Interest on general debt	5.0
Parks and recreation	4.7
General control	3.0
Housing and urban renewal	2.8
Financial administration	1.7
General public buildings	1.7
All other functions	17.3

S O U R C E : *1978 Statistical Abstract.*

Thinking about these activities rapidly leads to another insight about local governments. They are labor-intensive. They deliver services that require the hiring of people—schoolteachers, police, highway construction and maintenance crews, firemen, doctors, nurses, orderlies in hospitals, and ground crews in parks. A reliable estimate is that from 60 to 70 per cent of all local government funds go directly for personnel or for personnel-related costs (health plans, insurance, pension plans). As inflation forces wages and personnel costs up, the costs of local government rise greatly without much change in the *levels* of services.

In a well-documented example, describing Oakland, California, Meltsner and Wildavsky report that "the city budget has expanded to meet the increased costs of operation, not to meet the needs of Oakland's deprived population."[5] In that city, personnel costs constitute 70 per cent of the total budget. Between 1960 and 1968, the number of positions expanded only 1 per cent per year, from 3,014 to 3,254. Taking into account the costs of merit increases and pension plans, and with only a 5 per cent salary increase to meet general inflationary pressures, if other costs go up as little as three per cent, a city such as

[5] Arnold J. Meltsner and Aaron Wildavsky, "Leave City Budgeting Alone!: A Survey, Case Study, and Recommendations for Reform," in *Financing the Metropolis,* ed. by John P. Crecine (Beverly Hills: Sage Publications, 1970), p. 325. See also Meltsner's book about Oakland, *The Politics of City Revenue* (Berkeley and Los Angeles: University of California Press, 1971).

Oakland can have a built-in eight per cent growth rate in annual city expenditures. Because of the nature of the work and the way it is organized, urban services resist productivity changes. The Oakland story is typical.

Table 4-3 indicates the distribution of employees in various local government activities within the 72 largest SMSAs in the United States. Teachers account for more than half of the employees, with police, hospitals, and fire protection next. Most local government employees—and expenses—are hardly in the class of frills or amenities. The people and the money are in basic quality-of-life activities: education, police protection, health, and fire protection.

Table 4-4 indicates that the patterns of employment within the larger metropolitan areas are different from those of other areas. The number of employees is greater: 331.1 per 10,000 citizens, compared

TABLE 4-3. Local Government Employment in the 72 Largest SMSAs by Function

Function	Local Government Employment (full-time equivalents)	
	Number (thousands)	Per Cent
Total	3,532	100.0
Education	1,780	50.4
Police protection	275	7.8
Hospitals	217	6.1
Fire protection	126	3.6
Local utilities other than water supply*	125	3.5
General control	119	3.4
Highways	113	3.2
Public welfare	109	3.1
Parks and recreation	91	2.6
Sanitation other than sewerage	77	2.2
Water supply	63	1.8
Financial administration	62	1.8
Health	51	1.4
Housing and urban renewal	46	1.3
Correction	41	1.2
Sewerage	41	1.2
Libraries	38	1.1
All other functions	158	4.5

SOURCE: *Local Government Employment in Selected Metropolitan Areas and Large Counties: 1971* (Washington, D.C.: U.S. Bureau of the Census, 1972), p. 1.

 * Electric power, transit, and gas supply systems.

TABLE 4-4. Comparison of Local Government Employment
Inside and Outside the 72 Largest SMSAs

Function	Full-Time Equivalent Employment per 10,000 Population	
	Inside 72 SMSAs	*Outside 72 SMSAs*
Total	331.1	299.3
Education	167.0	184.6
Highways	10.6	17.0
Public welfare	10.2	5.2
Hospitals	20.4	19.7
Health	4.8	2.8
Police protection	25.8	13.9
Fire protection	11.8	7.5
Sewerage	3.8	2.5
Sanitation other than sewerage	7.2	4.6
Parks and recreation	8.5	3.2
Housing and urban renewal	4.3	1.4
Correction	3.8	1.4
Libraries	3.6	2.0
Financial administration	5.8	6.1
General control	11.2	10.6
Water supply	5.9	4.7
Local utilities other than water supply*	11.8	3.6
All other functions	14.8	8.7

SOURCE: *Local Government Employment in Selected Metropolitan Areas and Large Counties: 1971* (Washington, D.C.: U.S. Bureau of the Census, 1972), p. 2.

 * Electric power, transit, and gas supply systems.

to 299.3 outside of large cities. The difference is partially attributable to such activities as airports, ports, or terminals that are not available in other areas. In addition, the greater population density and complexity or the urban areas lead to more employees for police, fire protection, and parks. In the less-urbanized areas, on the other hand, there is a higher ratio of employees in highways and in schools.

VARIATION IN MUNICIPAL ACTIVITIES: CONSTRAINTS AND OPPORTUNITIES IN THE LOCAL ENVIRONMENT

Scholars wonder what causes variation in local expenditures from community to community. A first question seems to be, What is the role of available resources in how much a locality can spend? A parallel query is, What control does a locality have over what wealth is available to it? Chapter 1 indicated that many important economic decisions affecting a locality are made outside that locality. Such decisions include whether or not a firm will locate in a community and what the employment levels of a firm that is nationally owned might be. Beyond these conscious decisions, however, there is still another way in which vital economic forces are beyond the control and, perhaps, even influence of any local government.

For example, the prosperity of a local region is largely dependent on the private industrial and commercial activity within it. Local governments as such are a small economic input in total local economic activity. They cannot independently influence prosperity and growth, as the federal government can. Local governments also lack regulatory powers over other variables that might influence local prosperity, such as growth in the money supply and control over interest rates.

Private industrial and commercial activity prosper according to complex variables. One variable is the national economy, within which regional economies are subsystems. But identifiable factors also operate within regional economies. A traditional view is that local growth is determined by the ratio of export industries (those whose product is sold outside the local area) to local service industries (whose economic activities are solely within the area). This view shrinks the Keynesian model of national economies to fit the local scene. In it, export industries, because of their greater multiplier effect in creating local jobs, are the key to local prosperity. A more recent view is that local economies benefit most from having newer, more innovative industries within their borders.[6]

The advantages of innovative industry to localities are numerous, but also cyclical. Innovative industry attracts higher-paid workers. The high wages increase income equality in the whole area and have a roll-out effect of raising incomes through the entire local economy. Innovative industries pay higher wages because of the work skills needed, so such industries enjoy a temporary competitive advantage, a monopoly of sort, in the national marketplace. This advantage gives them monopoly pricing power and higher profit margins, which are passed on, in part, to local labor.

At the same time, demands for products change and competitors can catch up. The rate at which local advantages decline depends in part upon the product. The demand for some products is income-

---

[6] See Wilbur Thompson, "Internal and External Factors in the Development of Urban Economies," in Crecine, *Financing the Metropolis*, op. cit., pp. 27–50, and also Thompson's *A Preface to Urban Economics* (Baltimore: Johns Hopkins Press, 1965).

elastic because spending for such products is discretionary and rises as overall national income rises. Wilbur Thompson explains how this economic process operates:

> A local export sector which emphasizes either new products or income-elastic products will tend to experience a greater than average expansion in output and in demand for labor. A steadily rising national per capita income acts directly to stimulate the growth of localities producing income-elastic products.[7]

Thompson argues that larger areas have built-in advantages for industrial innovation. They are more likely to produce individual innovators than are smaller communities, to have support facilities, and to have diverse industries that allow them to weather the inevitable cycle of up and down. He notes that:

> all products wax and wane, and so the long-range viability of any area must rest ultimately on its capacity to invent and/or innovate or otherwise acquire new export bases. The economic base of the larger metropolitan area is, then, the creativity of its firms and financial institutions, the persuasiveness of its public relations and advertising agencies, the flexibility of its transportation networks and utility systems, and all the other dimensions of infrastructure that facilitate the quick and orderly transfer from old dying bases to new growing ones.[8]

CAUSES OF VARIATION IN MUNICIPAL ACTIVITIES: SOME FINDINGS

Given that many factors affecting a local community are beyond local control, what do we know about the relationship of different variables to levels of expenditures? The search for the determinants of such expenditure levels has a long scholarly history in social science.[9] Sophisticated statistical techniques allow researchers to identify how much of the variation in a dependent variable (expenditures) is accounted for by various independent variables (such as income, urbanization, population density, per cent of low-income people), taken collectively or singly. Simon Fabricant pioneered the determinant literature in his *The Trend of Government Activity in the United States*

---

[7] Thompson, "Internal and External Factors," *op. cit.*, p. 36.

[8] Ibid., p. 38.

[9] For a review of this extensive literature, see Gail Wilensky, "Determinants of Local Government Expenditures," in Crecine, *Financing the Metropolis*, op. cit., pp. 197–218.

Since 1900.[10] Analyzing state and local expenditures in 1900 and 1942, Fabricant found income, urbanization, and population density account for 70 per cent of the variation. Income was the most important. In analyzing trends between 1900 and 1942, he concluded that "the chief cause of rising per capita expenditures would be rising income."[11]

Harvey E. Brazer applied essentially the same form of analysis to five sets of cities in a 1959 study (using 1951 data): an inclusive sample of 462 cities; samples of cities in California, in Massachusetts, and in Ohio (to control, in effect, for the particular impact of state laws, geography, and tradition); and the 40 largest cities.[12] Brazer analyzed not only total expenditures, but also individual services, including police and fire. In the analysis of all cities, income was a major factor on all specific policy expenditure levels, as was intergovernmental revenue. Density of population was significant for all activities except recreation and highways. Other than for police expenditures, total population was not important.

Brazer noted the wide variation among the 462 cities in both total expenditures and for particular services. There were differences by region and by type of city. When the analysis was confined to the cities in each of the three states, more variation was explained, but the same variables were not always related to the same services in the same way in each state. Confronting all of this diversity, he observed, "there is no facile means of explaining the tremendous range of differences in the levels of city expenditures."[13]

In a similar study, Louis H. Massotti and Don R. Bowen found three variables—socioeconomic status (a synopsis of income), the age of the city, and the mobility of its population—accounted for most of the variation in expenditure levels of 18 Ohio cities with populations of more than 50,000.[14]

An interesting finding of Brazer's work was that the suburbs might in some way have an impact on the fiscal dilemmas of the central cities. He found central city expenditures associated with the central city share of the SMSA population. The smaller the central city's proportion of the SMSA population, the larger its per capita expenditures, suggesting that as the suburban fringe grew larger, it increased central city costs. A similar finding emerged from Kee's analysis of expendi-

---

[10] (New York: National Bureau of Economic Research, Inc. 1952).

[11] Ibid., p. 136.

[12] *City Expenditures in the United States* (New York: National Bureau of Economic Research, 1959).

[13] Ibid., p. 68.

[14] "Communities and Budgets: The Sociology of Municipal Expenditures," *Urban Affairs Quarterly,* 1:2 (December 1965), 39–58.

tures in 36 SMSAs. He found the main variables explaining total expenditures to be state aid, the ratio of central city population to its SMSA population, and per capita income.[15] The stimulative role of state aid was also uncovered in an analysis by Campbell and Sacks.[16]

These studies are cited to indicate again how forces external to local politics may influence the activities of local governments. The determinant studies are voluminous and only a few are mentioned here. They indicate how the environment in which a governmental unit exists sets constraints or provides opportunities.

CAUSES OF VARIATIONS IN MUNICIPAL POLICIES: SOME RESERVATIONS

Quantitative studies of variation in municipal expenditures have real value. They demonstrate how the socioeconomic and demographic (population) environment forms constraints and opportunities for local governments. One must, however, keep in mind some limitations of such inquires.

Expenditures do not measure everything important or necessarily the most important activities of local government. For example, the impact of expenditures may be more important than their levels.[17] The same amount of money can be used to be highly redistributive to different income groups, ethnic groups, or neighborhoods on a geographic basis, or not redistributive at all. Within one highway department budget, choices are made as to whose roads get paved and who is hired to do the job. Within one school budget there are numerous ways to spend the funds, for standard instruction or special programs, for some schools more than others, for new materials, or for custodial help. Studying expenditure levels sheds no light on allocative effects.

In addition, studying expenditure levels cannot help in evaluating the quality of particular services. Knowing how much money is spent cannot tell us whether a police force is efficient and fair or not, or whether the street cleaning funds do in fact result in clean streets. To analyze these outcomes, we must utilize case studies of individual cities or survey data from many cities. Expenditure data do not tell us about activities that involve no money. What about the positions that governments bestow—paid or unpaid—on individuals? What about the ceremonial honors, the recognition? The distribution of nonmate-

[15] See Woo Sik Kee, "Central City Expenditures and Metropolitan Areas," *The National Tax Journal*, **18**:4 (December 1965), 337–353.

[16] See Alan K. Campbell and Seymour Sacks, *Metropolitan America: Fiscal Patterns and Governmental Systems* (New York: Free Press, 1967).

[17] See Brian R. Fry and Richard F. Winter, "The Politics of Redistribution," *The American Political Science Review*, **64**:2 (June 1970), 508–522.

rial values has rarely been measured. Yet people care a great deal about such values and fight bitterly for them.

People also contest for nonmaterial values in the form of cultural dominance. These struggles concern

1. Whether materials taught in public schools will be permissive or traditional, or whether teaching methods will be experimental or traditional.
2. Whether or not a community will put fluoride in the water to prevent dental cavities (a hotly fought issue in many localities).
3. Whether law enforcement will be tolerant or permissive toward vice and pornography.
4. What kinds of new construction or development will be permitted under the zoning laws (including, for example, which neighborhoods will be zoned for apartments, which for single-family residential uses, and which for commercial or mixed uses).

This list is illustrative but not exhaustive. In local politics, as in life, money is important, but it is not everything. There are always *additional* aspects of local government activity that are not measured by such studies.

As a final point, some scholars maintain the determinant studies assume an unproved model of local politics. The studies share "the implicit assumption that something called the political process acts as translator . . . that local government and its officials are a passive entity through which inputs like wealth are converted to outputs like police or recreation expenditures."[18] It is assumed that per capita wealth is converted into effective demand for local government services; that expenditures then satisfy these demands.[19] The models, critics charge, do not indicate how the demands are generated, how the political system processes them, or whether citizens feel satisfied with the outcome. Nor do such models indicate whether the local system takes account of all needs or systematically filters some out.

THE ACTIVITIES OF MUNICIPAL GOVERNMENTS: THE IMPOSITION OF COSTS

Governments that distribute benefits also impose costs. Again a caveat must be interjected. Not all costs involve money. For example,

[18] Meltsner and Wildavsky, op. cit., p. 312.
[19] Ibid., p. 312.

the following are among various nonmonetary costs local governments can impose:

1. Through their police powers, they can initiate proceedings in the civil justice system that will put in jeopardy a person's property; they can initiate proceedings in the criminal justice system that will put in jeopardy a person's freedom.
2. Through the use of *eminent domain*, the power to take private property for public use, local governments can take a person's property, as long as the person is compensated. (But the person might not want to move or sell at any price.)
3. By the location of a facility or the initiation of a program, the government may impose costs of inconvenience or even danger upon some people in a neighborhood (the location of a public jail, a narcotics treatment center).
4. Through the use of zoning, and especially zoning variances, the government may give others permission to build private facilities—liquor stores, parking lots, movie theatres, smelly factories—in neighborhoods in such a way as to impose inconvenience or even money costs on many people.

All local governments impose the basic cost, money, too. Let us now turn to how they do that and what routes they choose. Figure 4-2 illustrates graphically how local governments raise their money. The property tax is the main source of income. The importance of federal and state aid is very clear in this chart. Other taxes that local governments use vary from community to community. Some localities have income taxes and the rates on these range, according to the community, from 0.2 per cent up to a high of 3 per cent in Philadelphia.[20] Local income taxes are found in only 10 states, and primarily in cities in Kentucky, Maryland (largely imposed by county governments), Michigan, Ohio, and Pennsylvania, where usage is virtually universal. Local sales taxes are more common, appearing in municipalities in 22 states and ranging in rates from 0.5 per cent up to as high as 3 per cent.[21] Other local taxes are levied on amusements, hotel space, restaurant meals, and various forms of licenses. In addition, various amounts of revenues are raised from user charges at locally operated museums, parks, stadiums, hospitals, and other facilities.

But however one slices the pie, the property tax is the mainstay of the local government revenue structure. The property tax provides

[20] See Advisory Commission on Intergovernmental Relations, *State and Local Finances: Significant Features 1967 to 1970* (Washington, D.C.: 1969), pp. 110–121.

[21] Ibid., pp. 86–87.

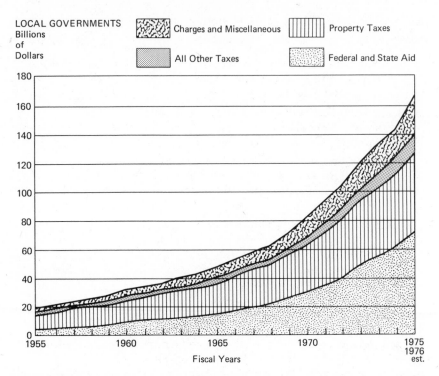

FIGURE 4-2. Sources of Local Government Revenue, 1955–1976. SOURCE: Advisory Commission on Intergovernmental Relations, Significant Features of Fiscal Federalism, 1976–1977, Vol. II (Washington, D.C.: U.S. Government Printing Office, 1977), p. 15.

81.6 per cent of the total revenue from taxes of local governments. Dependence on the property tax varies somewhat among types of local governments, with municipalities having the most fruitful alternative sources. Smaller local governments (townships), county governments, school districts, and special districts use the property tax as virtually their sole system of taxation.

The property tax as assessed by local governments involves a complicated process. The tax is assessed on real estate, on business equipment, and inventories. A first decision is on the *rate* of taxation, expressed as x-dollars for each thousand dollars of assessed valuation. A corollary decision is the *level* of assessed valuation. Will property throughout the community be assessed at full market value (in which case a lower rate will produce a desired set amount of revenue)? Or will property be assessed at a low fraction of its full market value (requiring a higher rate to bring in that desired amount)? In addition, local government must distribute the property tax burden among commercial and residential properties.

State law limits some local discretion with property taxes, but generally considerable discretion remains. A great deal of political decision making revolves around this tax. Local officials know well the connection between expenditures and property taxes. Because the property tax is such a large percentage of local revenue, unless funds for a program come in as "free money" from the federal or state governments, then any new expense means some increase in the property tax. Local officials are also aware that prospective residents and firms choose among localities on the basis of the tax/service mix.

Finally, decisions about industrial and commercial rates and assessments are very sensitive. Businessmen who decide where to locate rarely have to pick any one particular locality and, thus, bargain hard as they deal with communities. Often national firms with multimillion dollar resources and vast experience in building facilities such as shopping centers bargain with the amateur, part-time officials of the outer suburbs of a metropolitan area over tax terms.

Local businessmen frequently argue that because residential users require heavier service expenses from local governments—for schools, for street maintenance, for police protection, for garbage collection—homeowners should bear more of the burden. And it is true that most commercial and industrial properties provide a tax "profit" to localities, whereas residences, especially single-family residences with children residing within them, are much more expensive to service and are a loss in a simple tax sense. Nationwide, residential property accounts for 52 per cent of all local property tax collections, and businesses for 48 per cent.

After decisions are made on rates, levels of assessment, and commercial/industrial versus residential allocations of burden, there remains the enormously difficult job of assessing each separate piece of property for tax purposes. Individual properties may be difficult to assess, especially commercial properties or complicated industrial equipment. In a rapidly inflating real estate market, a fair market value is hard to set without the benchmark of a recent sale. On the other hand, when properties are not reassessed except at the time of a sale, gross inequities result from allowing old assessments to remain in effect.

The inequities work in different directions. If the desirable properties of owners inflate in value without reassessment, then those owners are paying less than they should because the properties are undervalued. But for those same owners of desirable real estate, if there is constant reassessment in an inflating market, they may be forced to pay steeply increased assessments on purely paper increases in value. That experience triggered the property owners' revolt in 1978. Then, California voters passed Proposition 13, which rolled back property tax levels and narrowly limited future increases except when an individual piece of property was sold.

Still a different set of inequities in the property tax falls upon those who live in poorer neighborhoods. In declining neighborhoods, whenever there are not reassessments, property taxed at its old values is overvalued and thus overtaxed. Poorer and working-class persons often pay more in residential property taxes than they should. This painful situation occurs whenever property values are changing quickly in a metropolitan area, with some sites becoming more desirable and some less. One federal study of 10 cities showed low-quality housing in blighted neighborhoods to be overassessed.[22] In Baltimore, Chicago, and Philadelphia, for example, properties in blighted areas carried 10 times the tax burden of property in upward transitional neighborhoods. Such tax policies contribute to urban blight by making property in poorer neighborhoods more expensive and less marketable and thus discouraging investment and rehabilitation.

MORE ON THE DISTRIBUTION OF COSTS

Most urban politics texts deal little with the costs of local government. But downplaying this aspect of politics overlooks a strong force in local government. From the citizens' point of view, local government costs shape many attitudes about every other aspect of local life. Within localities, citizen resistance to more tax restrains spending on services. For individuals, the amount of local tax they must pay determines how much income will be available for other uses and needs. Within metropolitan areas, tax levels influence choices of where people will live and where businesses will locate.

Tax policy has such impact because local taxes are substantial. As a national average, property taxes on single-family residences take 4.9 per cent of all personal family income.[23] In the Northeast and the far West, areas of greatest taxpayer resistance, property taxes take 6.9 and 5.4 per cent of personal income, respectively. Resistance heightened during the 1970s as property values increased rapidly because of national real estate inflation, and also because local tax rates increased at the high annual rate of 7.9 per cent a year. At the start of this decade, tax rates are still higher within the central cities than in the suburbs, but that gap is closing rapidly.

[22] "A Study of Property Taxes and Urban Blight," Subcommittee on Intergovernmental Relations, 93rd Congress, 1st session (Washington, D.C., 1973).

[23] Advisory Commission on Intergovernmental Relations, *Significant Features of Fiscal Federalism 1976–1977*, Vol. II (Washington, D.C.: 1977), p. 106.

At the same time that local tax costs reach record highs for the citizens, local governments find themselves nonetheless having difficulty making ends meet. Fiscal strain on local governments matches the tax pressure on citizens. New York City required federal assistance through loans and loan guarantees to avoid bankruptcy, and other cities are feeling the pinch. Professor Terry N. Clark[24] derives an index of local government fiscal strain, based on the amount of per capita long-term debt; per capita short-term debt; per capita expenditures for nine common local services; and the ratio of total revenue from local sources to the sales value of local taxable property. His index is reproduced as Table 4-5, with cities at the top under the greatest "strain."

Clark found that size, growth, age, and region of the country were not related to fiscal strain. The size of the tax base and the percentage of low-income persons were related to fiscal strain. Most important were the percentage of Irish persons in the population (apparently leading to a political style of greater spending) and leadership variables. Cities with moderately strong mayors but weak business interests, with collective bargaining agreements with employees, with high ratios of employees to citizens, with low tax collection rates, and with high capital budgets, showed higher fiscal strain.

Focusing on the cost side of local government reveals the burden side of providing local services. For citizens, the tax burden is high, and resistance grows. For local governments, the available funds do not meet the possible demands, and local budgets strain. As budgets expand, citizens and businesses compare costs elsewhere and move. That reduces resources even further for the local government, and a cycle of crisis and decline begins. Demands for services and resistance to taxes provide the environment for local decisions. Collective bargaining and the budget cycle are the daily immediate points of choice making. We turn now to those topics.

DECISION PROCESSES IN LOCAL POLITICS

Local governments have considerable control over their own decision-making processes. Local governments have evolved into three main types; each is discussed in Chapter 5. At any point in time, when a community already has one system, change may be difficult. But in most states, newly formed communities are given some choice among systems. Once an initial structure is established, localities either have some discretion to make changes or may obtain approval for changes from their state governments. Localities regularly estab-

---

[24] "How Many More New Yorks," *New York Affairs*, Vol. 3, No. 4 (Summer/Fall 1976), pp. 18–27.

TABLE 4-5.   Fiscal Strain in Selected Cities

	Municipal Fiscal Strain Index		Municipal Fiscal Strain Index
New York	165.03	Tampa, Fla.	44.27
Boston	128.82	Phoenix, Ariz.	42.38
Newark, N.J.	105.91	Tyler, Texas	40.89
San Francisco	102.97	Charlotte, N.C.	39.95
Albany, N.Y.	102.88	South Bend, Ind.	39.24
Buffalo, N.Y.	89.00	Waco, Texas	38.67
Atlanta, Ga.	87.29	Indianapolis	38.65
Cambridge, Mass.	81.44	Fort Worth	38.65
Malden, Mass.	81.13	Euclid, O.	36.64
Seattle	79.34	Santa Monica, Cal.	35.39
Waterbury, Conn.	78.88	Schenectady, N.Y.	32.68
Jacksonville, Fla.	73.69	Bloomington, Minn.	32.33
Utica, N.Y.	72.41	Irvington, N.J.	32.04
Los Angeles	68.27	St. Petersburg, Fla.	32.03
Akron, O.	63.57	Hamilton, O.	30.80
Memphis, Tenn.	60.28	Hammond, Ind.	30.60
Birmingham, Ala.	60.08	Berkeley, Cal.	29.81
St. Louis, Mo.	58.76	Clifton, N.J.	27.85
Manchester, N.H.	58.20	San Jose, Cal.	25.95
Palo Alto, Cal.	55.67	Duluth, Minn.	25.32
Chicago	55.33	Gary, Ind.	21.21
Pasadena, Cal.	54.47	Waukegan, Ill.	20.70
St. Paul, Minn.	54.16	Warren, Mich.	20.43
Minneapolis	51.35	Salt Lake City	18.99
Long Beach, Cal.	49.67	Amarillo, Texas	18.05
Pittsburgh	48.35	Fullerton, Cal.	13.25
Milwaukee	45.38	Santa Ana, Cal.	10.53

SOURCE: Terry Clark, "How Many More New Yorks," *New York Affairs*, Vol. 3, No. 4 (1976), p. 21. Reprinted by permission.

lish new departments, boards, and commissions, as well as new staff positions in their executive branches, new judgeships, and new committees for their local councils. There is room for argument about where ultimate power to make these decisions lies, but localities have, at the minimum, a strong input. Local officials risk the highest stakes in such arrangements and then assert the leading role in such decisions.

Local decisions are made by processes that the reader will surely recognize. For example, almost all local governments possess some sort of formally democratic process. The word *almost* is used advisedly. The United States, in the nineteenth and early twentieth centuries, contained proprietary local communities, "company towns" where everything was owned by one private corporation that also governed its property and inhabitants.[25] There are few, if any, of these left, at least in form, although it is an interesting question whether those development corporations that are building "new towns" in America are planning to share with residents the formal authority to govern these properties. Most apparently are, but will only pass control of zoning and other crucial property issues over to the inhabitants over a long time period.

Following are some of the processes for making local decisions that will be found almost everywhere:

1. *Referenda.* Almost all American localities permit citizens to decide directly on some policy questions. The issues are framed as propositions on the ballot, and citizens choose among alternatives to vote "yes" or "no." Voting on increased property tax rates to finance school expenditures is especially common, but there is little practical or theoretical limit to the kinds of questions that sometimes appear as referenda.

2. *Elections.* Almost all American localities permit citizens to pick local officials through periodic and regular elections. What offices are to be filled varies, depending on the system of government and the locale. In the council-manager system, for example, citizens elect the council members who then hire a manager. Some localities elect literally dozens of local officials, down to recorders of deeds, certain clerks, and— especially in the county system—even chief law enforcement officers such as sheriffs. Almost all localities provide for universal suffrage, although some New England towns require ownership of property as a prerequisite to voting in fiscal town meetings (where issues are decided rather than officials chosen). The shape of local election districts varies from place to place, and so does whether elections are run as nonpartisan or with party labels.

3. *Citizen access to officials through lobbying.* Almost all local governments accept the ethos of democratic government that citizens should have the right to lobby officials to achieve their goals. There is even a common cliché about local governments that they are "closer to the people," which supports the ideological legitimacy of this process. How well this works out, who lobbies, who gets what, what does it matter—all these are important theoretical and empirical questions.

4. *Executive politics.* Most local governments exhibit what we might call, after the national model of the presidency, execu-

---

[25] For an account of one such community, Gary, Indiana, see Edward Greer, *Big Steel, Little Steel* (New York: Monthly Review Press, forthcoming).

tive politics. Executive power is most pronounced in the largest partisan cities. In big-city mayors one finds the whole panoply of executive devices: extensive staff, use of media, a central location in the entire local political process. Executive politics is most muted in council-manager systems (where in theory the chief executive—the manager—is the top employee of the council) and in small towns.

5. *Legislative politics.*   The common styles of American legislative politics are found in local city councils. Partisan councils in big cities are often mini-Congresses, dealing with an odd mix of substantive issues and day-to-day service and patronage concerns of constituents. The nonpartisan councils of the suburbs perform various representational roles and, internally, engage in processes of bargaining and coalition formation that characterize legislative bodies everywhere.

6. *Judicial politics.*   Local courts rarely make law in quite the same way as federal courts or state courts, perhaps because serious crimes come under the jurisdiction of these two higher-level court systems, as a rule. But there is an extensive process surrounding these courts,[26] which handle matters of great importance to many people: certain crimes (including drunkenness, vagrancy, prostitution, petty theft) and certain important civil matters (especially probate for estates). The processes of interaction between lawyers and local court officials, from prosecutors (with whom they bargain over pleas) to judges (from whom they seek lucrative executorships in estates) are similar to the judicial processes at other levels.

7. *Regulatory agency politics.*   No local regulatory agency has the magisterial quality or the impact of, say, the Interstate Commerce Commission, which regulates all trucking rates and railroad freight rates for the entire nation. But the local zoning board with its commissioners, its semijudicial procedures for hearings and appeals, and its case-by-case decision making within a framework of broad and often vague rules is a close cousin to its state and national counterparts. As in national politics, those most regulated, such as real estate interests, seek to place their people on the boards.

8. *Bureaucratic politics.*   Bureaucratic politics are organizational politics, the internal decision-making processes of per-

---

[26] For a seminal study of local courts and local judicial behavior in several sharply different cities, see Martin A. Levin, *Urban Politics and the Criminal Courts* (Chicago: University of Chicago Press, 1977).

manent public institutions with large numbers of employees, with professional traditions and codes of conduct, and with goals and constraints of their own. We are familiar with talk about Pentagon politics, or the bureaucratic politics of the federal executive departments. These processes go on at the local level among teachers, police, social welfare workers, clerks, highway engineers, all the technicians who make up the modern urban civil payroll. Often militantly unionized, these local employees, because of their values, their numbers, and their continuing strategic position in day-to-day local government, have great influence almost everywhere.

Local politics has some special historical characteristics and some special qualities. But by and large it resembles other American political processes far more than it differs from them. Two related processes, local bureaucratic behavior and municipal budgeting, are critical for all other local decisions and to the total size of expenditures.

LOCAL BUREAUCRATIC BEHAVIOR

Personnel costs are the largest expense of local governments, which deliver labor-intensive services. The large numbers of local employees become an important interest group within the community, especially as they seek to influence public policy affecting their own wages and working rules.

In addition, who gets hired for certain jobs and what their attitudes are will affect how the services are delivered. Administration of any policy is never a cut-and-dried, completely neutral act. All laws, including local ordinances, are framed in general terms. The administration of these laws applies them to particular circumstances and individual cases. There is always room for discretion. The policemen on the beat makes a decision when he sees a minor infraction whether to make an arrest, issue a warning, or ignore it. The schoolteacher in the classroom makes dozens of decisions about the work and treatment of students every day. On a day-to-day basis, the government that citizens see is the permanent government of nonelected clerks, functionaries, policemen, teachers, garbage men, and others.

From the citizens' perspective, what matters about local bureaucracies is the quality of service and the costs. Four factors affect service, quality, and cost: (1) selection system, (2) professionalism, (3) the work subculture, and (4) collective bargaining.

Selection System.   City employees obtain their jobs in one of two ways: through patronage or through civil service. In a patronage system, persons are hired because they have the support of local party officials. Other qualifications may help, but political support determines. Loyalty is to that party organization. Patronage systems have waned in most places, but the mayor of Chicago still controls some 30,000 local positions. Top appointments in every city still work this way. By contrast, under civil service systems, persons obtain jobs because of formal qualifications and tests. They cannot be fired except for cause. Insulated from politics, and some might say from accountability, workers become loyal to the agency employing them, and their focus turns inward.

Professionalism.   Professionalism implies formal training before entry or on the job plus a set of methods or body of practice that is commonly developed, understood, and used. Professionalism also implies mobility among practitioners, because there is a set of standard problems and standard responses, so people can move from place to place without great difficulty.

Professionalism among local employees is most developed in larger, more specialized agencies. Professional standards are also more developed in some local services than in others. Schoolteachers, engineers, and social workers may be the most professionalized, with police and firemen in the middle, and highway workers and clerks, least. The schoolteacher learns his/her standards from the state college and the state certification board. Professional associations link practitioners in each field, bring them together at annual meetings, and publish journals about the field. Schoolteachers and police may have more understanding of and sympathy with their counterparts in other cities than with the goals of city planners or housing inspectors or elected officials in their towns.

The Work Subculture.   The work subculture has several aspects. Sayre and Kaufman describe how tradition operates in New York City to pattern recruitment into the great bureaucracies of that city.[27] In New York City, historically, the police department is an Irish enclave, the sanitation department belongs to the Italians, the school department to the Jews, the nonmedical hospital positions to blacks and Puerto Ricans. Such patterns are not unique to New York, but typical of how agencies develop, although the ethnic dominance is peculiar to that city.

[27] See Wallace S. Sayre and Herbert Kaufman, *Governing New York City* (New York: Norton, 1965, 1960).

Most important, the work subculture creates informal rules for behavior of the employees, which may or may not coincide with the formal regulations. The informal rules, the mores of the office of the agency, or the school, or the police force are passed on from those already at work to newcomers who are "taught the ropes." That may involve nothing more complicated than learning the patterns of time taken for coffee breaks. It may also pass on a complete set of attitudes toward the agency's clientele or the outside world. Within the uniformed forces, especially, an "us versus them" spirit develops toward all those who are not part of the tightly knit paramilitary organization.

Collective Bargaining. Table 4-6 lists the numbers of city employees in the 15 largest cities. Collective bargaining introduces an entirely new element, no matter how the city charter arranges work or

TABLE 4-6.   City Employees in Fifteen Largest U.S. Cities

	Total Population	Fire	Police	Education	Other
New York	7,781,984	13,855	31,839	93,233	177,616
Chicago	3,550,404	4,771	12,813	40,093	22,274
Los Angeles	2,479,015	3,393	6,914	43,888	27,113
Philadelphia	2,002,512	2,940	8,255	18,257	21,951
Detroit	1,670,144	1,930	4,776	20,408	19,806
Baltimore	939,024	2,137	4,069	13,460	14,815
Houston	938,219	1,388	1,727	14,973	5,329
Cleveland	876,050	1,387	2,638	10,705	10,617
Washington, D.C.	763,956	1,447	3,173	12,509	20,314
St. Louis, Mo.	750,026	1,271	2,818	7,403	9,063
Milwaukee	741,324	1,101	2,063	7,145	6,124
San Francisco	740,316	1,762	2,121	7,070	14,659
Boston	697,197	2,092	2,757	6,881	12,740
Dallas	679,684	1,272	1,726	11,186	6,659
New Orleans	627,525	945	1,594	7,300	7,016

SOURCE: *1967 Census of Governments: Employment of Major Governments.*

the agency is structured by the elected officials and top administrative personnel. Increasingly, local employees are organized into bargaining units.[28] Sometimes, the bargaining units are local fraternal or professional societies, and sometimes, local unions.

[28] For a more thorough discussion of this issue, see *The Scope of Public-Sector Bargaining,* W. J. Gershenfeld, J. Loewenberg, and B. Ingster, eds. (Lexington, Mass.: D. C. Heath, 1977); *Public Employee Unions: A Study of the Crisis in Public Sector Labor Relations,* A. L. Chickering, ed. (Lexington, Mass.: D. C. Heath, 1976); and Sterling D. Spero and John M. Cappozzola, *The Urban Community and Its Unionized Bureaucracies* (New York: Dunellen, 1973).

Collective bargaining opens up many crucial issues and settles them outside the political arena and outside the decision making of administrative officials. These issues include the standard labor-management concerns of wages and hours. They also often involve working conditions. Police may negotiate how they are scheduled in shifts, and the union membership position could differ from the preferences of elected officials or the public. Teachers could negotiate pupil loads or even the content of what would be taught.

Collective bargaining at the local level, although already widespread and spreading every year, remains a very sensitive process. There used to be a firm legal doctrine that public employees could not strike. The reasoning was that public employees were different from employees of private industry and had special responsibilities. The special responsibilities flowed from the crucial nature of their work to the well-being, orderly functioning, and safety of the community. It is easy to see the dangers posed to communities if police and firemen go out on strike. Health can be endangered by a strike of unionized garbage men, and both parents and children can be seriously inconvenienced by a strike of teachers. Another argument about the special nature of public employment *vis-à-vis* the right to strike is that because they have great job security, local employees are different from workers in private industry.

In practice, state laws come up against harsh realities. On the one hand, strikes are generally prohibited. On the other is the reality of an increasing number of either strikes in defiance of state law or of "job actions" in which employees slow down their work or call in sick all at once. These actions have continued in the face of court injunctions and of the jailing of union leaders in cities as different as Philadelphia, New York, and St. Louis. Local employees are becoming increasingly more organized, more militant, and more prone to settle their disputes through the familiar processes of industrial labor-management relations. Local union militancy has brought great money gains for employees, increased costs and taxes and, frequently, strained community feelings. As local taxes rise, pressure on elected officials to "get tough" with unionized employees increases.

MUNICIPAL BUDGETING

Within local governments, the annual budget cycle brings together all the choices. How much will be spent and for what? Who will pay and how much? Each budget has two broad categories. The capital budget is for physical plant, facilities whose useful life is more than one year. The operating budget is everything else: wages, salaries, pension and fringe benefit costs, supplies, smaller equipment, and interest charges on municipal debt. Budgets reveal little about the distribution of nonmaterial benefits and costs, or how new or unanticipated items come onto the expenditure agenda.

THE CRECINE MODEL OF BUDGETARY DECISION MAKING

The most exhaustive study of local budgeting has been done by John P. Crecine.[29] He postulated a model of budgetary decision making having three main elements: a departmental process; a mayoral or executive process; and a city council process. After testing his model against actual expenditures in Cleveland, Detroit and Pittsburgh, he extracted a series of conclusions about how the process works:[30]

1. Whatever budget emerges for any locality is a sum of smaller decisions. The sequence contains these elements: the revenue or level decisions; the budget or allocation decisions; and the actual operating decision (the task is actually done). Each decision in the sequence constrains what follows—the level decisions limit the allocation decisions that limit what tasks can be performed. Dividing the elements in time makes the yearly problem of allocating municipal resources humanly manageable.

2. The patterns of decision (for the departments, the executives, and the councils) appear to be consistent over the time and among cities (at least the larger cities). Only the specifics of particular historical problems vary from community to community.

3. Three institutional rules appear dominant. One is that the city charter requires a balanced budget, which means that funds will have to be raised at that point in time to pay for whatever is allocated. No deficit or forward funding is usually permitted local governments, thus denying them one of the great flexible luxuries of federal budgeting. Second, almost all municipalities request budget proposals from departments each year, and this technique forces historical comparisons. The departments indicate how a request compares with what has been historically allocated or is currently allocated for the same purpose. Third, almost all municipalities try to pursue a uniform wage policy.

[29] *Governmental Problem-Solving* (Skokie, Ill.: Rand McNally, 1969).
[30] Ibid., pp. 218–19.

Three of Crecine's conclusions are quite controversial:

4. The strategies of municipal officials, the personal choices, and procedures they follow are internalized and insulated from external pressures.
5. Limits on taxation link the budget process and the larger external socioeconomic environment. Officials anticipate what the public purse will bear.
6. The decision responds primarily to special revenue opportunities, to long-run, cumulative political pressures, or to short-term catastrophic events.

Other findings are less in dispute than those about internal responsiveness:

7. Municipal operating budgets demonstrate a great deal of inertia, which makes last year's budget the best predictor of this year's budget.
8. The municipal decision maker faces many uncertainties about future events coupled with many restrictions on his freedom to act.
9. Last year's budget is the base because it provides continuity for an equilibrium of forces in making this year's budget. This year's budget marginally adjusts last year's budget.
10. Finally, local decision makers perceive their budget situations as unique. They do not view the budget experiences of other cities as a guide. Thus, there are few alternatives to using historical experience as the primary reference point for current decisions.

The budget process is what political scientists and organization theorists label *incrementalism*,[31] doing what you did before plus or minus a little, depending on what money is available and what needs to be done. There is argument in the field of public administration about whether incrementalism is the best way to go about matters. Many administrative science theorists call this process irrational, and propose devices to replace it, and others propose other systems.[32] Zero-base budgeting assumes each budget year should begin from

[31] The classic expression of this viewpoint is Robert A. Dahl and Charles E. Lindblom, *Politics, Economics, and Welfare* (New York: Harper & Row, 1953).

[32] Here, again, there is a voluminous literature. For a good review, see the section "Budgetary Reform and the Restructuring of Public Expenditure Determinants," in Crecine, *Financing the Metropolis*, op. cit., pp. 247–362.

scratch and all programs justified anew. Planning/Programming/
Budgeting System (PPBS) requires formulation of budget alternatives
for each activity each year.

In practice, most municipalities stick with incremental systems.
What may seem irrational to professional planners seems sensible to
municipal officials. Existing budgets represent a political equilibrium
among departments and external interests. Any system that would
open everything up from scratch for yearly debate would increase the
conflict level enormously by multiplying uncertainty. In addition, it is
hard to quantify much of what cities do, because so much of their
expenditures go for services. Efforts to improve the efficiency or output
of workers often conflict with both civil service rules and union rules.
Further new systems require costly additional bureaucrats. So most
municipalities resist administrative reforms.

In the budget process, some items are increased first and cut last
or, the other way around, cut first and increased last, depending on
what funds are available. The order is as follows (for the add-first-or-
cut-last ranking, read in order listed; for cut-first-and-add-last ranking,
read the list in reverse order):

1. Administrative salaries.
2. Nonadministrative salaries and wages.
3. Operating expenses, supplies, materials.
4. Equipment.
5. Maintenance.

Thus, in a deficit situation, maintenance and equipment are the
first to be cut. That is why many city buildings and facilities often look
run-down. Even in the direst fiscal situation, administrative salaries
are never reduced. Other steps are taken, such as leaving vacant positions vacated by retirement and resignation, and by postponing raises.
Mass layoffs of city personnel are uncommon. In those rare years when
surplus funds are available, administrative salaries are raised first,
maintenance needs last.

Municipal governments always strive to increase revenues. They
are voracious seekers after new monies from the federal and state
governments. But failing in the external hunt and perhaps being un-
blessed by naturally increasing local tax sources such as new plants,
shopping centers, and high-rent apartments, then the need arises to
consider an increase in taxes. Tax increases are not the problem of city
departments. They are supposed to do some job or deliver some service. Traditionally, the mayor or manager or the city council worry
about raising the money. Their choices are not very great. They can

increase the rate of existing taxes; expand the base of some existing tax (by, for example, increasing the level of assessed valuation for the property tax); or they can add some new tax.

Other considerations limit tax choices. Any change in tax rates must be within the limits allowed by the state government, or the politicking necessary to raise the rates must be undertaken. Any new tax must also be allowable under state laws, or the municipality must seek new state legislation. As a general rule of politics, and as a practical consideration for the local treasury, officials have to impose the tax on those who have the money to pay it. Taxing the unemployed, the retired, or the impoverished is not feasible. Municipalities try to find a way that the additional revenue will come from everyone who uses the facilities (which for a central city means all in the metropolitan area), rather than from residents or property owners in general. Finally, officials avoid raising property or equipment taxes on businesses to prevent firms from moving.

The perspectives in the budgetary process of the departments, the executive, and the council are different. Using Crecine's model expressed as a computer flow chart, the departmental process is illustrated in Figure 4-3. The department process, as indicated in Figure 4-3, is an abstraction of the procedures generally followed for most departments—schools, police, health, highways, sanitation, and others—in most large cities. If school departments possess independent taxing authority, the main outlines will be similar, with the exception that the request goes to a school board instead of to a chief executive.

Departments try to get what they can. The executive, the mayor in Figure 4-4, but also the manager in council-manager cities, has the task, personally and through the use of his personal staff, to balance the budget. The process involves putting together a rough estimate of how much more money will be needed than was required for the preceding year coupled with an estimate of available additional funds. Salaries cannot be predicted with accuracy whenever they are determined by collective bargaining.

In working toward balancing the budget, the executive's office uses a variety of techniques. The usual procedure is to prune and cut departmental requests. Tax rates can be raised or new taxes added if there is going to be a deficit. Or expenditures can be brought into balance with revenues by cutting the lower-priority items such as maintenance and equipment. If there is a surplus, then some supplemental requests can be granted, or the most undesirable taxes eliminated or reduced. Figure 4-4 presents the review steps taken, the points at which decisions have to be made, and how the existing reve-

FIGURE 4-3. The Municipal Department Budget Request Process. SOURCE: John P. Crecine, *Governmental Problem-Solving: A Computer Simulation of Municipal Budgeting,* © 1969 by Rand McNally and Company. Figure V-1a, "General Dept. Request Decision Process," pp. 55–56. Reprinted by permission of the author.

1. Budget letter and budget forms received from mayor containing
   (a) current appropriations for all account categories in the department;
   (b) current total appropriation; (c) previous year's expenditures in various account categories; (d) estimate of allowable increase over current appropriations implied from the "tone" of the mayor's letter.

2. Trend of departmental appropriations —direction and magnitude of recent changes in amounts of appropriations in departmental account categories.

3. Department, using information from 1 and 2, formulates a "reasonable" request for funds in its existing account categories, using current appropriations as a base or reference point and adjusting this estimate (for some accounts, an increase for the current year means a decrease for next year, e.g., equipment; for others, an increase for the current year indicates another increase next year), and the difference between last year's expenditures and appropriations.

4. Using reasonable requests calculated in 3, a preliminary department total request is calculated.

5. Is the total department request outside the guedelines set by the mayor's office (implied from the tone of the mayor's budget letter)?

no

yes

6. Check to see if there are any increases in salary accounts over current appropriations.

7. All department requests in all categories are adjusted so that any increase (proposed) over current appropriations is submitted as a supplemental request. Go to 6 to check for salary increases.

no increase

increase

8. Make regular request equal current appropriations and put increase in as supplemental request.

9. Calculate total of regular departmental request.

10. Send regular requests and departmental total to mayor's office along with supplemental requests.

FIGURE 4-4. The Mayor's Budget Recommendation Model.
SOURCE: John P. Crecine, *Governmental Problem-Solving: A Computer Simulation of Municipal Budgeting*, © 1969 by Rand McNally and Company. Figure VI-1a, "General Mayor's Budget Recommendation Model," pp. 75–78. Reprinted by permission of the author.

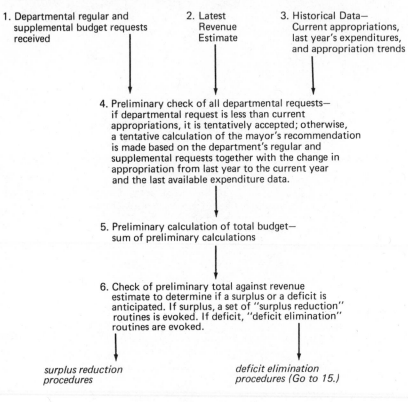

1. Departmental regular and supplemental budget requests received

2. Latest Revenue Estimate

3. Historical Data— Current appropriations, last year's expenditures, and appropriation trends

4. Preliminary check of all departmental requests— if departmental request is less than current appropriations, it is tentatively accepted; otherwise, a tentative calculation of the mayor's recommendation is made based on the department's regular and supplemental requests together with the change in appropriation from last year to the current year and the last available expenditure data.

5. Preliminary calculation of total budget— sum of preliminary calculations

6. Check of preliminary total against revenue estimate to determine if a surplus or a deficit is anticipated. If surplus, a set of "surplus reduction" routines is evoked. If deficit, "deficit elimination" routines are evoked.

surplus reduction procedures

deficit elimination procedures (Go to 15.)

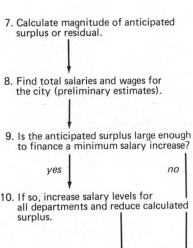

7. Calculate magnitude of anticipated surplus or residual.

8. Find total salaries and wages for the city (preliminary estimates).

9. Is the anticipated surplus large enough to finance a minimum salary increase?

yes   *no*

10. If so, increase salary levels for all departments and reduce calculated surplus.

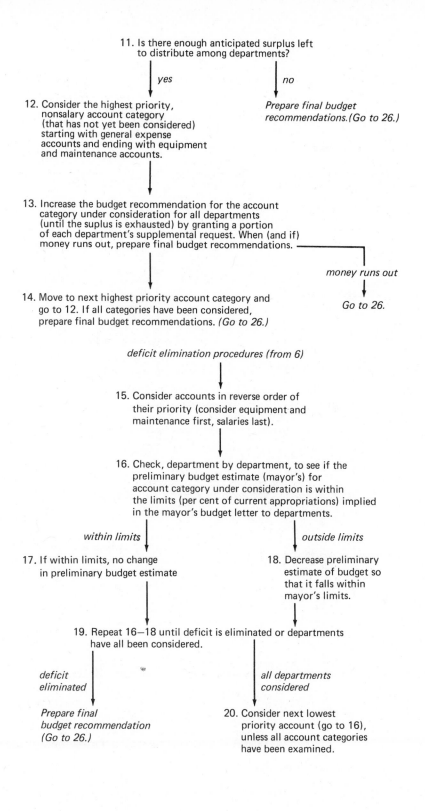

11. Is there enough anticipated surplus left to distribute among departments?

   yes   *no*

12. Consider the highest priority, nonsalary account category (that has not yet been considered) starting with general expense accounts and ending with equipment and maintenance accounts.

Prepare final budget recommendations.(Go to 26.)

13. Increase the budget recommendation for the account category under consideration for all departments (until the suplus is exhausted) by granting a portion of each department's supplemental request. When (and if) money runs out, prepare final budget recommendations.

money runs out

14. Move to next highest priority account category and go to 12. If all categories have been considered, prepare final budget recommendations. *(Go to 26.)*

Go to 26.

deficit elimination procedures (from 6)

15. Consider accounts in reverse order of their priority (consider equipment and maintenance first, salaries last).

16. Check, department by department, to see if the preliminary budget estimate (mayor's) for account category under consideration is within the limits (per cent of current appropriations) implied in the mayor's budget letter to departments.

within limits   *outside limits*

17. If within limits, no change in preliminary budget estimate

18. Decrease preliminary estimate of budget so that it falls within mayor's limits.

19. Repeat 16–18 until deficit is eliminated or departments have all been considered.

deficit eliminated   *all departments considered*

Prepare final budget recommendation (Go to 26.)

20. Consider next lowest priority account (go to 16), unless all account categories have been examined.

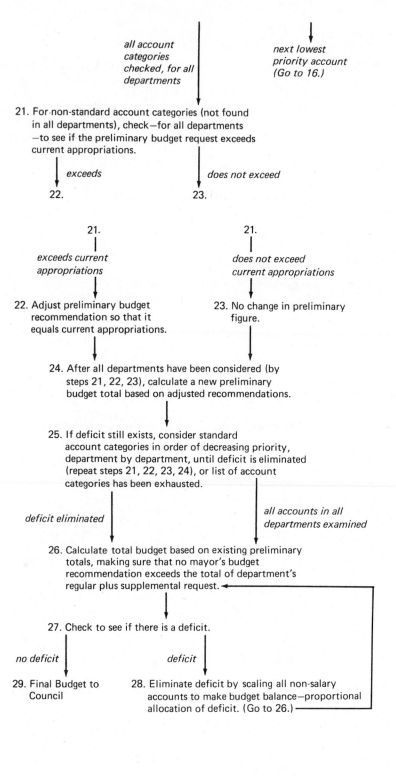

all account
categories
checked, for all
departments

next lowest
priority account
(Go to 16.)

21. For non-standard account categories (not found
in all departments), check—for all departments
—to see if the preliminary budget request exceeds
current appropriations.

exceeds

22.

does not exceed

23.

21.

exceeds current
appropriations

21.

does not exceed
current appropriations

22. Adjust preliminary budget
recommendation so that it
equals current appropriations.

23. No change in preliminary
figure.

24. After all departments have been considered (by
steps 21, 22, 23), calculate a new preliminary
budget total based on adjusted recommendations.

25. If deficit still exists, consider standard
account categories in order of decreasing priority,
department by department, until deficit is eliminated
(repeat steps 21, 22, 23, 24), or list of account
categories has been exhausted.

deficit eliminated

all accounts in all
departments examined

26. Calculate total budget based on existing preliminary
totals, making sure that no mayor's budget
recommendation exceeds the total of department's
regular plus supplemental request.

27. Check to see if there is a deficit.

no deficit

deficit

29. Final Budget to
Council

28. Eliminate deficit by scaling all non-salary
accounts to make budget balance—proportional
allocation of deficit. (Go to 26.)

nue and expenditure possibilities condition these expenditures. The crucial decision-making role of the executive's office is quite evident.

The third element in this model of municipal budgeting is the city council. Faced with a detailed budget from the executive's office, the council possesses very few choices. Changing one portion of the budget means that at least one other portion must be altered to compensate for the first change. Any increase in the salary account means a tax increase. Most city councils do not have the professional budgetary staff or the personal expertise to undertake changes of magnitude. The best time for individual councilmen to make an impact on budget increases is by influencing what the executive will present during the preparation of that document. Another difficulty for councilpersons is the sheer detail of expenditures presented in line item budgets, often down to $25 items.

Of course, councilpersons can and do make small cuts and small additions. The role of councils in appropriations has not been studied with the scrutiny of the same process in the Congress or the state legislatures. But the consensus is that their role in this process is, beyond a ritualistic one, not great. Figure 4-5 diagrams in flow chart form the council role in the budgetary process.

FIGURE 4-5. The General Council Appropriations Model. SOURCE: John P. Crecine, *Governmental Problem-Solving: A Computer Simulation of Municipal Budgeting*, © 1969 by Rand McNally and Company. Figure VII-1a, "General Council Appropriations Model," pp. 103–104. Reprinted by permission of the author.

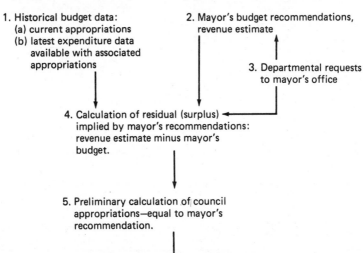

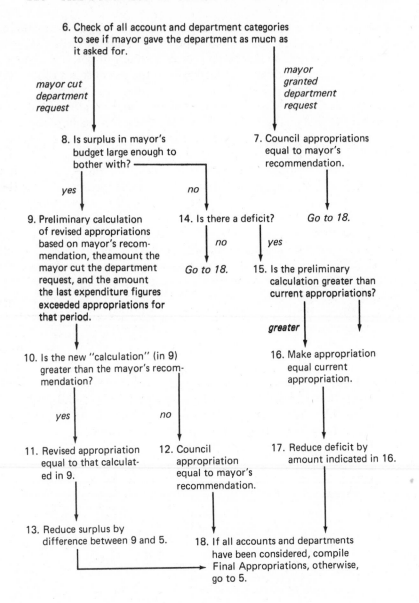

6. Check of all account and department categories to see if mayor gave the department as much as it asked for.

mayor cut department request

mayor granted department request

8. Is surplus in mayor's budget large enough to bother with?

7. Council appropriations equal to mayor's recommendation.

yes   *no*

9. Preliminary calculation of revised appropriations based on mayor's recommendation, the amount the mayor cut the department request, and the amount the last expenditure figures exceeded appropriations for that period.

14. Is there a deficit?   *Go to 18.*

no   *yes*

Go to 18.   15. Is the preliminary calculation greater than current appropriations?

10. Is the new "calculation" (in 9) greater than the mayor's recommendation?

greater

16. Make appropriation equal current appropriation.

yes   *no*

11. Revised appropriation equal to that calculated in 9.

12. Council appropriation equal to mayor's recommendation.

17. Reduce deficit by amount indicated in 16.

13. Reduce surplus by difference between 9 and 5.

18. If all accounts and departments have been considered, compile Final Appropriations, otherwise, go to 5.

A CONCLUDING COMMENT

This chapter focused on policy types and policy outputs of local governments, as well as on one policy process, municipal budgeting. Chapter 5 discusses the governmental structures through which various policies are carried out. It is hoped that this chapter persuades the reader that local governments remain important producers of public policy. We can argue about what *important* means, or even about what *public policy* means. But by producing large-scale benefits as measured by money spent and large-scale costs as measured by taxes imposed, it certainly seems that local governments remain important policy units.

5 URBAN GOVERNMENTS: THE STRUCTURES OF LOCAL AUTHORITY

THE SIGNIFICANCE OF STRUCTURE

How any institution is organized may be to the advantage or disadvantage of different elements in the community. Constitutional politics, the conflict over basic government organization, becomes a regular part of public life. Such politics characterizes nations whenever fundamental questions are unresolved. Constitutional politics played a major role in the early years of our own American republic.

The federal government has, however, achieved a level of public acceptance for its basic form of organization. Its three-part structure of executive, legislative, and judicial branches, for example, is not seriously subject to challenge. Constitutional issues in federal politics are questions of the proper balance among the three branches and the power of government versus the liberties of individual citizens. Few ever propose a new constitution with a new form of government organization.[1] In addition, the procedures for altering the basic structure, as outlined in the U.S. Constitution, by amendment or by the as yet never-used convention mechanism, are formidable and difficult to surmount.

---

[1] For one such proposal, see Rexford G. Tugwell, *A Model Constitution for a United Republic of America* (Santa Barbara, Calif.: Center for the Study of Democratic Institutions, 1970).

118

Similarly, the structures of state governments, for a variety of reasons, have been relatively difficult to alter.[2] With a few exceptions, such as Nebraska's unicameral legislature, the states have imitated the federal structure. They have not experimented with alternative forms, such as cabinet government or nonpartisan government (although one state has a nonpartisan legislature). There has been experimentation with a great variety of independent boards, commissions, and regulatory agencies. These arrangements have changed over time, especially with the explosion in government activities in the twentieth century. Yet the basic formats remain intact. No state has considered eliminating the governor, replacing him/her with a hired executive responsible to the legislature, or electing all the legislators from one big state-wide district on a nonpartisan basis. Yet, something of this sort results from the reform model of local nonpartisan council-manager government.

In contrast, at the local level, fundamental constitutional politics is a continuing process, for a number of reasons. For example, as metropolitan settlements spread, there are numerous opportunities to form new incorporations or to alter the charters of rapidly changing small towns turning into suburbs. In addition, it is not difficult to alter a city charter.

The structure of local government exists in a different political context than constitutional questions at the federal or state level. Since the end of the nineteenth century, there have been alternative structural systems, each with their users and advocates, for American local governments. Different political groups have clear expectations about what difference it makes which system a locality utilizes.

THE POTENTIAL IMPACT OF STRUCTURE

No method of organizing any institution is completely neutral in its impact on all those who might be affected by it. Any arrangement is likely to be more beneficial to some than to others. After one arrangement has been in place for many years, its continuation carries an advantage to those who are most familiar with it, who know the rules, who know how to make the machinery run, who know the players. Conversely, a wide-scale change introduces, at the minimum, uncertainty and, at the maximum, shifts the advantage to those who best understand the new rules.

[2] See Elmer E. Cornwell, Jr., Jay S. Goodman, and Wayne R. Swanson, *State Constitutional Conventions: The Politics of Revision in Seven States* (New York: Praeger Publishers, 1975).

Consider some specific stakes of alternative systems of local government:

1. What will be the organization of the government and the distribution of authority among branches and units?
2. What offices or positions will there be in the government?
3. How will people be chosen for the offices or positions, by election or appointment?
4. If officials are chosen by election, who will be eligible to vote?
5. If officials are chosen by election, what will be the nature of the districts from which they are selected?
6. If officials are chosen by election, will there be party labels on the ballots or not?
7. If officials are appointed, who will appoint them?
8. Should people who are appointed be chosen on the basis of civil service criteria (formal qualifications and written examinations)?
9. Should people who are appointed be chosen upon the endorsement of other officials (patronage) with or without formal qualifications?

These alternatives have significant ramifications. To use a simplistic example, if only property holders with $50,000 or more in net assets could vote, what would the electoral winners likely deliver in city services for the poor? Some ramifications are more complicated. Under a civil service system, city employees are hired by announced written examinations and formal qualifications for each position. That seems to be a technique of fairness, removing questions of personal affiliations or racial or ethnic identity. Such was the rationale behind civil service systems when they were first introduced at the turn of the century. But contemporary critics view them differently. They argue that such formalistic systems make it difficult for unskilled persons to get better jobs (on which they might learn the requisite skills) and also that such tests are difficult for people who come from cultural backgrounds different from those of the administrators who design and grade the tests.

Thus, how the structural arrangements of a local government are designed may affect very real values for people and groups. Further, these values extend to public policy. If a city manager is responsible only to an elected council, is she likely, because of the way her constituency is legally defined, to be more insulated than a mayor, who is, after all, elected by the public at large? And will such insulation result in a manager taking different stands on policy issues and going about her activities in a different way?

Here is the format for this chapter. First, we will trace the development of our major forms of urban government, because contemporary structures are, in part, a product of past controversy. American local government has been a hotly contested area, at a philosophical and at a practical level, for more than 100 years. The second section of the chapter describes the differing systems now in existence, how they are organized, and how they are distributed among the thousands of local communities in America. Finally, we will describe some of the socioeconomic and policy correlates of the use of different governmental forms by different urban communities.

THE DEVELOPMENT OF URBAN GOVERNMENT

American local governments were patterned originally on those of the British mother country. At the time of the colonies, British communities elected local legislative councils, which, in turn, conducted local affairs. That is still the basic structure in Britain today. The first American local governments took this form. Then, during the 1820s, in open imitation of the structure of our national government, localities introduced the popular election of mayors, instead of having the mayor chosen by the council. At this time also, many communities also started electing officeholders at lower levels, such as town clerks and treasurers. Nonetheless, the council retained the primary power for whatever services were provided, and those were very sparse. In New England towns, the town meeting of all citizens set policy for the council to follow. Elsewhere, even mayors were largely figureheads in what we would now call the weak mayor-strong council system.

Early local governments initiated rudimentary forms of record keeping, license granting, tax assessment, and order keeping. The councils appointed city officials and watched budgets and expenditures. Where there were mayors, they had ceremonial responsibilities such as presiding over council meetings. Pre-Civil War America was a country dominated by the individualistic ethos. Government at all levels was weak and devoted primarily to various forms of encouraging enterprise and subsidizing developmental activities. The nation was primarily agricultural and in contemporary terms underdeveloped.

After the Civil War, major changes in local governmental forms and a vast expansion of local government activity began. In terms of form, the cities, again imitating the federal and state governments, began to divide their councils into two-unit or bicameral bodies. By 1900, about one third of the larger cities had two-house, or bicameral, councils. The trend toward bicameral local legislatures was accompanied by an expansion of their size. There were 149 members, for example, in Philadelphia's Common Council.

During this same post-Civil War period, the movement to strengthen the powers of the executive at the local level began, another local reflection of what was happening in state and national politics. What we now call the strong mayor-council system emerged. Under this system, a popularly elected mayor had appointment authority over department heads and, often, a legislative veto. The rise of the mayor in city governments occurred simultaneously with some other changes. Most important in political terms was the establishment of the political machine.

NINETEENTH-CENTURY URBAN POLITICAL MACHINES

The post-Civil War city was ideal for the political machine. There were huge new populations. More than half the population of New York was foreign-born in 1860. In 1890, at least a quarter of the adult population of the entire country was foreign-born, and the proportion in most large cities was much higher.[3] The immigrants had special problems and special needs. Most were unskilled, and because the big post-Civil War waves were not from England, except for the Irish, they did not speak English. They often came from rural, peasant, traditional societies, where social ties were based on religion and kinship. It was not only the nature but the quantity of immigrant needs that helped fuel city building.

Between 1850 and 1900, urban populations increased 600 per cent. The average rate of growth was 45 per cent per decade.[4] The physical needs were immense for roads, buildings, bridges, docks, schools, sewers, and transit systems. The weak, limited urban governments of the time were not prepared for the influx. Because the activities of the state and federal governments were limited and of minimal help, there was no place to look for help. There was no welfare system to speak of, except small municipal funds for the most destitute and private charity. Furthermore, the prevailing value system was the individualistic idea of every man for himself, with a touch of social Darwinism, emphasizing the survival of the fittest. These values pervaded national and state governments and early American capitalism, which was completely unregulated.

Some avenues of success were closed. To become a successful industrialist required capital, business skills, and commercial con-

---

[3] For a description of the overall organizing challenge facing machines, see Seymour J. Mandelbaum, *Boss Tweed's New York* (New York: Wiley, 1965).

[4] See Ernest S. Griffith, *A History of American City Government: The Conspicuous Failure, 1870–1900* (New York: Praeger Publishers, 1974), p. 149.

nections. Professional status required family ties and education. But political power required only sufficient shrewdness to organize one's countrymen into voting blocs that would support you or your allies. Politics thus became a route for personal mobility, a way out of the dreadful slums, escape from heavy manual labor and sweatshops, and a way to power and wealth.

The question was, how would politics become the route? The practical answer was through party organization at the grass roots level. By controlling local party offices, individuals could control the nominations of those who would run for electoral positions or obtain these positions themselves. Once the party organization controlled the electoral positions of city government, it then had access to enormous material resources. All city jobs in this era were patronage jobs, and these could be allocated to party officials and dispensed to loyal supporters. All city contracts and franchises for utility and transport routes could be allocated on a political basis to those businessmen who were willing to contribute and kick back to the party.

STRUCTURE AND FUNCTION OF THE POLITICAL MACHINE

A variety of possible political solutions could have emerged in response to urban possibilities. But into the breach of this tough, chaotic urban world, the result was the political machine. Research indicates that even the most powerful machines emerged over a long period of time, after decades of public conflict and internal, factional feuding, before achieving a centralized, hierarchical form.[5]

Simply defined, the machines consisted of the party structure and the men who ran it. The structure was arranged hierarchically. At the bottom, party men had grass roots contact with their supporters at the block level (a system of organization modern political parties desperately wish they could re-create).[6] Thus, the base was the immigrant voters and the block captain of the party who made contact household by household. Over the block captain was the precinct captain, and over the precinct captain was the ward chairman. The wards might be consolidated into clubs that covered several such units or that brought together one big citywide or countrywide structure. At the top was the

[5] See Martin Shefter, "The Emergence of the Political Machine: An Alternative View," in *Theoretical Perspectives on Urban Politics* (Englewood Cliffs, N.J.: Prentice-Hall, 1976), pp. 14–44.

[6] See Fred I. Greenstein, *The American Party System and the American People* (Englewood Cliffs, N.J.: Prentice-Hall, 1970), pp. 43–54; and the classic, *Machine Politics* by Harold Gosnell (Chicago: University of Chicago Press, 1968).

county or city party chairman, the "boss," often holding no public electoral office, but commanding the entire elaborate party apparatus. The overall system was the same, although details of the structure might vary from place to place. Describing New York during this era, Arthur Mann recounts:

> In New York City the smallest unit is the election district committee, headed by a captain. Many election districts make up an assembly district, headed by a leader in charge of still another committee. The assembly district leaders constitute the county executive committee, headed by a chairman. Assembly district leaders are elected in party primaries, and in turn, choose their own election district captains and elect the party chairman. At its height in the twentieth century, the New York City Democratic organization numbered 32,000 committee men spread over five counties, and Madison Square Garden was the only place large enough in which to hold a meeting.[7]

In return for their votes, the immigrants received a number of *quid pro quo* returns. They got friendship and help from the organization, and in a language they could understand. They got "recognition"—the psychological satisfaction that comes from seeing a few of their own background make it to the top of wealth and power. And, in a larger sense, the machine played a role in assimilating the newcomers into American society, through helping them find jobs, through social events, and through building schools for their children.

The machine professionals got their own rewards. Most of the fuel was economic, money. For those at the lower- and middle-levels of the organization, there were jobs on the city payroll. In New York City alone in the 1880s there were some 12,000 municipal jobs to give and an annual payroll of $12 million, a larger operation for that era than the iron and steel works of Andrew Carnegie. Whether those jobs were performed honestly or performed at all was not of much concern.

For those at the very top of the machine, the rewards were greater: millions of dollars (and this was before the personal income tax). Of the 18 bosses studied by Zink, 10 left fortunes of at least a million dollars.[8] In an era of business development, entrepreneurs were willing to pay and to cut top machine leaders in on monopolies for municipal transit

[7] In William L. Riordan, *Plunkitt of Tammany Hall* (New York: E. P. Dutton, Inc., 1963), pp. xi–xiii.
[8] See Harold Zink, *City Bosses in the United States: A Study of Twenty Municipal Bosses* (Durham, N.C.: Duke University Press, 1930), p. 37.

systems, waterworks, or utilities. The machine sold everything that could be sold: licenses, contracts, permission for illegal gambling and prostitution gangs to operate. The behavior of the machines, however dishonest, kept faith with the dominant values of the day, which were to make a "buck" no matter how. These values were enthroned throughout the society and even in a famous evangelistic religious sermon of the era, which urged as the highest goal that young men "get rich."

SOME MAJOR BOSSES OF POLITICAL MACHINES

The top of the machine was occupied by a boss who frequently held no public office and who often tried to avoid the limelight.[9] One classic study showed about an equal number of city bosses to be Democrats and Republicans.[10]

"King" McManes of Philadelphia.   "King" Jim McManes, the boss of Philadelphia from 1865 to 1887, derived his power from control of the "gas trust," a municipal body that operated the city's gasworks. He also was party leader of the Seventeenth Ward. The gas trust position gave him control over 800 to 1,000 jobs and annual supply purchases of $2 million. Other positions he held, including head of the city's street railways, gave him control of more than 5,000 public jobs. McManes, a Republican and a Presbyterian, was an Irish immigrant who made good.

Plunkitt of Tammany Hall.   Perhaps the classic machine was in New York City. Its base was a political club called Tammany Hall, which still exists. One of the most colorful leaders of the Hall was George Washington Plunkitt, who cheerfully admitted to having saved a million dollars from what he called "honest graft" obtained in real estate speculation and construction. A Tammany District leader, a state senator, and an alderman, Plunkitt held court daily on a bootblack stand at the New York County Court House. His conversations and ruminations on politics were reported by a journalist of the era.[11] To get a flavor of the machine, they are worth quoting at length. First, here is Plunkitt on "honest graft":

> Everybody is talkin' these days about Tammany men growin' rich on graft, but nobody thinks of drawin' the distinction between

---

[9] For a general survey, see *The City Boss in America: An Interpretive Reader*, ed. by Alexander B. Callow, Jr. (New York: Oxford University Press, 1976).

[10] Zink, op. cit.

[11] Riordan, op. cit.

honest graft and dishonest graft. There's all the difference in the world between the two. Yes, many of our men have grown rich in politics. I have myself. I've made a big fortune out of the game, and I'm gettin' richer every day, but I've not gone in for dishonest graft—blackmailin' gamblers, saloonkeepers, disorderly people—and neither has any of the men who have made big fortunes in politics.

There's an honest graft, and I'm an example of how it works. I might sum up the whole thing, by sayin' "I seen my opportunities and I took 'em."

Just let me explain by examples. My party's in power in the city, and it's goin' to undertake a lot of public improvements. Well, I'm tipped off, say, that they're going to lay out a new park at a certain place.

I see my opportunity and I take it. I go to that place and I buy up all the land I can in the neighborhood. Then the board of this or that makes its plan public, and there is a rush to get my land, which nobody cared particular for before.

Ain't it perfectly honest to charge a good price and make a profit off my investment and foresight? Of course, it is. Well, that's honest graft.[12]

Then there is journalist William L. Riordon on a record of a day's work by Plunkitt, based on the politician's diary:

2 A.M.

> Aroused from sleep by the ringing of his doorbell; went to the door and found a bartender, who asked him to go to the police station and bail out a saloon-keeper who had been arrested for violating the excise law. Furnished bail and returned to bed at three o'clock.

6 A.M.

> Awakened by fire engines passing his house. Hastened to the scene of the fire, according to the custom of the Tammany district leaders, to give assistance to the fire sufferers, if needed. Met several of his election district captains who are always under orders to look out for fires, which are considered great vote-getters. Found several tenants who had been burned out, took them to the hotel, supplied them with clothes, fed them, and arranged temporary quarters for them until they could rent and furnish new apartments.

[12] Ibid., p. 3. Reprinted by permission of E. P. Dutton, Inc.

8:30 A.M.

Went to the police court to look for his constituents. Found six "drunks." Secured the discharge of four by a timely word with the judge, and paid the fines of two.

9 A.M.

Appeared in the Municipal District Court. Directed one of his district captains to act as counsel for a widow against whom dispossess proceedings had been instituted, and obtained an extension of time. Paid the rent of a poor family about to be dispossessed and gave them a dollar for food.

11 A.M.

At home again. Found four men waiting for him. One had been discharged by the Metropolitan Railway Company for neglect of duty, and wanted the district leader to fix things. Another wanted a job on the road. The third sought a place on the Subway and the fourth, a plumber, was looking for work with the Consolidated Gas Company. The district leader spent nearly three hours fixing things for the four men, and succeeded in each case.

3 P.M.

Attended the funeral of an Italian as far as the ferry. Hurried back to make his appearance at the funeral of a Hebrew constituent. Went conspicuously to the front both in the Catholic church and the synagogue, and later attended the Hebrew confirmation ceremonies in the synagogue.

7 P.M.

Went to district headquarters and presided over a meeting of election district captains. Each captain submitted a list of all the voters in his district, reported on their attitude toward Tammany, suggested who might be won over and how they could be won, told who were in need and who were in trouble of any kind and the best way to reach them. District leader took notes and gave orders.

8 P.M.

Went to a church fair. Took chances on everything, bought ice cream for the young girls and the children. Kissed the little ones, flattered their mothers, and took their fathers out for something down at the corner.

9 P.M.

At the clubhouse again. Spent $10 on tickets for a church excursion and promised a subscription for a new church bell. Bought tickets for a baseball game to be played by two nines from his district. Listened to the complaints of a dozen pushcart peddlers who said they were persecuted by the police and assured them he would go to Police Headquarters in the morning and see about it.

10:30 P.M.

Attended a Hebrew wedding reception and dance. Had previously sent a handsome wedding present to the bride.

12 P.M.

In bed.[13]

Boss Tweed of Tammany Hall. The most famous boss of Tammany, which did not really lose its influence until the 1950s, was the "Honorable" William M. Tweed, "grand sachem" from 1868 to 1871 (Figure 5-1).[14] Tweed did not run for public office, but held posts out of public view. He held key party offices and appointed city jobs, such as Deputy Street Commissioner of New York and City Public Works Commissioner. At the top, Tweed organized a "ring" of City Hall insiders who charged all those doing business with the city a straight 65 per cent commission in return for the commitment that any bill submitted to the City Board of Auditors would be accepted. At the bottom, Tweed stayed in office through an army of patronage workers, most on the city payroll, who got out the vote. At one time Tweed men—the Tammany candidates—simultaneously held the mayoralty, three crucial municipal judgeships, and all the other city elective offices plus the governorship of New York and many seats in the state Assembly.

The Decline of McManes and Tweed. McManes lost his power gradually. Tweed ended his career in jail, after he was brought down by a series of "muckraking" exposés in the *New York Times* and after long battering from the political cartoons drawn against him by Thomas Nast. Bosses flourished in roughly similar fashion in many other large cities, including Cincinnati, Jersey City, New Orleans, San Francisco, St. Louis, Pittsburgh, and Chicago. Increasingly, they came under attack. Lincoln Steffens, a pioneer investigative journalist, pre-

---

[13] Ibid., pp. 91–93. Reprinted by permission of E. P. Dutton, Inc.

[14] See John M. Allswang, *Bosses, Machines, and Urban Voters: An American Symbiosis* (Port Washington, N.Y.: Kennikat Press, 1977), pp. 36–59, and Zink, op. cit.

pared a stinging series of revelations for the popular *McClure's Magazine* between 1900 and 1904.[15]

THE REFORM ATTACK

Today we realize that the machines flourished because of certain basic conditions—rapid urbanization, the arrival of new populations, and a harsh economic environment. However one views politics without issues, based on material exchanges and ethnic loyalties, the machines built the physical infrastructures of the largest cities and assimilated huge new populations in a period of great social stress and tension. The availability of political processes gave the new populations a way to improve their condition short of violence and miles short of revolution. The machine effectively forced from power the "nativists," the economic notables of Anglo-Saxon descent who had previously dominated city politics when it was a gentleman's pursuit and a genteel calling.

However, the blatant corruption of the machines with their political power base in the immigrants—the "newer races" as James Michael Curley, mayor of Boston, liked to call them—generated a reform movement. This movement involved, beneath its rhetoric, a struggle over dominance in local politics and over the shape of local policy. Reform also offered drastic proposals to change the structure of urban government. The reform attack aimed at the partisan party system. The remedy was a change in the rules.

REFORM ORGANIZATIONS AND THEIR ACTIVITIES

The movement to cut them down began as soon as the machines began to gather real power.[16] For example, the Citizens' Municipal Reform Organization and the Committee of One Hundred were active in Philadelphia in the 1870s. At the core of the antimachine drive were middle- and upper-class people of nativist, Anglo-Saxon stock. The struggle had a reform-versus-corruption tinge plus encompassing the ethnic, religious, and class rivalries that have carried over to the present day.

THE NATIONAL MUNICIPAL LEAGUE AND THE SHORT BALLOT LEAGUE.

Founded in 1894 and still active today in promoting municipal reform and "good government," the National Municipal League was

[15] *The Shame of the Cities,* reprint (New York: Sagamore Press, 1957).

[16] See the articles in *The Age of Urban Reform: New Perspectives on the Progressive Era,* ed. by Michael H. Ebner and Eugene M. Tobin (Port Washington, N.Y.: Kennikat Press, 1977).

the most important organization in the reform movement. The League helped start reform organizations in many cities. It coordinated local reform associations across the country. Another reform group was the Short Ballot League, which had Woodrow Wilson as its president at one point. The Short Ballot League believed that the machine won because citizens could not choose properly when confronted with a long list of candidates for local office. Citizens would choose better officials if only a few candidates were elected and all other positions were filled by appointment.

The spirit behind the Short Ballot League was a young New York advertising man, Richard S. Childs. Childs was intensely concerned about municipal reform, and in 1917 he managed to bring the Short Ballot League into the National Municipal League and persuaded the new, larger creation to endorse his own idea, a new system of local government called "council-manager" government.[17] Childs sold his new system by widespread personal appearances around the country and through a heavily circulated National Municipal League booklet, the *Model City Charter*. Childs' personal career in local government reform spanned from the turn of the century until the late 1960s.

Program of the Municipal League. The municipal reform movement sought to eliminate the machine by destroying local political parties. This concept was merchandised as a new form of "direct democracy," in which no parties would intervene between citizens and officials and no dirty "spoils politics" would mar the day-to-day conduct of local government. The reform ideology drew heavily on the model provided by the large corporation, which had come into its own in the 1860–1920 period. The reform ideology *idealized* how the corporation worked. The idealized values were efficiency, stockholder democracy, but a management free to run things as long as its performance was good. In an era that was discovering the efficiency expert and the time-management expert in industry, transporting these values over to local government had considerable appeal.

The local government reform movement linked itself to the national Progressive movement, by ideology and by personnel. National Progressive goals, aimed at eliminating national corruption, were transposed to the local agenda: procedures for purchasing, contracting, and auditing of city expenditures, and, above all, the civil service system for the selection of municipal employees.

Childs and the Municipal League possessed a clear program. They portrayed the goal of urban governments to be simply provision

[17] See John Porter East, *Council-Manager Government: The Political Thought of Its Founder, Richard S. Childs* (Chapel Hill, N.C.: University of North Carolina Press, 1965).

of routine services, such as police and fire protection and water. In a simplified, business administration, the customary machine considerations of ethnic loyalty, party support, or financial gain would play no part. These reformers conceded only reluctantly that there might be some matters of urban policy about which there was conflict or disagreement. But where they recognized the possibility of conflict, they responded that in the "public interest" a policy could be found that would not benefit or penalize any one group.

With these philosophical positions about urban governments came a complete set of structural reforms. The short ballot would eliminate voter confusion, voter reliance on party tickets, and the fragmentation of authority within government. Another plank was to elect council members from at-large districts rather than from small, territorially defined wards or districts. The goal here was to eliminate the control that clustered minorities had over council seats under the ward system. An ethnic minority might be 80 per cent of the population of one of nine wards, for example, and thus automatically win one council seat. But in the entire city population that minority might be only 20 per cent, and if all seats were at-large, there would be no guarantee of winning any seats. This same device is often used to minimize Hispanic and black representation on city councils today. The reformers, however, in response to the alignments of the era, had in mind primarily the Irish, and secondarily other Catholic ethnic groups and also Jewish immigrants from Eastern Europe.

The key plank was nonpartisan election. Nonpartisan election embodied the reform goal of government without "politics." It was sold as a system for beating the machine and for electing the "best men." Clearly, of course, if party influence was to be battered down in the cities, but government had to go on, someone and some other source of political power would replace the machine. The someone was to be the "best man," usually a person with impeccable upperclass credentials. The alternative source of power was to be the civic organization, dominated by businessmen, newspapers, and other nonparty bastions of the middle and upper classes.

Another key element was the council-manager system. Under this system, described in greater detail later in this chapter, an elected council hired a manager to run the municipal government, in the same way elected corporate directors hire a company president. Childs apparently derived his concept of the council-manager system from thinking about the corporate model and about the experience of cities that did not use the mayoral system. Numerous communities had councils that made policy collectively and then each member—called a commissioner—administered a department of the city government.

This was and is called the commission system of municipal govern-ment. Childs was also aware that some cities, such as Staunton, Vir-ginia, in 1908, had hired professional managers to run some municipal programs. Childs called his council-manager system a marriage of the manager concept and the commission system.

The reform movement in municipal government succeeded. Many of the structural changes in municipal governments urged by the reformers won adoption. The first city to use the nonpartisan ballot was Louisville, Kentucky, in 1888. Dallas accepted it in 1907, and the first eastern community to adopt it was Boston in 1909. The national Progressive movement also favored nonpartisanship, and as a part of this alliance, *all* urban governments in California were made nonparti-san in 1914. They remain that way to this day. The first thorough count of local electoral systems became available in 1929, showing the ex-tent of the reform success: 57 per cent of all cities with more than 30,000 population utilized the nonpartisan ballot.[18]

The council-manager system was also adopted by various munici-palities, beginning with Sumter, South Carolina, in 1912. In 1914, after extensive efforts by Childs, Dayton, Ohio, became the first large city with more than 100,000 people to adopt the plan. The dramatic Dayton victory led to 100 more adoptions in the succeeding five years. Until the end of World War II, there was substantial, but not spectacu-lar, growth in the use of the council-manager systems. After World War II, the rapid formation of new, middle-class suburbs resulted in in-creased use of the council-manager plan.

POLITICAL MACHINES TODAY

Reports of the demise of highly structured urban machines are exaggerated. Strong party organizations persist in some cities. The Democratic machine in Chicago controls 35,000 patronage jobs plus lucrative contracts. It is flexible in its attitudes toward tax assessments and zoning regulations. Despite occasional deference to "good gov-ernment," Chicago remains the classic of the genre, of serious, patronage-oriented politics.[19] Until strong federal prosecutions put the leaders in jail in the early 1970s, many New Jersey cities were ruled by powerful, traditional bosses.

[18] See Eugene C. Lee, *The Politics of Nonpartisanship* (Los Angeles: University of California Press, 1960).

[19] The patterns set by the late Mayor Richard J. Daley appear to continue. For analyses of the Daley years, see Edward C. Banfield, *Political Influence* (New York: The Free Press, 1961); Mike Royko, *Boss: Richard J. Daley of Chicago* (New York: E. P. Dutton, 1971); and Miton L. Rakove, *Don't Make No Waves—Don't Back No Losers* (Bloomington: Indiana University Press, 1975).

One condition regarded as an underpinning for the machine is still met in many places, namely, a newly urban population. There are hundreds of thousands of blacks and Spanish-speaking citizens who are, relatively speaking, recent immigrants to the larger core cities. In several, Newark, New Jersey, and Gary, Indiana, blacks have already come to power through machinelike organizations. In many other cities, what might be called submachines are in control of parts of the territory. For example, although Tammany Hall may be almost gone in Manhattan, the Democratic machines of the boroughs of the Bronx, Brooklyn, and Queens are powerful enough to overcome various reform challengers and elect an organization man, Edward Koch, mayor of New York. This occurrence recalls Plunkitt's comment that reformers are "mornin' glories," whom the organization always outlasts.[20]

Similarly, as Raymond E. Wolfinger has pointed out, it is possible to separate two aspects of machine politics.[21] One is the structure of party, or the organization. The other is a system of politics based on material exchanges and benefits, rather than on issues or ideology. It is quite possible to have the latter without the former. The prime constituency for machine politics may not be the poor at all, but those with the greatest potential for economic gain and loss from authority. Wolfinger reminds us how much of the early machine activity was underwritten by businessmen, who provided the money for large-scale corruption by paying bribes and kickbacks for favors on every kind of contract, street car purchase or franchise, paving job, school construction, or utility facility. He notes:

> machine politics served the needs not just for poor immigrants, but also of the generation of businessmen who exploited the foundation of urban America. But after the first great rush of city building, the essential facilities and utilities had been supplied and business interest in local government declined.[22]

Today, business interests that once turned to municipal governments for opportunity and action may turn to the federal government. Smaller commercial interests, however, still find city and suburban contracts of great interest. The larger business firms who have shifted their focus upward have not abandoned their concern with material exchanges and substituted a politics of issues. They have simply shifted their geographical focus. We know that businesses dealing with

[20] Riordan, op. cit., pp. 17–20.
[21] "Why Political Machines Have Not Withered Away and Other Revisionist Thoughts," *The Journal of Politics*, Vol. 34, No. 2 (May 1972), 365–398.
[22] Ibid., pp. 390–391.

the federal government seek preferred treatment and "pull." Being middle-class and upper-middle-class citizens, however, they act in a discreet manner, using campaign contributions and other devices as the transmission mechanisms.

We conclude that some machines still exist in terms of both structure and the *quid pro quo* basis of politics. The material basis exists even where the structures are not fully present. While lower-class people are more commonly identified with machine politics, people of all classes appear to use politics for their own material benefit. At the same time, there are some paradoxes. Many urban areas have large ethnic and immigrant populations, but no machine politics. For example, in 1960, the West Coast cities of San Francisco, Los Angeles, and Seattle had 44, 33, and 31 per cent foreign stock, respectively, but none of the characteristics of machine politics. Especially in the Southwest and West, different historical traditions, modes of settlement, and perhaps substantially different attitudes about what is acceptable in politics, prevail.

REFORM POLITICS TODAY

Nationwide, the reform movement has fought machine politics to a draw, if not to a close win. The ideals of the reform movement—honest government and merit civil service—took such hold that few argue against them publicly. Wherever there is politics based on favors and corruption, there are more intensive efforts than in the old days to hide the transactions. The reformed governmental structures have been widely adopted.

At the same time, reform has not fared equally well in all contexts. In the largest cities, reform movements have been part of an alliance that has frequently paired upper-class liberals and lower-class blacks in a coalition against lower-middle-class white ethnics. Good government and efficiency wed the drive for social progress. The archetype of this alliance occurred in the tenure of John V. Lindsay as mayor of New York from 1966 to 1974.

Lindsay was a WASP lawyer, a naval officer, a Yale graduate, and a successful liberal Republican congressman from Manhattan when he ran for mayor in 1965. He ran on a classic reform notion: stop the behind-the-scenes broker politics of the Democratic machine and substitute efficient government. In addition, he had a visible sympathy for blacks and the underprivileged. To top it off, he was handsome and charismatic. Lindsay succeeded in the beginning, particularly in toning down the steaming racial tensions of the city. But he was in trouble from the beginning in dealing with the municipal unions, because of his stern moralism.

When he ran for reelection in 1969, Lindsay had to run on the label of a third party, the Liberal party, because he had lost the primary of his own Republican party. His enemies piled up. Citizens resented the decline of such municipal services as snow removal and street cleaning. They objected to his favoritism toward minorities in controversies over public school decentralization and the placing of low-income housing in middle-class neighborhoods. In the end, there was little support for his view that "there are overriding city needs that have to take precedence over particular local needs, and I believe local communities will accept these."[23] At the end, 60 per cent of New Yorkers thought his regime was working poorly, and only 9 per cent rated it good. Lindsay switched to the Democratic party, ran unsuccessfully for its presidential nomination in 1972, and then retired from politics.

The Lindsay case is not definitive proof that reform never works in the larger cities. Many larger cities, especially outside the Northeast and Midwest, have successful reform-style governments. Los Angeles, for example, exhibits many of the characteristics of reform politics: nonpartisanship, heavy volunteer participation in campaigns, weak parties, reliance on issues, stress on honesty, efficiency, and professional management.

The greatest triumph of reform, and where it burns most brightly today, is in middle-, upper-middle-, and upper-class suburbs. There the reform style and values come together in homogeneous communities. In these communities, especially where affluence is greatest, patronage jobs do not appear attractive. The idea of receiving favors through "pull" is abhorrent. Efficiency and quality-service delivery are highly valued. Further, the amateur politics of volunteers and issues fits into the socioeconomic setting of such communities. Reform has had its ups and downs in the largest cities, but found a natural home in other kinds of communities.

THE CONTEMPORARY DISTRIBUTION OF SYSTEMS OF URBAN GOVERNMENT

Decisions about systems of government structure are not made anew each year, but register the outcome of previous conflicts, opportunities, and the balance of forces at prior times. Systems adopted long ago remain. The three main forms are those that have had, historically, constituencies and precedents: the mayor-council, the council-

[23] Quoted in Jeff Greenfield, "Reading John Lindsay's Face," *New York Times Magazine*, July 29, 1973, p. 43.

TABLE 5-1.   Forms of Municipal Governments

City Size	Number of Cities	Mayor-Council		Commis-sion		Council-Manager	
		No.	%	No.	%	No.	%
More than 1,000,000	6	6	100	—	—	—	—
500,000–1,000,000	18	13	72	—	—	5	28
250,000–500,000	34	17	50	2	6	15	44
100,000–250,000	105	40	38	8	8	57	54
50,000 –100,000	253	98	39	11	4	144	57
25,000 –50,000	564	203	36	37	7	324	57
10,000 –25,000	1354	677	50	56	5	621	45
5,000 –10,000	1540	939	61	40	3	561	36
Totals	3874	1993	51	154	4	1727	45

S O U R C E : Table derived from data in Table 3, *1978 Municipal Yearbook* (Washington, D.C.: International City Managers Association, 1978), used by permission.

manager, and the commission systems. Table 5-1 shows the present distribution of these systems in the entire country.

Larger cities use mayor-council systems with strong mayors, and medium-sized communities favor manager-council systems. In the 24 largest cities with populations of more than half a million people, 19 use the mayor-council system, and of the 34 cities in the 250,000–500,000 range, 17 use the mayor-council structure. Of these 36 of our largest cities, in all but two the mayor-council system is the strong mayor variation. That is, the mayor possesses the powers at the local level that are associated with those of the top elected political executives, governors and the president at the state and federal levels. Only Minneapolis and Los Angeles among these large communities use the weak mayor variation of the mayor-council system. Major cities—New York, Boston, Philadelphia, New Orleans, Pittsburgh, Detroit, St. Louis, Houston, Chicago—all have mayors who stand in relation to the rest of the apparatus of local government much as the president stands at the federal level.

As city size decreases, usage of the council-manager structure increases, except in the very smallest communities. The council-manager system is most popular in the 25,000–100,000 population range, which marks it primarily as a governmental system for suburbs. Five large cities that use the council-manager system are Kansas City, San Diego, Dallas, Cincinnati, and San Antonio. All adopted it before they reached their present size. Nonetheless, that some 40 per cent of all local governments use the council-manager system is impressive testimony to the political acumen, impact, and power of the constituency represented by the reform movement.

Manager cities almost uniformly use the rest of the reform package.[24] Eighty-five per cent have adopted the nonpartisan ballot, 81 per cent choose councilmen from at-large districts, and 70 per cent have both these features in combination. Even cities that have retained the mayor-council system of government have adopted other reform features. About half of them have nonpartisan ballots, 29 percent elect their councilmen-at-large rather than from wards, and 18 per cent have adopted both these reform devices at once.

HOW LOCAL GOVERNMENTS ARE ORGANIZED

No governmental system functions exactly as it is portrayed in a chart. Still, it is useful to understand the formal structures of government. We outline here an ideal-type model of the several types of municipal government: the strong mayor-council system, the council-manager system, and the commission system.

THE STRONG MAYOR/COUNCIL SYSTEM

The strong mayor-council system, portrayed in Figure 5-2, re-creates the familiar federal model, with several exceptions. Nothing at the municipal level approximates the Supreme Court, with its power of judicial review. Municipal courts generally deal with minor offenses, such as traffic violations. So instead of a three-way, court-legislature-executive separation of powers, there is a two-way, council-executive separation. Both the council and the mayor are popularly elected. The council is analogous to the Congress at the federal level. The council shares in policy making with the mayor. It engages in oversight—review and examination—of the various service departments of the city. In practice, there are few powerful councils under the strong mayor-council system. In theory, however, the council has a veto over all policy initiatives, from expenditures and taxes to policy on public parks.

The mayor has a strong legal—and actual—position in the strong mayor-council system. He has veto power over acts (called ordinances) of the council. He recommends policy. He has authority to appoint all the heads of city departments, from the police and fire chiefs to the tax assessor, and to fire them. In some cities, either civil service systems or municipal unions give employees in service departments beneath the policy level some tenure protection. But in many cities, all employees

---

[24] See Raymond E. Wolfinger and John Osgood Field, "Political Ethos and the Structure of City Government," *American Political Science Review*, **60**:2 (June 1966), p. 313.

FIGURE 5-2. Mayor-Council Form. SOURCE: National Municipal League. Reproduced by permission.

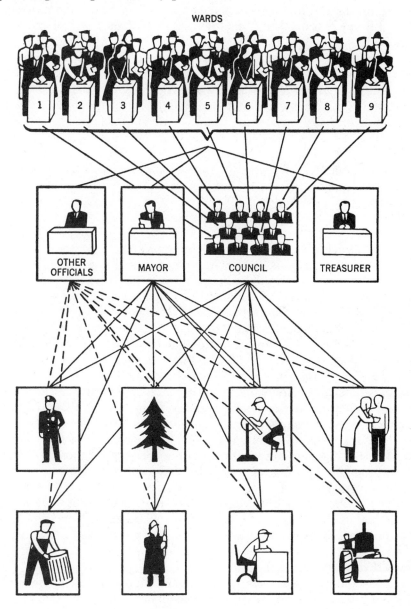

are dependent on the mayor's patronage for their jobs. The mayor prepares the budget and is expected to determine overall spending and taxing rates. Most big cities have now developed budget offices, staffed by professionals and modeled after the Office of Management and Budget (OMB) in the White House.

In addition to his formidable array of legal tools, the mayor in the strong mayor-council system has other political assets. He is usually a full-time, fairly high-paid official with all the accoutrements of office: the limousine, professional staff, and aides. The councilmen, in contrast, are frequently part-time and have no staff except in the rarest exceptions. The mayor, as head of the urban government, obtains visibility in the local media. That visibility plus his location at the center of government makes him the focus of all that goes on. Thus, in theory and often in practice as well, the mayor is the key man in the strong mayor-council government.

THE COUNCIL-MANAGER SYSTEM

The council-manager system, diagrammed in Figure 5-3, seeks to combine public responsibility with corporate-style professional management. As in other municipalities, there is little division of political labor with the courts. The council is usually small, part-time, and elected at-large on a nonpartisan basis. In theory, the council makes policy and the manager carries it out. The manager has the authority to appoint and to fire department heads. The day-to-day operation of city services belongs to him. In the beginning, most managers had engineering training (most mayors and councilmen come from backgrounds in small business, local law practice, and politics). Early professional doctrine for managers, as put forth by the International City Managers Association, held that managers should not get involved in politics. They should simply carry out whatever the elected council wanted. But the line between presenting recommendations, promoting a program, and politics is very thin. Recent professional doctrine for managers holds they have a duty to guide the council in the "best" policy direction. How political the job of manager becomes depends a great deal on the individual's orientation toward his role and on social and political forces in the community.

THE COMMISSION SYSTEM

The commission system, portrayed in Figure 5-4, was the form originally favored by reformers before council-manager systems were devised. First worked out by Galveston in 1900, 108 cities utilized it by 1910, but not a great deal more than that use it today. Yet, the commission system has some interesting characteristics. It resembles

FIGURE 5-3. Council-Manager Form. SOURCE: National Municipal League. Reproduced by permission.

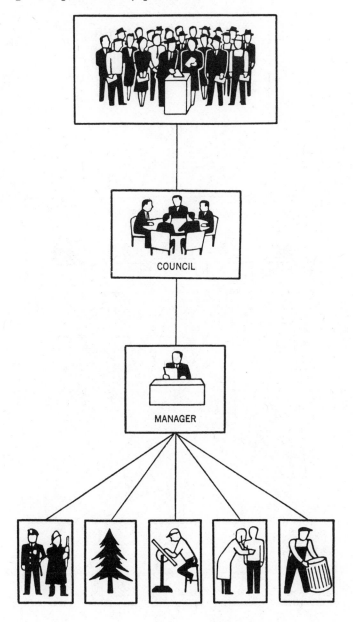

FIGURE 5-4.   Commission Form. SOURCE: National Municipal League. Reproduced by permission.

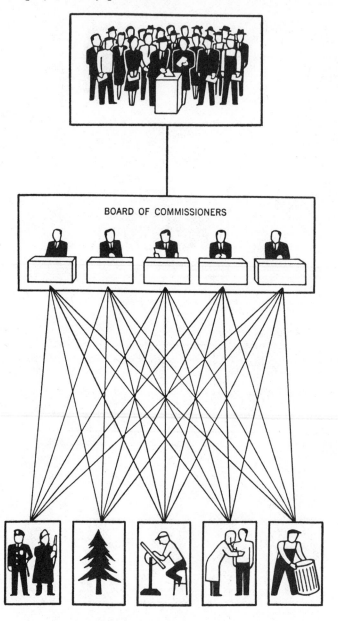

contemporary local governments in Britain. The commission system is drastically different from the potentially centralized strong mayor-council and council-manager systems. It is deliberately decentralized. A set of elected commissioners acts as a general legislature. Moreover, each man or woman commissioner is responsible for the day-to-day running of a department of the city government. A kind of log-rolling—if you do not meddle in my department, I will not interfere in yours—must operate among the commissioners. Because we live at a time when various forms of geographical decentralization of governments are being proposed for cities, the commission system is interesting as an already existing type of decentralization, with sharing of authority by design.

OTHER STRUCTURAL ASPECTS OF LOCAL GOVERNMENT

Strong mayor-council governments, council-manager governments, and commission governments are not the only units of local legal authority. Overlapping the authority of the systems so far described are still other purely local units.

SPECIAL DISTRICTS

Within many of the larger units there exist special districts, limited purpose governments, with considerable legal autonomy. Set up in an almost unclassifiable set of ways, and insulated from much public influence, special districts operate everything from bridges to transit systems. In the Midwest and West, there is a tradition of school board independence. Members of a school board may be elected separately and have independent taxing authority. Special districts often provide services across the boundaries of multipurpose, ordinary government units. Chapter 7 discusses such special districts.

COUNTY GOVERNMENTS

A pervasive local government structure is the county. There are 3,042 county governments in the United States, but only about 15 per cent, or slightly more than 400 of them, are in the urbanized areas, the SMSAs. Empirical research into political behavior within these units is not extensive. We will consider their activities in relation to metropolitan governments in Chapter 7. At this point, we offer descriptive generalizations about what county governments do and how they are organized.

County governments are perhaps the most important units of local government in rural areas. They are more highly developed in the

South and the West than in the Northeast, in the services they offer and the complexity of their organization. They often expand rapidly as suburban populations expand into formerly rural areas. Every metropolitan area includes at least one (and frequently more than one) county government. It is difficult to generalize about their scope of responsibility, which depends on how many people are in the county. Cook County, Illinois (more than 5 million population), Los Angeles County (more than 6 million), and Wayne County (which includes Detroit and more than 2.7 million people) contain very active county governments.

Table 5-2 suggests what county governments do and separates their services into those provided to all the residents within their jurisdiction and those provided only to residents who live in unincorporated areas within their territories. Unincorporated areas are not within the boundaries of any other municipal government. For the unincorporated areas in many large SMSAs, the county governments are *the* main providers of roads, police, parks, and libraries. Such are the traditional services of American counties, along with keeping legal records, property deeds, marriage and divorce records, birth certificates, and forming the jurisdictional units for state courts and law enforcement agencies. The use of county boundaries as a basis for a jurisdiction of local government goes back to early British practice.

The traditional governmental structure of county government is an elected board—called the Board of Commissioners, Board of Supervisors, or Commissioners Court—which has almost exclusive

TABLE 5-2. Delivery of Services by County Governments in Counties over 100,000 Population

Service	Per Cent of Counties Entire County	Providing Services to Unincorporated Areas
Police	33.0	68.8
Fire	5.4	24.4
Street construction	20.4	50.7
Street lighting	1.4	17.6
Recreation	21.3	37.5
Parks	33.0	42.9
Garbage collection	2.3	12.7
Public housing	1.4	6.8
Libraries	28.9	45.2
None	23.5	4.1

SOURCE: *Municipal Year Book, 1962* (Washington, D.C.: International City Managers Association, 1962), p. 64.

control over various functions. This system, diagrammed in Part *A* of Figure 5-5, corresponds to the commission system of local government previously described. Typically, also, a large number of county officials are elected independently, especially the sheriff and the county attorney. Rule by the county board and its commissioners is the major structure used in county government. More than 80 per cent of all counties use the system.

As citizen demands on county governments accelerate, many develop executive systems. Some 450 now use executive systems, and these alternatives are diagrammed in Figure 5-5. Part *B*, the county manager plan, is a county version of the manager-council system. Part *C*, the elected county executive plan, is a county version of the mayor-council system. More than 250 counties now have elected chief executives. Among them are St. Louis County, Missouri; Nassau, Westchester, Suffolk, Eire, Onondaga, and Oneida counties, New York; DeKalb County, Georgia; Jefferson Parish, Louisiana; and Milwaukee County, Wisconsin.

GOVERNMENTAL FORM AND COMMUNITY CHARACTERISTICS

Local government structures are not immune from change because the rules of the game are part of the regular politics. This condition raises many issues. For example, can we see the past alignments of local politics in the present distribution of governmental forms? Most analysts believe the machine versus reform controversy lined immigrants and poor on one side against the nativists and the middle and upper classes on the other. Do these relationships between local government system and community socioeconomic characteristics still exist?

In addition, political scientists suggest that there should be a relationship between government form and the public policies pursued.[25] The mayor-council system, for example, distributed the symbolic and tangible rewards that city governments controlled. With direct election of the mayor, and its council selected on a territorial basis to maximize the representation of homogeneous class and ethnic groups, this system was believed responsive to ethnic, racial, and class demands. Because of their lack of political insulation from demands, mayor-council governments would be relatively big spenders on local services.

---

[25] For a survey of this literature, see Brett W. Hawkins, *Politics and Urban Policies* (Indianapolis: Bobbs-Merrill, 1971), especially Chapter 2.

FIGURE 5-5. Three Different Forms of County Government Organization. SOURCE: Herbert S. Duncombe, *County Government in America* (Washington: National Association of Counties, 1966). Reproduced by permission.

A. County Government by a Board of Commissioners

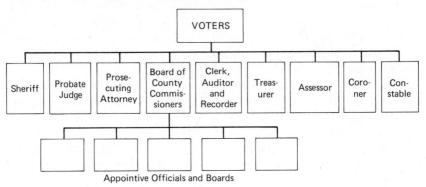

B. The County Manager Plan

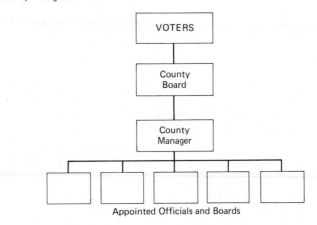

C. The Elected County Executive Plan

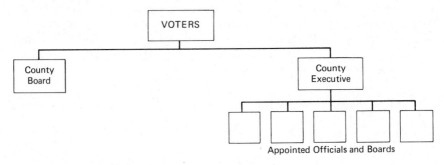

In contrast, the manager-council system, with its insulation of the manager and its emphasis on professionalism and efficiency, is hypothesized as less responsive to such ethnic, racial, and class needs. One argument of the reformers who devised council-manager government was that it would be cheaper. Individual groups would not be bought off by machine rewards and "administration" would replace politics. Do we have any evidence that council-manager systems are less responsive to group demands, or that they spend less?

GOVERNMENTAL FORM AND SOCIOECONOMIC CHARACTERISTICS

Let us consider first social characteristics of communities and form of government. The nineteenth-century machine was closely associated with large immigrant populations and ethnic solidarity. Does this association persist in the choice of mayor-council or council-manager systems? Evidence for such persistence would be an association between ethnicity, operationalized as the percentage of the city that is foreign-born, and the mayor-council system. Daniel N. Gordon's research indicates that the percentage of foreign-born was correlated with the mayor-council form in 1933 and was still a correlate of that form in 1960.[26] His study encompassed all cities in 1930 with more than 30,000 people, 94 per cent of 1950 cities with more than 25,000, and 75 per cent of 1960 cities with more than 50,000.

Gordon's correlations persisted even with controls for region, city, economic base, population size, and population change. His results suggest that the immigrant-ethnic influence over the rules of the urban government lasted over a substantial time period. There is no way to prove whether this occurred because the ethnics in city politics were able to fight off overt challenges to the system believed most responsive to their needs, or whether, once the form was established, they exerted enough influence to keep it.

Other studies came to similar conclusions. Alford and Scoble found foreign parentage associated with the mayoral form of government.[27] They also found connections between population diversity and the mayor-council system, and noted that "ethnically and religiously diverse, but nonmobile industrial cities are highly likely to be mayor-council cities."[28]

[26] "Immigrants and Urban Governmental Form in American Cities, 1933–1960," *American Journal of Sociology* (September 1968), 158–171.
[27] Robert R. Alford and Harry M. Scoble, "Political and Socioeconomic Characteristics of American Cities," in *The Municipal Yearbook* (Chicago: International City Managers Association, 1965), pp. 82–98.
[28] Ibid., p. 95.

If the hypothesis is correct, council-manager cities should have reverse social characteristics. Various studies show council-manager systems do exist in communities with less social diversity and greater income and educational rank. A study of 300 suburbs in the 25 largest metropolitan areas concluded that council-manager communities have fewer blacks, fewer elderly persons, more people in white-collar jobs, more educational attainment, and faster population growth.[29] This supported a later conclusion that "white, Anglo-Saxon, Protestant, growing, and mobile cities are highly likely to be manager cities.[30] In another analysis, of 74 Chicago suburbs, 18 of the top 20 with the most expensive homes had council-manager systems. None of the 31 suburbs with the least expensive dwellings, in contrast, used this system.[31]

Not all studies come to the same conclusions. Wolfinger and Field studied 309 cities with more than 50,000 population.[32] In the Northeast, the mayor and manager forms had about the same ethnic concentrations. In the Midwest and West, mayor-run cities had slightly higher ethnic concentrations. Region predicted best what kind of government a city would have. Region is a summary variable that includes local political culture and patterns of settlement.

Another analysis, by Lineberry and Fowler, of 200 cities with more than 50,000 population also found fewer differences in the population characteristics of mayor-council and council-manager cities than expected.[33] On the variable of class, cities with reformed systems were not particularly the habitat of the white middle class.

It would be helpful if studies of urban governmental form and population characteristics were more conclusive. The studies, it seems, show at least remnants of the original conflicts over structure in the form of more diverse, more highly ethnic populations in mayor-council cities, especially the largest cities. If this is so, the present arrangement of structures is a residue of the past conflicts. Further, the ethnic and class relationship to governmental form is supported by finding council-manager systems in middle-class suburbs, many of which were begun in the 1920s as upper-class communities.

[29] See Leo F. Schnore and Robert R. Alford, "Forms of Government and the Socio-economic Characteristics of Suburbs," *Administrative Science Quarterly,* 8 (June 1963), pp. 1–17.

[30] Alford and Scoble, op. cit., p. 95.

[31] Edgar Sherbenou, "Class, Participation, and the Council-Manager Plan," *Public Administration Review,* 21 (Summer 1961), pp. 131–135.

[32] Wolfinger and Field, op. cit.

[33] Robert L. Lineberry and Edmund P. Fowler, "Reformism and Public Policy in American Cities," *The American Political Science Review,* 61 (September 1967), 701–716.

GOVERNMENTAL FORM AND PUBLIC POLICY

An equally interesting set of questions arises about the relationship of the policies governments pursue and the forms of government they use. The political science literature states the situation as follows. Mayor-council government, especially when coupled with partisan elections and ward boundaries for council elections, is designed to be responsive to group demands. Because every group can achieve control over at least some council seats[34] and because party machines will bargain with constituents for their votes, these structures should be willing to spend more, and perhaps tax more, for local services. The mayor-council system is also said to be better able to manage political conflict, because the mayor and councilmen respond to group demands by paying off with patronage and programs. In contrast, the council-manager system was explicitly designed to avoid such responsiveness. By implication, wherever this kind of urban structure confronts a socially heterogeneous population, it will be less capable of managing conflict.

There is no way to test hypotheses about managing conflict under the different structures, apart from case studies. Scholars have, however, provided empirical tests of the relationships between the form of urban government and responsiveness.

Once again, the evidence does not all go one way. Wolfinger and Field concluded region was a better predictor of expenditure for certain programs than was the form of city government.[35] They found no relationship between protecting city employees by civil service systems and ethnicity. They found no significant relationship between type of government and expenditures for city planning or executing urban renewal projects, both presumed to be more amenable to manager-council systems and their constituents than to mayor-council systems.

On the other hand, Lineberry and Fowler found mayor-council cities more responsive to socioeconomic cleavages in their populations in taxing and spending. They arranged cities into four categories, the least-reformed having mayor-council systems, partisan elections, and ward districts, whereas the most reformed cities had a manager, nonpartisan elections, and at-large districts. As reformism increased, with a few exceptions, the link between social characteristics and policy decreased. The correlation between ethnicity and higher taxes is

[34] For evidence that blacks win greater representation in district systems, see Clinton B. Jones, "The Impact of Local Election Systems in Black Political Representation," *Urban Affairs Quarterly*, Vol. 11, No. 3 (March 1976), pp. 345–356.

[35] Wolfinger and Field, op. cit.

greater in the least reformed cities. The same relationship holds for expenditures. Reform structures appear to mediate between the public policy in the form of lower expenditures for services.

These scholars concluded that:

> The more important difference between . . . cities is in their behavior rather than their demography. . . . The translation of social conflicts into public policy and the responsiveness of political systems to class, racial, and religious cleavages differs markedly with the kind of political structure.[36]

LOCAL GOVERNMENT STRUCTURES AND POLITICS: SOME CONCLUSIONS

Local governments, unlike those at the state and federal level, have not been constitutionally secure units of authority. Basic structure became the basis of political controversy, which reached a peak in the 1860–1920 period. During the height of the battle, alternative systems of local government developed. Serious social conflicts underlay the struggle.

Some of these conflicts remain in the landscape of local governmental systems—the distribution of mayor-council and council-manager forms of government. Still other remnants, reminiscent of the deep underlying causes of these conflicts, are seen in the political behavior of the new immigrants to the big cities—the blacks and the Hispanics. These groups have developed and are still developing the kind of group consciousness that precedes organization for political power. Group consciousness takes the form of self-help organizations and, ultimately, political organization. That is not to say that the community organization of today among blacks or Spanish-speaking persons will lead to the machine politics of the 1880s Irish. The country is different. Whatever the symbolic rewards of control, the material incentives are less in the battered central cities. But there are similarities in the process and the goals, because there are still some similarities in the conditions of settlement. Finally, some conflicts between suburbs and central cities in a metropolitan area are transformations of the old fight over control, exclusiveness, rewards, and costs.

Any discussion of local governmental form leads inevitably to analyzing who participates, who cooperates with whom, who fights with whom, and who wins and who loses. Chapter 6 explores who the participants are and attempts to survey a voluminous theoretical and empirical literature aimed at answering the question, "Who runs this town?"

---

[36] Lineberry and Fowler, op. cit., p. 715.

6
POWER AND PLANNING
IN LOCAL POLITICS

This chapter analyzes questions of power in local politics. A number of models purport to give the answers. Then, the text turns to another dimension of local government. What about the role of rational planning in the local community? There are planning departments in almost all urban governments and in most suburbs and county governments as well. How do they work and what is their role? Finally, this chapter introduces the student to some normative questions. Who *should* rule in the local community? How *should* governments be arranged?

POWER IN LOCAL POLITICS

Analyzing power in local politics extends the process we undergo all the time in thinking about national politics. We talk about parties, the role of the president, the power of interest groups such as the oil industry or organized labor. Although there are arguments about the distribution of power in national politics, there is at least a minimal consensus about what the resources and the stakes are. We draw on our knowledge of national politics to specify what is useful to local activists (resources) and what difference it makes (stakes).

RESOURCES OF POWER

Let us inventory the potential resources that could be used by individuals, officials, groups, or parties to achieve outcomes they desire.

151

Position. Position, or authority, comes to mind first. However trivial the office of city councilman or city judge or town selectman or even mayor, if one is concerned about policies under the purview of these positions, being in office yields a vantage point. Is what someone wants a special zoning permit? The votes on the council are almost always necessary. A change in police practices? It will help to have a sympathetic judge. Someone to talk to about trash pickup? The selectman can help. Whether it is a special favor on a tax assessment for a commercial store or a general change in tax policy for the whole suburb, the mayor is a key man. He may not be able to obtain either one. But because of his central place in the institutional structure, there is very little chance of winning the favor or the policy *without* his support.

To talk about the power of position is only to summarize what political scientists and sociologists have been noting about modern government since the turn of the last century. Position confers upon its occupants more than varying degrees of legal authority. It gives them experience, a full-time means of support to work at politics, a stake in outcomes, and exposure and status. Not just elected officials but also bureaucrats draw on the power of office. Zoning policy goes through civil servants in the planning board. Civil servants comprise the lower and middle echelons of the police department. Professionals, many of them with tenured or life positions, run the school system. These people work under the local laws or ordinances, but they interpret general language to fit specific needs and cases. They are protected in their employment. They have time as well as expertise on their side. Their power, especially to delay, is enormous.

Wealth. A second resource is wealth. Wealth as a local-level political resource takes many forms. Sometimes wealth serves private citizens, who contribute to campaigns in return for expected favors, or who bribe officials, from building inspectors to police.

Sometimes wealth controls jobs, a control that provides political power for retail and industrial firms. Jobs support citizens, and the taxes generated finance services. This kind of wealth creates deference in local officials, who try to be helpful at best or, at least, not damaging. The political influence of local business almost always derives from its economic resources.

Private wealth is not the only kind that appears in local politics. Local governments control substantial wealth. They spend substantial amounts on a wide range of goods and services. Each may be the largest *single* economic unit in its particular community. That wealth makes local government both a prize to be captured and a power in its dealing with others.

Numbers. A third resource of power is numbers. Numbers matter wherever offices are filled or issues decided on the basis of voting by universal suffrage. The advantage of numbers comes into play, however, only when definite conditions are met. The potential constituency first has to be mobilized. For example, taxpayers defeat about half of all school bond referenda. If those voters were not made aware of the issues and did not go to the polls, their numbers would be irrelevant. Anti constituencies are notably volatile at the local level and easy to arouse. Pro constituencies for local spending or for changes in city charters are harder to turn out.

Or consider a different case. On a plan to change garbage collection from twice a week to twice a month in some suburb, those who decide ask themselves, "Will the housewives who notice this change most come together as a political force?" Will they complain directly to the town hall? Would they drop garbage on the Chief Sanitation Engineer's lawn as a protest? Does the engineer live in the community where they can get at him or her? Will whatever resentment that comes from this constituency be balanced off by taxpayer satisfaction with reduced costs? In other words, if those who are affected are not likely to want to do anything or not able to do anything, then, potential numbers do not translate into much.

Another situation limits the potential impact of numbers. In a referendum, numbers are an obvious advantage, when mobilized. Referenda put issues ranging from school and park construction, to fluoridation of water, to sewer construction directly to local citizens for decisions. But many areas are still the province of decision making by governmental institutions. Numbers bear on these decision-making centers only indirectly through elections. Many factors modify the linkage between elections and policy.

One system of local government, the council-manager system, is designed to mute the impact of numbers. A large percentage of council-manager systems select the council on a nonpartisan basis or from at-large districts, or both. In mayor-council cities, where the system is designed to respond to various voting blocs, other factors dilute citizen strength. Democratic theory holds that officials are most responsive to their constituents when there is competition for the job, in the initial election and for re-election. Suppose, however, that there is no two-party competition for office? We know that the Democratic party monopolizes the elective offices of most core cities and the Republicans predominate in the suburbs. Intraparty primary competition remains, but is it sufficient to give numbers political influence? Or, suppose, once elected, local officials are no longer politically ambitious. Suppose they do not care whether or not they are re-elected, or do not want to run again anyway? How can the anticipation effects of numbers operate here? Raising these dilemmas illustrates the complexities of translating numbers into power in local political settings.

Organization. Another resource in local politics is organization. Organizations provide structure for the potential or actual mobilization of numbers, permit the use of spokesmen who can devote more time to a cause than can ordinary citizens, and add visibility and permanence to any cause. Organization does not materialize unless people have interests they need advanced. Organization requires other resources—time, money, ability, motivation. Officeholders understand the effort needed to create organizations and respect it. Organizations gain power in local situations because their existence regularizes politics for officials by providing a stable system of bargains and exchanges. This text describes local political groups in Chapter 8.

Control over Sanctions. In the strictest sense, control over sanctions derives from the other resources of local politics. Control of police powers comes from control of local positions. Control over jobs comes from economic wealth. But sanctions, the ability to apply or to withhold some painful effect, merit separate mention. First, consider the sanctions available to local governments. The police power protects a person's property well or poorly. A suburb can have a reputation for vigilant patrolling and rigid prosecution of all crime, or as an easy place for burglars and drug dealers. The police can be fair to all citizens, or harass racial minorities or students. Through tax assessment, a local government can take part of a person's property unfairly, or it can assess all persons with fairness. City councils can include various buildings, blocks, or neighborhoods in urban renewal or highway programs. Then they take that land for the resulting public and private uses under the power of eminent domain, the ancient power of government to take property, with compensation, for public purposes. In other words, local governments control sufficient sanctions to interfere with the lives, liberty, and property of almost all citizens at some time, if they choose to so act.

Similarly, potential sanctions rest in the hands of private sectors of each community. An employer can always threaten to move his store or plant. His making good on the threat leaves citizens without jobs and the government without tax revenues. The sanction of violence is not the sole possession of government. Organized criminals represent the potential use of intimidation of citizens and officials and the possible use of lethal violence. Teen-age street gangs rule whole neighborhoods of some of the biggest core cities (Figure 6-1). Their power rests on extortion and violence.

FIGURE **6-1.** Bandit's Roost, New York street gang, circa 1900. (Photography by Jacob A. Riis, the Jacob A. Riis Collection, Museum of the City of New York.)

Expertise. Finally, expertise is a resource in local politics. Knowledgeability about government workings strengthens elected public officials and civil servants. Because the civil servants survive many administrations, they pit their knowledge against elected officials. Expertise is also a resource for local lawyers. Their experience with arcane issues such as zoning and building regulations and the workings of local zoning boards gives them a special place in community affairs. Expertise gives power to school officials, from the superintendent to the curriculum specialist, in their dealings with a concerned, but often mystified, public.

CONTROL IN LOCAL POLITICS: STAKES

To talk about resources is also to talk about the stakes of local politics. Almost anyone might make a different list in a different order from the one that follows. However, the following may be illustrative:

1. A physically safe or unsafe living environment.
2. Good schools or poor schools for one's children.
3. Expensive or less expensive taxes.
4. The opportunity or lack of it for public employment.
5. The opportunity or lack of it for private employment.
6. The opportunity or lack of it for commerce and profit.
7. A living environment of social homogeneity (comforting or stultifying) or of social heterogeneity (stimulating or terrifying).
8. A chance to influence local affairs or little chance to exert such citizen or activist influence.
9. A clean or dirty physical environment.
10. An aesthetically attractive or unattractive spatial environment.
11. Good or poor park and recreational facilities.

POWER IN LOCAL POLITICS: WHO'S GOT IT?

For 25 years, an intense argument has existed in the academic world over *who* has power in local politics? The discussion brings forth five serious models of community affairs. These models pay little attention to the *extra-local forces* that we analyzed in Chapter 3—the national government, corporations, and the state governments. The models deal with the question, "Who runs what there is to run in this town?"

Each model seeks to answer these questions. Which groups, classes, races, officials, or individuals possess the power to achieve their goals! How do they act to achieve their goals, or do they act at all? How do we compare the power to obtain desired goals in one area of concern—schools, police, taxes—with the power to achieve group or individual ends in other areas? The models consider which kinds of resources are characteristic of winning and losing participants. How do different ways of reaching decisions affect the weight of different resources for different participants? Do the winners in local controversies always come from the wealthy strata of the city—the bankers, old-line law firms, and retail businessmen? Or are there different types of winners on different issues, with lower-class people, despite their lack of large personal material resources or status, obtaining various kinds of benefits?

Should *all* decisions of a city government be considered the "pot" and be studied to see who plays in the poker game and who gets what? What about those resources that are never brought into the game but are still worthwhile, or thought so, by some segments of the local community? The power to stay out or keep something out may be a substantial power. And what about players who, everyone knows or thinks she knows, have the most money but are never brought into the game at all and cannot be either persuaded or coerced to play? Then the game consists of impoverished players sitting around the table fighting for leftovers.

Or, to further complicate the analysis, how does one weight the influence of governmental versus nongovernmental players? At the federal level, there is no question but that the White House is more powerful than any single corporation or union. But is the mayor more powerful than any single company when, as in the cases of United States Steel in Gary, Indiana, or the Cannon mills in Kannapolis, South Carolina, the company generates 60 to 90 per cent of all the economic activity in the town?

Perhaps what it all means is, How do you measure power? Despite centuries of effort, the success of political scientists has been only mixed. Power can be defined in the abstract. *A* is able to influence *B* to do what he, *A*, wants, in a context where *B* would not necessarily otherwise act that way. But how does one go to an operational concept in an environment as complex as an urban area? Even if we could identify a set of participants, what would be the criteria for assigning them power? Would we count the resources they started with, wealth, skill, status, experience, official position? Would we examine success on one issue, or some issues, or all issues? Would we look at actual interactions to see that *A* is influencing *B* directly, or would we take into account anticipated reactions when *B* figures out what *A* wants and does it with no contact? Would we weigh all issues equally? And what power would we attribute to someone who could, if she chose, make sure what she cared about most never appeared on any public agenda?

These are more than abstract questions. Let us look at several hypothetical examples. If one elite succeeds on all issues, then challenging groups must persuade or coerce that on-top elite. During the 1960s, that was the viewpoint of many civil rights activists who believed in a local power structure. The business-dominated elite would be brought around through marches, demonstrations, and implied threats to the business standing and respectability of the city. The business elite would then, presumably, line up city officials and others to whatever was agreed upon. But if there was no one elite that could influence hiring, schools, police, and other services all at once, then the efforts of the civil rights activists would be misguided. So, for them, knowing "who governs?" mattered.

Or consider a gang of organized criminals that operates gambling, prostitution, and drug enterprises in the city. Its view of how city politics operates may focus on the top elected officials and assume that if they can be corrupted, then lower-echelon employees, especially the police, will go along. But perhaps that view overlooks the professionalism of the police, or the importance of "good government" interests such as the local newspapers. If the gangsters err about a particular town, the mistake could put them out of business and in jail.

Think about one more hypothetical illustration. A group of businessmen want an urban renewal project. They manage to gain the support of the mayor, the newspapers, and the major university in the city, but citizens in the affected neighborhood resist. The project becomes an issue in a mayoral election. In response to what she thinks is voter objection, the mayor backs away from her earlier support. Here, the businessmen have assumed that top officials and civic notables who give their support can deliver. But the electoral politics of the case suggest that the voters possess a veto. In this case, the businessmen had an incorrect vision of the distribution of local power.

MODELS OF URBAN POWER DISTRIBUTIONS

In studies of urban power distributions, social scientists have developed (at least) five important models. Each model has its adherents. We summarize each model and then present a personal analysis. In the end, the student must reach his or her own conclusions. The five are the games model, the power structure model, the pluralist model, the nondecision model, and the political (or synthesis) model.

The Games Model. Almost 25 years ago, Norton E. Long, a famous urbanist, advanced the idea that "the local community can be usefully conceptualized as an ecology of games."[1] He noted that man is "both a game-playing and a game-creating animal, that his capacity to create and play games and take them deadly seriously is of the essence, and that it is through games . . . that he achieves a satisfactory sense of significance and meaningful role."[2]

---

[1] *The American Journal of Sociology,* **64**:3 (November 1958), 251.
[2] Ibid., p. 252.

Local politics is a very special game. Its structure and set of expectations condition how people behave and what they expect, much in the same way that the game of baseball determines what a third baseman will do and what fans expect from him, or the way that professional football has a pattern of behaviors and hopes for a quarterback. Within the territory of a local community, well-defined roles exist. These roles tell individuals who occupy particular positions how to act. There is a banker role, a civil rights leader role, a mayor role, a church leader role. The roles relate to each other. Each player pursues his own career but, at some point, needs some of the other players to achieve his or her own ends. At this point, collaboration becomes possible. The public watches the various individual career games and the big game, the civic game, where the roles overlap. Long says the public has "some appreciation for the standing of the players," who in turn "know how to behave and they know the score."[3]

The civic game has two special qualities. First, in a form of civic role playing known as top leadership, the leaders of particular private roles come together to govern or give the appearance of governing the community. The leaders of private sectors come together, much in the fashion of magicians in primitive societies, to meet and give the appearance of solving a problem. Yet, Long notes, they do not commit real resources to the civic endeavor, such as large amounts of their own time or heavy staffing. Rather, they meet sporadically and substitute publicity for action. The top leadership civic game for each player is secondary to his private role.

The behavior of the top leadership in the civic game dismays no one. The ritual alone satisfies the needs. Going through the motions adds status points without any costs to the businessman or the professor. For the local bureaucrat, a scheme for a welfare program or a highway receives an added legitimacy. For the public, the process provides reassurance that those who are respected in the private sector care about the public sector and are "doing something."

In a situation of continuous game playing, the answer to the question of who governs is, "no one." In the local ecology of games, there is no purposeful, planned rule and little conspicuous bargaining. Rather, there is anarchy. Particular problems either solve themselves with time, are not dealt with at all, or are solved on an *ad hoc* basis. Yet, this no-one-governs situation of low civic intensity is not necessarily all bad. The lack of order displeases those who think problems should be purposively solved. But that is not what the local ecology of games

---

[3] Ibid., p. 253.

provides. The system survives and "gives all the players a set of vaguely shared aspirations and common goals."[4]

The Power Structure Model. In the 1940s, studies of local politics simply described the formal duties of officeholders in local government. This formalistic social science departed from the realistic studies of the 1920s and early 1930s that had analyzed urban machines. Sociologists shattered the formalistic approach by applying new techniques to the study of urban politics. In reputational surveys, local leaders were asked who had power in general, and power over which specific decisions. The answers were then cumulated, and the scholars looked at the characteristics of those names.

The trail-blazing study was Floyd Hunter's *Community Power Structure: A Study of Decision-Makers.*[5] He analyzed "Regional City" (Atlanta) and found what he called a "power structure" and what other sociologists, particularly C. Wright Mills writing about national politics at the same time, called a "power elite."[6] Hunter found power structured such that elected officials of the "Regional City" government were nowhere near the top. Table 6-1 reproduces his listing of policy-making leaders. Of the 40 persons on the list, only four came from the formal offices of government. When Hunter arranged his list hierarchically on the basis of the number of times a leader was named by other leaders (the basis of the reputational methodology), only the mayor of Regional City ranked in the top 10 of community influentials, ranking fourth.[7]

Hunter's list of power-wielders in Regional City pointed to a very clear power structure. That power structure consisted primarily of those with local economic power, the owners and very top managers of local industry. The level of reported interactions was even more intense among a smaller group at the top of the 40, whose preeminence appeared to be recognized even within the structure. The leaders worked with each other through a complicated system of partially informal ties. They got together on political projects and also enjoyed overlapping memberships in social clubs and on civic committees.

The power structure cooperated with other elements of the community, but Hunter detected implicit understanding of where everyone ranked, who would make policy, and who could carry it out. He said that:

[4] Ibid., p. 261.
[5] (New York: Doubleday Anchor Books, 1963). Originally published by The University of North Carolina Press, 1953.
[6] *The Power Elite* (New York: Oxford University Press, 1956).
[7] Hunter, op. cit., p. 64.

TABLE 6-1. Policy-making Leaders in Regional City by Occupational Position

Type of Occupation	Name of Leader	Name of Organizational Affiliation	Position
Banking, Finance, Insurance	Hardy	Investment Company of Old State	President
	Mines	Producer's Investments	President
	Schmidt	First Bank	President
	Simpson	Second Bank	Vice-President
	Spade	Growers Bank	President
	Tarbell	Commercial Bank	Executive · Vice-President
	Trable	Regional City Life	President
Commercial	Aiken	Livestock Company	Chairman, Board
	Black	Realty Company of Regional City	President
	Delbert	Allied Utilities	President
	Dunham	Regional Gas Heat Company	General Manager
	Graves	Refrigeration Incorporated	President
	Parker	Mercantile Company	Executive Manager
	Parks	Paper Box Company	Chairman, Board
	Smith	Cotton Cloth Company	Manager
	C. Stokes	Oil Pipe Line Company	President
	Webster	Regional City Publishing Company	Managing Editor
	Williams	Mercantile Company	Chairman, Board
Government	Bamer	City Government	Mayor
	Gordon	City Schools	Superintendent
	Rake	County Schools	Superintendent
	Worth	County Government	Treasurer
Labor	Gregory	Local Union	President
	Stone	Local Union	President
Leisure	Fairly	None	Social Leader
	Howe	None	Social Leader
	Mills	None	Social Leader
	Moore	None	Social Leader
	Stevens	None	Social Leader
Manufacture and Industry	Farris	Steel Spool Company	Chairman, Board
	Homer	Homer Chemical Company	Chairman, Board
	Spear	Homer Chemical Company	President
	E. Stokes	Stokes Gear Company	Chairman, Board
	Treat	Southern Yarn Company	President
Professional*	Famer	Law Firm	Attorney
	Gould	Law Firm	Attorney
	Latham	Private Office	Dentist
	Moster	Law Firm	Attorney
	Street	Law Firm	Attorney
	Tidwell	Law Firm	Attorney

* Attorneys' affiliations not given. Without exception they are corporation lawyers.
SOURCE: Floyd Hunter, *Community Power Structure: A Study of Decision-Makers* (New York: Doubleday, Anchor Books, 1963), p. 75. Reprinted by permission of the University of North Carolina Press.

The leaders of Regional City tend to protect themselves from too many demands by channeling policy execution through an understructure on matters of policy. This understructure is not a rigid bureaucracy . . . but is a flexible system. . . . The men at each level are spoken of as first, second, third, and fourth rate by the power leaders, who operate primarily in conjunction with individuals of the first two ratings.[8]

Hunter offered some examples of personnel in the different categories:

First rate: Industrial, commercial, financial owners and top executives of large enterprises.

Second rate: Operations officials, bank vice-presidents, public relations men, small businessmen (owners), top-ranking public officials, corporation attorneys, contractors.

Third rate: Civic organization personnel, civic agency board personnel, newspaper columnists, radio commentators, petty public officials, selected organization executives.

Fourth rate: Professionals such as ministers, teachers, social workers, personnel directors, and such persons as small business managers, higher paid accountants.[9]

The implications of Hunter's findings took many people aback. Power in the urban setting did not belong to government officials, nor was it dispersed. Rather, power concentrated in an overlapped, interrelated set of economic notables who, because they held no public positions generally, exercised authority behind the scenes and informally. Other sociologists using similar methods came to largely similar conclusions in their research on other cities.[10]

The Pluralist Model.   Political scientists, differently oriented in their approach to politics, responded with critiques of the Hunter approach. They conducted studies of their own and, eventually, developed a different framework, the pluralist model. Their main criticism of Hunter was that he did not study power at all,[11] but studied who some people thought were influential. He did not look at actual cases of what kinds of decisions were made in Regional City, or who won or

---

[8] Ibid., p. 107.

[9] Ibid., p. 108.

[10] See John Walton, "Discipline, Method, and Community Power: A Note on the Sociology of Knowledge," *American Sociological Review*, 31 (October 1968), 648–689.

[11] See Nelson W. Polsby, *Community Power and Political Theory* (New Haven: Yale University Press, 1963).

lost in terms of benefits. How could one know about who had power without looking at its actual use and results?

The primary scholarly response was a detailed study of New Haven, Connecticut, by Yale University political scientists. The best-known volume emerging from this research was *Who Governs?* by Robert A. Dahl.[12] The political scientists relied on survey research, analysis of public records, and observation of activities of leading officials, who apparently took them considerably into their confidence. These researchers observed decision making in three areas, designated as key areas: nominations for public office (because the stakes were legal control over jobs, status, and contracts), public education (because the schools were central in the future of the life chances of the citizenry's children), and urban renewal (because New Haven had the most spectacular program in the country at that time and because the entire core area of the central city was affected).

In his historical reconstruction of New Haven's political past, Dahl concluded that at one time economic and political power overlapped. But domination by economic notables stopped in New Haven before the Civil War, when an entrepreneurial class challenged the old rulers. From the post-Civil War era to the present, Dahl found New Haven politics to be relatively open, constantly making room, often under pressure, for a stream of immigrants. In the three key areas, those who won on the decisions were not the same people as the economic elite.

In elections, the economic notables long ago abandoned both parties to the immigrants, so in New Haven a stable and pervasive pattern of ethnic voting developed.[13] In the area of urban renewal, the major figure was the mayor, Richard C. Lee. Lee persuaded and cajoled the major economic interests in the town into cooperating. Lee brought them onto a civic committee that ratified his plans and sold the idea to the restive lower-class populations and small businessmen who stood to be, and were, displaced.[14] On school policy, Dahl found:

> An examination of eight different sets of decisions taken between 1953 and 1959 indicates that there are three main centers for initiating or vetoing policies involving the public schools. These are the mayor, the Board of Education, and the Superintendent of Schools.[15]

[12] (New Haven: Yale University Press, 1960).

[13] See Raymond E. Wolfinger, "The Development and Persistence of Ethnic Voting," *The American Political Science Review*, **59** (December 1965), 896–908.

[14] See Dahl, op. cit., and Raymond E. Wolfinger, *The Politics of Progress* (Englewood Cliffs, N.J.: Prentice-Hall, 1974).

[15] Dahl, op. cit., p. 150.

Further, Dahl wrote:

> In eight different sets of decisions between 1953 and 1959, there were twenty-seven instances in which the initiation or veto of a policy alternative could be attributed to a particular individual, group, or agency. . . . Of the twenty-seven instances of successful action or policy, all except three were traceable to participants officially and publicly involved in the school system. Fifteen, or more than half, were traceable to the mayor or officials who were members of his educational coalition.[16]

Dahl found differences in levels of citizen participation in New Haven. He believed almost any group could win if it pursued an issue with sufficient intensity. Every group possessed potential political resources, and political leaders anticipated citizen reaction and tried to avoid losing support. The influence of the economic notables cited in Atlanta could not be seen, even in the matter of tax assessments. Dahl labeled New Haven a "pluralistic political system" and concluded it was democratic. Other political scientists applied similar methods to other cities by examining specific decisions, and they too found pluralistic systems.[17]

The Nondecision Model. It was not long before a very influential critique of *both* the power structure model and the pluralist model was forthcoming. In "Two Faces of Power," Peter Bachrach and Morton S. Baratz—one a political scientist, the other an economist—argued that both of the prior approaches were wrong.[18] The sociologists were wrong in not looking at actual decisions. And the political scientists overlooked what the critics called a nondecision. The definition was as follows:

> Nondecision making is a means by which demands for change in the existing allocation of benefits and privileges in the community can be suffocated before they are even voiced; or kept overt; or killed before they gain access to the relevant decision-making

[16] Ibid., p. 151.

[17] See, for example, Linton Freeman and others, *Local Community Leadership* (Syracuse: University College of Syracuse, 1960); and Edward C. Banfield, *Political Influence* (New York: Free Press, 1960), for such studies of Syracuse and Chicago, respectively.

[18] *The American Political Science Review,* **56** (December 1962), 947–952, reprinted in Bachrach and Baratz, *Power and Poverty* (New York: Oxford University Press, 1970), pp. 3–17.

arena; or, failing all these things, maimed or destroyed in the decision-implementing stage of the policy process.[19]

Bachrach and Baratz maintained that the primary method for sustaining any given arrangement in politics is nondecision making.[20] Different techniques prevent left-out groups in society from getting their share. Terror through intimidation, harassment, even murder keeps people from voicing complaints against the established order. Co-optation gives the challenging group the illusion of being a part of the political process, without altering policy. Invoking norms, precedents, rules, or procedures deflects challenges.

The nondecision model shifts the emphasis from how things are done and who does what to who benefits and who loses under the status quo. Early examples of nondecisions came in two forms. On the one hand, at the national level, the absence of significant civil rights progress between 1890 and 1945 could be pointed to, along with the way the passivity of southern blacks was encouraged by a mix of outright terrorism and more subtle techniques. On the other hand, local examples tended to be couched in the form of critiques of the pluralist method. For New Haven, for example, it was argued that economic notables could still rule, because the three issue areas Dahl studied were misleading. Why should economic notables care about public education or political nominations when they sent their own children to private school and lived outside the city? As for urban renewal, perhaps Mayor Lee so anticipated the reactions of the businessmen on his committee that they dominated him, rather than vice versa.

The only local study cited that appeared to substantiate a nondecision view of local politics was that of "Springdale," published as *Small Town in Mass Society,* by Joseph Vidich and Arthur Bensman.[21] Bachrach and Baratz conceded that studying nondecisions was difficult. They maintained, however, that nondecisions could be analyzed by watching decisions and talking to those who are aggrieved overtly or covertly, in a community. Only in one case, "if there is no conflict, overt or covert," could nondecision making not be studied.[22] In this instance, one would have to assume that there was consensus on the prevailing allocation of values. But, otherwise, nondecisions were researchable. In an effort to prove this point, they presented the efforts of the black minority in Baltimore to gain power between 1965 and

---

[19] Bachrach and Baratz, ibid., 44.
[20] Bachrach and Baratz, ibid., p. 44.
[21] (Princeton: Princeton University Press, 1958).
[22] Bachrach and Baratz, op. cit., p. 49.

1968. They used unstructured interviews, observation, and public documents as data. The focus began with efforts to organize the poor from a community base, and continued through reapportionment and antipoverty agency controversies. The conclusion was that the "prevailing mobilization of bias blocked black leaders' attempts to arouse their would-be constituents to political action and thereby assured that blacks would remain locked out of the political system."[23]

The Political Model. Still another model could be called the political model, which synthesizes elements of the power structure and the pluralist models. Robert H. Salisbury's article, "Urban Politics: The New Convergence of Power," is its clearest statement.[24] The essence is that various elements have power (pluralist), including business (elitist), but that the mayor as he chief political official occupies a central position in an "executive-centered coalition." Salisbury makes clear that he describes only the biggest cities, and notes "we should recognize . . . the shifting importance over time of public allocations to the total of allocations made in the community, and remember, too, that public and private actions are always mixed together, nowhere more than in the city."[25]

Salisbury finds a distinct historical pattern in the distribution of urban power. In eighteenth- and early nineteenth-century cities, the original power was in the hands of an overlapping social, economic, religious, and political elite—a true power structure. In the mid-nineteenth century, this elite was replaced by the merchantry, the newly rich entrepreneurs. In western cities there were no patricians from the start. Around the turn of the century, the immigrant impact began to be felt. Several factors facilitated the power of this new group, which shared power with the merchantry.

One factor was the emergence of the national corporation, which diminished the concern of the local entrepreneur for the local community. Simultaneously, the wealthy merchants, displaced in politics by newcomers, began to discharge their civic obligations through relatively insulated but high-prestige service on boards of libraries, schools, parks, and orchestras. Another factor was the city building carried out by urban machines and requiring an autonomous governmental sector. Now there were large numbers of city works. The displaced economic notables acquiesced in the rule of the urban boss

---

[23] Ibid., p. 80.

[24] *The Journal of Politics*, **26**:4 (November 1964), 775–797.

[25] Ibid., p. 777. Salisbury believes the model fits St. Louis, which he studied personally, and was also applicable to New Haven, Philadelphia, Detroit, Nashville, and Seattle.

because city activities were not that important to them. That is, "although government was far more formidable in this period than formerly, the major decisions allocating resources in the city were still made by private interests."[26]

Further changes occurred in the 1930s and 1940s. In the 1930s, big-city voters became overwhelmingly Democratic and, oddly, provided a cover for "good government" values that ended the machine. In the 1940s, businessmen reentered politics because of the economic threat to the central city posed by population change, suburbanization, and decay. These changes led to the new convergence of urban power:

> It is headed, and sometimes led, by the elected chief executive of the city, the mayor. Included in the coalition are two principal active groupings, locally oriented economic interests and the professional workers in technical, city-related programs. Both these groupings are sources of initiative for programs that involve major allocations of resources, both public and private. Associated with the coalition, also, are whatever groups constitute the popular vote-base of the mayor's electoral success. Their association is more distant and permissive, however. Their power to direct specific policy choices is severely limited.[27]

Under the new convergence, the mayor is the main figure. Only he has either the organizational support or charisma to get elected and only he stands at the center of the communications network and legal authority network of the city. The businessmen with major investments in the community know that what happens to the core city affects them—banks, department stores, the largest real estate firms, and newspapers. The technicians, city bureaucrats, have their own goals—a bigger department, more service for their clients, and so on. Yet, neither of these elements can move without the mayor. He possesses the legal authority and also the legitimacy that comes from popular election.

In the political model, the electorate is not as important as the other elements. The electorate votes directly on various bond issues and referenda, as well as public offices. But the initiative for the referenda comes from the coalition that makes up the convergence. A few demands, particularly on racial issues, come directly from the citizenry. The coalition then must respond or finesse these demands. But most issues and most day-to-day government operate under the

[26] Ibid., p. 782.
[27] Ibid., p. 784.

steam of the executive-centered coalition, without much being heard from the public. Councilmen and other local officials and group leaders play a secondary role. The chief executive's power in the coalition is, however, not very great, except in a relative sense:

> the mayor is influential only relative to other groups in the city. He is not powerful relative to the problems he tries to solve. The mayor cannot determine by fiat or, apparently, any other way that the economic resources of the city shall increase, that crime and poverty shall decline, that traffic shall move efficiently. He only has rather more to say about how the problems shall be approached than anyone else.[28]

LOCAL POLITICS: WHO CONTROLS? —A SUMMARY ANALYSIS

The games, power structure, pluralist, nondecision, and political models of local politics are not the only ones developed. For example, Agger and his associates concluded in their study of four local communities that any model of local politics would have to analyze closely the ideologies of local leaders, particularly their views about the proper scope of local governmental activities.[29]

Furthermore, the power structure versus pluralist versus nondecision model debate goes on intensely. Some believe, for example, that there is no way to prove or disprove the existence of a nondecision. Raymond E. Wolfinger notes, "It is easy enough to say today that women's rights was a nonissue in, say, 1949; the trick is to figure out a way to discover it *in* 1949."[30] On the other hand, Frederick W. Frey maintains that the nondecision concept raises topics "so crucial that great effort to resolve existing difficulties (in research methods) is warranted."[31]

Meanwhile, community research goes on apace. One publication lists a bibliography of 240 community studies.[32] Much research is in comparative studies. Some synthesize the data from many previous analyses. Others start fresh with comparable data from sets of cities, aggregate statistical data on social characteristics, political characteris-

---

[28] Ibid., p. 790.

[29] Robert E. Agger and others, *The Rulers and the Ruled* (New York: Wiley, 1964).

[30] "Nondecisions and the Study of Local Politics: Rejoinder," *The American Political Science Review*, **65** (December 1971), 1103.

[31] "Nondecisions and the Study of Local Politics: Comment," *The American Political Science Review*, **65** (December 1971), 1099.

[32] Willis D. Hawley and Frederick M. Wirt, *The Search for Community Power*, (Englewood Cliffs, N.J.: Prentice-Hall, 1969), pp. 367–379.

tics, and public policy, and others combine these techniques with more traditional observation or reputational devices.

Terry N. Clark, a sociologist, has been a critic and an analyst of different methods in community research. He has maintained that a comparative approach will be the most fruitful in understanding local power.[33] Table 6-2 is his schematic representation of three different approaches: Hunter's (the power structure model), Dahl's (the pluralist model), and his own (the comparative focus). In essence, Clark seeks to go beyond the earlier models. At one stage of his research, he proposed 34 specific propositions about urban communities for testing, most of them dealing with the distribution of power.[34]

TABLE 6-2.   Contrasting Approaches to Community Research

	Hunter + Followers	*Dahl + Followers*	*Comparative Researcher*
Method	Reputational	Decisional	Combined methods
Focus	Power-structure	Decision-making structure	Power and decision-making structures
Centralization	Monolithic	Pluralistic	Variation along a centralization continuum
Leadership	Generalized leadership by businessmen and certain professionals	Issue-specific leadership; political leaders more generally active	Variation by community
Guiding Questions	Who governs?	Who governs?	Who governs, where, when, and with what effects?

SOURCE: The table from "The Structure of Community Influence," by Terry N. Clark in Harlan Hahn (ed.), Vol. 6, *Urban Affairs Annual Reviews* (1972), p. 287, is reprinted by permission of the publisher, Sage Publications, Inc. (Beverly Hills/London).

He then tested his propositions in a separate study of 51 communities, using a wide range of techniques.[35] His findings support

[33] "The Structure of Community Influence," in *People and Politics in Urban Society*, ed. by Harlan Hahn (Beverley Hills: Sage Publications, 1972), pp. 283–314.
[34] "Power and Community Structure: Who Governs, Where, and When?" *The Sociological Quarterly*, 8 (Summer 1967), 291–316.
[35] "Community Structure, Decision Making, Budget Expenditures, and Urban Renewal in 51 American Communities," in Charles M. Bonjean and others, *Community Politics: A Behavioral Approach* (New York: Free Press, 1971), pp. 293–313.

some aspects of the previous discussion of mayor-council cities, as well as some parts of the pluralist and political models outlined in this chapter. For example, more diverse communities had more separated potential elites, and thus more decentralized decision-making structures. Decentralized decision making (consistent with either the pluralist or the political models) was associated with economic diversification, population size, and (slightly) with active civic voluntary associations. It was negatively associated with reformed governmental institutions.[36]

In another comparative analysis, Claire W. Gilbert reanalyzed 166 power structure studies and compared the findings of those from before 1944 and 1954 with subsequent ones.[37] She found strong evidence of political processes tending to be more pluralistic. At the same time, however, she found a rise of economic notables, reflecting changes in smaller communities dominated by a few industries.

What is the student to make of all this? Models, conflicting interpretations, complicated quantitative comparative studies. Five conclusions represent a conservative estimate of what research has established so far.

1. Beyond question, in some communities, local decisions are dominated by an economic elite that is close to the power structure model. We expect to find this pattern in cities dominated by one industry, or in cities where an absence of political competition or group organization makes open political processes weak.

2. In many communities there is a greater probability that the pluralist model fits the local reality best. We would most expect a pluralist local system where the city is larger and socially and economically more diversified. Further, whatever centralization of power exists takes the form of an executive-centered coalition, with the mayor as the chief elected public official at the center.

3. The nondecision model raises many questions. The most serious problem is whether a community can bring potential resources and issues into the public decision-making arena. Some of what the nondecision adherents believe to be the effect of local elites may instead result from the centralization of governmental and nongovernmental resources in national in-

---

[36] Ibid., p. 303.

[37] "Some Trends in Community Politics: A Secondary Analysis of Power Structure Data from 166 Communities," *Social Science Quarterly*, 48 (December 1967), 373–381, reprinted in Bonjean, op. cit., pp. 210–215.

stitutions. With local elites, the most serious methodological question is how to study what, by definition, does not happen visibly. Much in our society is done quietly or is legally protected from public scrutiny. Conceivably, a method could be devised to study nondecisions. But social science research so far leaves this model in the realm of theory, perhaps intuitively or ideologically seductive, but unprovable.

4. At the minimum, we can specify who wins and loses in local politics on particular local controversies, or on continuing areas of concern, such as the distribution of services or the imposition of taxes. Comparative studies collect such data from many cities and compare spending and taxing, and these, in turn, with underlying social, economic, and governmental variables. Case studies remain the best way of studying particular struggles.

5. We can describe the participants in local politics at some level of generality. We can describe how economic interests usually act. We can describe how elected officials, mayors, city councilmen, and city managers see their jobs and how they behave. We can describe how various bureaucrats act.

PLANNING IN LOCAL LIFE

No model discussed here suggests that power is used in a planned, ordered way to achieve some vision of the Beautiful City or the Good City or the Virtuous City. No one who studies American local politics would suggest that whatever happens, however it happens, reflects a centralized planned order in which all physical and social actions are coordinated under government to achieve ends agreed upon in advance. Yet, such a planned local environment is a theoretical possibility. What's more, as a possibility, the idea of the planned city has intrigued human minds for thousands of years. In American urban history, we have many instances of planned cities. Some of these cities were built piecemeal by private or governmental organizations along the lines of plans drawn up by architects and urban planners. Others were built whole, and then owned and operated by private corporations. Today, all major cities and most communities of more than 10,000 population have planning departments, and almost all of the major metropolitan areas have some sort of areawide planning body. Thousands of people are employed as city planners.

From our perspective, planning raises a number of interesting questions. What is the philosophical basis of public planning as one means of achieving ends in our cities? What has been the history of efforts to plan American cities? How have past and present planning tied in to our political processes? What kinds of controversies do techniques and outcomes of planning generate? What are the future uses of planning for American cities?

THE PHILOSOPHICAL BASIS OF PLANNING

There are many different kinds of urban planning, ranging from specific plans for transportation or street layout or a civic center to what is sometimes called "the urban general plan" or "master plan." The classic definition is as follows:

> The general plan is the official statement of a municipal legislative body which sets forth its major policies concerning desirable future physical development; the published general plan document must include a single, unified general physical design for the community, and it must attempt to clarify the relationships between physical-development policies and social and economic goals.[38]

The components of the plan, as defined, usually emphasize physical development but take into account also social and economic forces in the community. The underlying philosophical principle is that decisions about the future of the community are too important to be left to the disconnected decisions of private businessmen, real estate developers and speculators, or individual citizens. The concept, thus, is exactly the opposite of the idea that the free market leads to the best outcome for all. Instead, the idea of planning is that the free market may very well lead to outcomes that are undesirable. As the alternative, goals are supposed to be spelled out by the highest elected officials, acting on the carefully put-together advice of objective experts, whose plan is frequently reconsidered and revised.

The experts in this process are the trained city planners, who are supposed to bring to their roles specialized skills that allow them to view the overall public interest among various alternative possibilities and to work out plans based on their overview and their skills. Their techniques depend for execution on the legal power of the community to regulate and prescribe various kinds of land uses, building standards, and other forms of activity.

In practice, planning meets with a mixed reception and mixed success. That does not alter the stark difference between its philosophical basis and other models of urban decision making. In the other

---

[38] T. J. Kent, Jr., *The Urban General Plan* (San Francisco: Chandler, 1964), p. 18.

models we considered, no one governed, or an elite governed, or there was a pluralist system, or a political leadership system, or there was a restriction of the agenda of politics in the interest of one sector. The processes involved are role playing and the exercise of various forms of resources—wealth, position, number, intensity of concern. In concept, these processes rest either on random forces or on the conscious exercise of power to achieve personal or group ends. Planning is different in that what is exercised is an expert vision of the Good City. The process involves no less than centralized design and execution. The interest to be served is, philosophically, a general interest.

The widespread presence of planning agencies at the local and metropolitan level is anomalous when we consider how contrary planning is to the political culture of individualism and the free market. Planning at the national level has existed since the New Deal, but has been of low-visibility in the executive bureaucracy, or in the White House. It often comes packaged as efficiency techniques, such as the zero-based budgeting technique. Local planning adopts various camouflages to overcome or to outflank charges of socialism or power grabbing that might be leveled at it. One frequent criticism of some planning techniques such as zoning is that they operate too much to protect private property values. Nonetheless, as we look at planning in detail, two remarkable aspects stand out: here is a system of decision making totally unlike other theoretical models; and here is a general system of decision making that runs counter to the American cult of individualism.

A BRIEF HISTORY OF AMERICAN PLANNING

Planning for physical aspects of American cities dates from colonial and immediate post-colonial times.[39] For example, there were systematic plans for Williamsburg, Virginia (in 1699), and for Philadelphia (in 1682). James Oglethorpe in 1733 designed a gridiron with open-space plan for Savannah, Georgia, that guided the growth of the community until 1856. The most famous early plan was that of Major Pierre L'Enfant, a French artist and engineer, for Washington, D.C., in 1791. L'Enfant drew on baroque and French classical elements and provided for a combined system of diagonal and radial streets superimposed on a gridiron plan. His basic plan for the nation's capital remains today.

[39] See John W. Reps, *The Making of Urban America* (Princeton: Princeton University Press, 1965); and James G. Coke, "Antecedents of Local Planning," in *Principles and Practice of Urban Planning*, ed. by William I. Goodman and Eric C. Freund (Washington, D.C.: International City Managers Association, 1968), pp. 7–28.

The years 1800 to 1865 saw rapid urban growth and great technological development, but urban planning vanished, buried in wild land speculation and individualism. One observer noted that "GAIN! Gain! Gain! is the beginning, the middle, and the end, the *alpha* and *omega* of the founders of American towns. . . . "[40] At the end of that period, various movements developed toward planning separate aspects of urban life. In New York, under the leadership of Lawrence Veiller, laws regulating tenement construction passed, culminating in the Tenement House Act of 1901. Such laws recognized a public interest in the design, safety, and sanitation features of privately owned housing. From 1860 onward, a systematic movement built major urban parks. This movement, led by the famous Frederick Law Olmsted, believed that large, well-designed parks would help mediate the tensions and facelessness of the cities by adding a touch of rural landscape. Between 1870 and 1900, New York developed Central Park; St. Louis, Forest Park; and new systems were developed in Baltimore, Philadelphia, Cincinnati, Chicago, Minneapolis, and Boston, all of which still stand as the core of these cities' parks today.

A major planning movement began near the turn of this century. The design of the Columbian Exposition at the Chicago Fair of 1893 inspired an interest in physical design, especially classical features. The movement emphasized civic beautification. Washington's park plan, completed in 1901, led to the development of the Lincoln and Jefferson Memorials and the groupings of public buildings that exist there today. Plans in this "City Beautiful" movement stressed open spaces, impressive public buildings, and wide thoroughfares. Daniel Burnham, a leader of the movement and author of its major document, *Plan of Chicago* (1909), wrote that "a city plan must ever deal mainly with the direction and width of its streets."[41] By 1913, there were 43 civic improvement plans, and 233 communities working on some sort of civic betterment project.

The City Beautiful Movement is regarded as a mixed achievement for planning. On the positive side, it dramatized the power and vigor of the new American industrial cities, built an impressive number of civic plazas and monuments, and recognized the connection between physical aspects of a city and the socioeconomic facets of urban life. On the negative side, the planners avoided the inherent philosophical clash between private action in the city and a larger public interest by applying their planning only to parks, boulevards, and civic centers. As James G. Coke notes:

[40] Quoted in Reps, op. cit., p. 349.
[41] Quoted in Reps, op. cit. p. 517. See also Mel Scott, *American City Planning Since 1890* (Berkeley and Los Angeles: University of California Press, 1969).

This choice of a focus had two unintended consequences. It made sure that the claims of the polity did not become an issue, since the achievement of these limited goals required public investment, rather than controls. At the same time, the choice created a special upper-middle-class constituency for planning. By nature suspicious of governmental controls, particularly at the local level, this group would respond enthusiastically to an all-rewarding objective like beautification through public investment.[42]

Straws in the wind signalled the concerns that are now central to contemporary planning. Many planners recognized the need to deal with social and economic as well as physical problems. More important, at the local legislative level, a legal basis developed to assert public control. In 1916 New York City adopted the first zoning ordinance. Zoning allowed local governments to specify land uses for areas of their territory: residential only, commercial only, industrial, mixed, and other classifications. Zoning passed its constitutional test in 1926. By 1931, 800 cities had comprehensive zoning systems. The Depression slowed local planning, as simple survival became the problem, but that era also marked initial efforts to establish some form of federal planning processes.

CONTEMPORARY PLANNING SINCE WORLD WAR II

The impetus to post-World War II planning has been another spurt of physical development, this time financed by federal programs, ranging from airports, to urban renewal, to housing, to highways, to "model cities," to mass transit. The legislative history of these various federal programs does not indicate what role planners played as the acts went through the Congress. One thing, however, is certain. All the acts, beginning with the 1949 urban renewal program, included federal funds for local planning. From the federal side, requiring planning as part of local projects achieves control over standards and quality, as well as setting up channels between local and federal officials. From the local side, the federal planning funds are first, a prerequisite to the big money for actual projects, and, second, "free money" to hire professional planners at no cost to local taxpayers. From the perspective of the planners at the local level and as an organized group in the American Institute of Planners nationwide, federal programs provide employment, tasks, and influence.

Spurred on by the proliferation of federal programs, almost all local communities set up planning agencies. By 1964 every city with

[42] Coke, op. cit., p. 21.

more than 100,000 people maintained a planning agency, and so did more than 90 per cent of those cities with more than 10,000 population. The first large program was the Urban Planning Assistance Program of the Housing Act of 1954, which in its first five years funneled planning money to more than 11,000 municipalities in 94 urban regions. At one stage, more than 20 categorical grant federal programs provided funds for local planning. Federal regulations now require that all local applications for federal grants or loans for specific projects, including facilities such as airports, hospitals, sewerage and water supply installations, and open space acquisition, be submitted to an areawide agency for clearance and approval before funds are forthcoming. This proviso, added to the availability of separate funds for metropolitan planning, results in a proliferation of regional and metropolitan planning agencies that operate alongside the purely municipal planners.

Although accurate counts are difficult to obtain, approximately 350 commissions, including countywide agencies, do some metropolitan planning. Some 175 metropolitan agencies are approved by the federal Office of Management and Budget to review local applications for federal grants. Some of these areawide planning agencies exist by compact among the localities. Others exist within regional councils of government, areawide assemblies of local governments, discussed in Chapter 7.

Areawide planners have so far been limited to preparing guidelines for future development, collecting information, and approving federal grant proposals. Their direct influence over local behavior is not concrete. The municipal planners, on the other hand, have had a larger grant of authority. Use of planning devices to control development is widespread, especially zoning and subdivision regulation. Zoning, according to one authority, "is probably the single most commonly used legal device available for implementing the land-use plan of a community."[43] Generally based on the guidelines of the 1924 Standard Zoning Enabling Act of the U.S. Department of Commerce, zoning is a system of dividing the municipality into districts for residential, commercial, industrial, or mixed uses, and then setting regulations within those districts, based on (1) the height and bulk of buildings and other structures; (2) the area of a lot and the size of required open spaces; (3) the density of population; and (4) the use of buildings and land in terms of purposes.

Zoning is a substantial regulatory power. Zoning generates considerable friction in local politics:

[43] See Robert M. Leary, "Zoning," in Goodman and Freund, *Principles and Practice of Urban Planning,* op. cit. p. 403.

1. Over the original definition of usage and regulations.
2. Over "variances" (legal permission to operate differently from what the ordinance provides).
3. Over conflicts in usages among nearby communities (it does not help one community to prevent construction of anything but single-family residences on one-acre lots if the next town upwind consists of packinghouses).

Zoning has been accepted in the United States, despite its clear control over private property, because its *usage* has been to *protect* property values. By excluding certain kinds of usages—such as factories, or multifamily housing, or federally supported low-income housing for minorities—zoning ordinances bulwark the existing social values of a community. Zoning is the critical tool for suburbs in maintaining social homogeneity. Through setting large-lot, single-family regulations, they prevent alternative uses of land and keep minorities out, practices the United States Supreme Court has approved.

Zoning sometimes is the province of a special local zoning board, sometimes of the whole city council, or sometimes of a special zoning committee of the council. However final power is allocated, planners play a major role in setting zoning standards and in enforcing them.

Subdivision Development

Closely related to zoning, subdivision regulation establishes land uses and community standards. Most modern cities were built before zoning regulations were widely adopted, so that regulation of whole sectors of cities prior to construction was rare; hence, there was mixed usage of land in older cities. But subdivision regulation has been a major planning device in constructing the suburbs. Subdivision regulation rests on the police power of the locality to control certain kinds of development. Regulation of subdivision development follows a standard procedure outlined in the 1928 Standard City Planning Enabling Act of the Department of Commerce. City councils or planning boards or commissions exercise it under state enabling acts. All 50 states have enabling legislation, and about 85 per cent of cities with more than 10,000 population include this device as part of their planning programs.

The most common procedure requires, in order to convert raw land into building sites, that a developer first receive approval of the proposed design of the subdivision. He or she files a plat or map that indicates street layout and the standards to be followed in the construction of streets, sewers, and utilities. Potentially, then, this is another device to exert a public interest, managed by planners, over urban development. The scattershot reality of American suburban growth suggests, however, that the device was applied in greatly varying ways and against greatly varying requirements throughout the country. As so much else in the concept of planning, the gap between the concept and the institutional structures on the one hand and the real world of local activity on the other often seems great.

CONTROVERSIES IN PRESENT-DAY PLANNING

Present-day planning contains harsh controversies. The main issues include where planning programs should be located within the city government, the role of social planning, the role of advocacy planning, and the philosophical and ethical basis of planning. Planners disagree among themselves about their proper role. Should they operate as parts of independent planning commissions or should they be staff in the executive office of the mayor, providing the special assistance that other staff give modern executives? Or should they serve as policy advisors to the city council? The answer to the location questions is a strategic one of where they can most maximize their own influence in the local political process. Actual arrangements across the country differ, with about 40 per cent of all planners in executive departments, 40 per cent attached to independent commissions, and the rest in some mixed mode.

Social planning means that planners now collect and analyze data and make recommendations in areas such as health, community and family organization, education, housing, recreation, and the local economy. The legitimacy of social planning is now widely accepted. An earlier unstated assumption of the planning movement—that the shape of the physical environment determined the social environment—has been largely modified or abandoned. In analyzing social problems, planners often open up the intrinsic internal conflicts between different local activities. What if local attitudes, now carefully surveyed, violently oppose a new highway that will displace citizens and wreck existing low-income housing? How does this affect traditional close relationships between highway planners and the city planning office? Clearly, it will cast social planners as defenders of the poor, and physical planners as defenders of "progress" in the form of new and better roads. The same conflicts come into play when social planners seek to integrate low-income housing into middle- or upper-class neighborhoods. Social planners then set themselves against traditional standards for zoning and against those planners whose job is to protect zoning systems and existing property holders.

Advocacy planners represent the interests of those who are likely to be affected by some aspect of urban development—housing plans, highway plans, urban renewal plans, school or hospital building plans. Usually the advocacy planners work for private community action groups, or perhaps for federally or state-funded community groups. They put themselves in an adversary position to the plans of local government. Usually, they represent poor people or minorities whom they feel need the same expertise on their side that the government has at its end. Advocacy planners bring ideological and social commitment to their work.

It is easier to grasp the basic issues that advocacy planning raises than it is to know how many advocate planners there are or what their impact has been. The implication of advocacy planning is that there is no one public interest that expert planners can present for local needs. If this is the state of the world, however, the question logically arises, What special claims to anyone's attention should planners have? Precisely, this question is the basis of a seminal critique by Alan A. Altshuler.[44]

A CRITIQUE OF PLANNING

Altshuler identifies the theoretical problem of ever obtaining a comprehensive view of all the variables involved in a city. He questions whether planning is not by its very nature committed to greater and greater extension of governmental power, with bureaucratic aggrandizement. His main concern, however, is that planning cannot separate itself at an ethical level from any other form of public activity and, thus, can never achieve objective professionalism.

The ethical problem is that planners cannot avoid politics if they are to achieve their program goals. Experts in the field advise them to be confidential advisors to political executives or policy advisors to elected city councils. But political advisors of any stripe cannot take independent positions, at least in public. They must fight for the program their leader adopts, once that decision is made. Their expertise then becomes part of a political defense. Altshuler notes:

> Planning in the service of discrete political clienteles can of course be justified quite plausibly in theory. It is possible to argue that such planning is the only kind which can be effective in the American governmental system, and that concentration on this kind of planning would at least aid government to pursue goals on

---

[44] *The City Planning Process* (Ithaca: Cornell University Press, 1965).

which there is consensus with greater efficiency than at present. Further, specialized planning of this sort would affect controversial values only haphazardly, much as corporate planning does today.[45]

Planners go along with politics in part to get done things they want done. They also follow the pull of politics because of the inadequacy of planning theory itself. Planning possesses no hard core of ideas that cannot be compromised. This absence of rock-bottom theory separates planning from other professions, which have some principles that cannot be altered and are even enforceable on practitioners by formal or informal means. The result is that planning, especially when it steps into realms where there are conflicts of values and outlooks, becomes a handmaiden to different and competing groups. And, at that point, it loses any claim to represent a special rational "overall" view of the public interest.

PLANNING: A SUMMARY

Planning continues to be an activity of local and metropolitan government. But planning will not be the basis for ordered design of communities. There is no philosophical reason for placing such control in the hands of planners and, practically speaking, few political leaders will do so. A frank recognition of the contradictions involved in their role is characteristic of modern planners, who often become political staff in the service of particular clienteles.

Other countries with different systems or urban government and different patterns of political culture, especially Great Britain and the Scandinavian countries with their "New Towns," or the socialist countries and France for national planning, rely more heavily on planning than do American cities. Ironically, planning reaches its apogee of power in the design of American cities not in the public sphere, but in the service of private developers. The corporate and speculative builders of the Levittowns, Reston (Virginia), and Columbia (Maryland)—all very different communities—have had very clear conceptions of what they wanted to build. They exercise strong planning control over all aspects of design and the daily social and economic life of their creations, including retaining political power in their own hands. Privately employed planners have also had enormous impact on a smaller-than-the-whole-city scale. They design gigantic suburban shopping centers. They rehabilitate central city shopping areas. Private sector city planning affects every locality.

[45] Ibid., p. 400.

CONTROL, POWER, AND PLANNING: SOME CONCLUDING NORMATIVE QUESTIONS

All political decisions involve normative decisions, value judgments about what should be done, about what steps are best. Normative decisions require choice and rest on personal values, preferences, and ways of looking at the world. Normative decisions are inescapable, in national politics or in local politics. So far, this chapter has dealt with questions that could be resolved by empirical methods: What are the resources and stakes of governmental power? Who does govern? What has been the role of rational planning as a means of urban decision making. For all these questions, there is another side, the normative side. Each student will have to make up his or her own mind about what *should* be done, who *should* hold power, how issues *should* be resolved. What we can do here, however, is list some of the major normative issues and the alternatives for each. Such a listing follows:

1. Who should hold power in urban governments? Should it be elected public officials? Or should it be those with the most resources, such as the wealthy with their property stake in the local community? Or should it be those who care the most intensely, the most involved groups? Or should it be those who actually work in the city—the organized teachers, city engineers, and policemen? Or should it be the general public, the unorganized but directly affected purchasers and consumers of local government services? Or should it be those who know the most about the cities, such as the planners with their expertise?

2. What is the relationship between city structures and city power? If changing the structure of government benefits some more than others, would that be proper? Suppose the most beneficial structures for some interests or values were individual neighborhoods? Or suppose they were entire metropolitan areas?

3. What is the proper role of planning? To what degree is there a right way to do things in an urban area and to what degree is such expertise possessed by those with planning credentials? How does one balance the claims of experts to know what is best against the claims of representative, democratic government, which argues that the people choose, even if they may not choose wisely?

4. Why should local affairs be part of politics in any case? What

are the benefits of local autonomy? We can easily imagine an administrative city, where political decisions are made by higher authorities at the national or state level and carried out by appointed bureaucrats. There are models of this type of city in other nations. In other words, why look to the local scene for any exercise of governmental power at all?

The student will surely think of more normative issues that are raised by the material in this chapter. Many issues transcend the boundaries of local communities. In Chapter 7 we examine metropolitan political patterns and issues.

7

METROPOLITAN POLITICS: SYSTEM OR CHAOS?

Anyone driving out from a central city soon discovers seemingly endless suburbs. Each has its own name. Each is a legal entity with independent governmental authority to tax and to perform police functions, subject only to the general laws of each state. We first review numerical aspects of government in metropolitan areas; then look at forms of metropolitan government, from the most decentralized to the most unified; and finally, survey four theoretical models, each offering a different viewpoint on American metropolitan areas.

A LANDSCAPE OF GOVERNMENTS

Local governments cover the American landscape. There are more than 18,000 municipalities, 18,000 townships, 3,000 counties, more than 30,000 independent school districts, and more than 18,000 special districts. Special districts perform one particular function, such as fire protection or sewage disposal. They serve parts of the territory of one community, or a group of communities, or even, areawide, all localities in the metropolitan area.

Multiple governments are the norm for all American metropolitan areas. More than 20,000 local governments operate within the SMSAs, and the average is 91 per SMSA. The number, however, varies greatly from metropolitan area to metropolitan area, from 1,214 in Chicago to only 4 in Honolulu. Older areas possess a greater number of individual

183

governments. Scholars suggest that the number of such governments is a function of aging, rather than of legal rules, such as the ease of annexation.[1] With annexation, one governmental unit, usually a central city, takes control of and blends neighboring territory into its own. Annexation occurs under state enabling legislation, which sometimes requires that voters approve by referendum. Frequent annexation would result in central cities with larger territories and in fewer separate governments.

SMSA AGE AND THE MULTIPLICITY OF INDEPENDENT GOVERNMENTS

Thomas R. Dye studied annexation and population growth in 212 SMSAs between 1950 and 1960.[2] Boundary lines were more stable in the older than in the newer communities. For those 35 cities that attained the 50,000 population mark between 1950 and 1960, 22.3 per cent of their 1960 population came from annexations. But for the 49 cities that had 50,000 people for 70 years or more, only 4.2 per cent of their populations came from annexation. That relationship produced a simple correlation of -.39, a strong connection between increasing age and decreasing use of annexation. For both manager and nonmanager cities considered separately, as age went up, the annexation score went down.

The relationship of age to development is very suggestive. The rigidity of boundaries of the older urban areas reflects what happens with time. Over the decades people and organizations adjust to arrangements as they find them, including accepting the legal boundaries of suburbs or small towns now enveloped in metropolitan sprawl. Life-styles and economic and social interests harden. In the older, usually northeastern urban areas, the suburbs have a higher socioeconomic status population than the core city. In the newer areas of the Southwest, West, and Rocky Mountain region, the differentiation is less, or may even be reversed, with a higher-status population in the central city. Further, in the older communities, housing in the central city is likely to be wearing out and unattractive to middle-class, family-oriented buyers. In the newer cities, the housing stock in the central city is newer and attractive to middle-class families. Dye notes,

[1] See Leo F. Schnore, "Forms of Government and Socioeconomic Characteristics of Suburbs," in his *The Urban Scene* (New York: Free Press, 1965), and Thomas R. Dye, *Politics in States and Communities* (Englewood Cliffs, N.J.: Prentice-Hall, 1977), pp. 326–327.

[2] "Urban Political Integration: Conditions Associated with Annexation in American Cities," *Midwest Journal of Political Science*, 8 (November 1964), pp. 430–446.

"Social class distance favoring the suburbs appears to be a distinct barrier to successful annexation efforts by central cities."[3]

If a developmental concept about multiple independent suburbs is correct, then several predictions follow. The likelihood that older metropolitan areas will reduce the number of governments is remote. The possibility that the newer metropolitan areas will have more governments as they, too, age is a real possibility. All that would alter that picture for the newer metropolises of Houston, Dallas, Denver, or Atlanta is if social processes in the 1980s somehow differ from those of the previous 100 years.

METROPOLITAN GOVERNMENT: MANY FORMS

In an abstract, hypothetical sense, one could imagine two polar forms of metropolitan governance. There could be one government for the entire metropolitan area, whether it was 10 square miles of people and industry or 400 square miles. You would have a centralized integrated mechanism for the area, like the national government. An opposite polar form would be multiple autonomous governments for the metropolitan area. As long as tasks somehow got done, we could still call this decentralized, unconnected arrangement, "governance."

A metropolitan government is any government that serves more than one identifiable local community. Starting from this definition, Figure 7-1 diagrams the alternative forms from the "least radical" to the "most radical." Least radical has nothing to do with the ideology of the political left or right. It refers to how much the form departs from a starting point of complete local autonomy. The most radical alternatives are the most centralized and unified.

The more radical metropolitan alternatives bring their substantial changes in the existing arrangements and affect larger and larger numbers of people. In the less radical alternatives, as Figure 7-1 indicates, the mode of decision making is usually purely governmental.[4] One unit of government agrees to buy services from a county government, for example, or joins with other units of government in a special district to provide sewers for an entire metropolitan area. However, as one moves across the line into the more radical areas that affect the crucial values of the community, the mode of decision making shifts to requiring approval by the voters. We now look at examples of each of the different modes.

[3] Dye, op. cit., p. 326.

[4] Professor Thomas M. Scott developed this schema. See his "Metropolitan Governmental Reorganization Proposals," *Western Political Quarterly*, **21**:2 (June 1968), pp. 498–507.

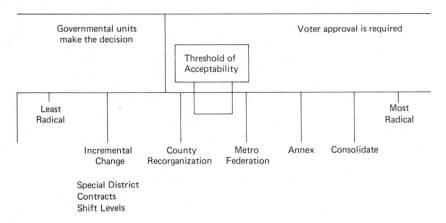

FIGURE 7-1. Continuum of Radicalness of Metropolitan Governmental Forms. (SOURCE: Thomas M. Scott, "Metropolitan Government Reorganization Proposals," *Western Political Quarterly*, 21:2 (June 1968), p. 500. Reprinted by permission.)

I. INCREMENTAL CHANGE: FOUR FORMATS

There are four organizational formats for incremental change: (1) the special district, (2) interlocal cooperation, (3) the contracting urban county, and (4) councils of governments.

Metropolitan Special Districts. Metropolitan special districts deliver at least one service to two or more localities within a metropolitan area. They may serve as few as two localities, a large portion of all the localities or, in the case of areawide metropolitan districts, all the localities. There are numerous such districts in existence, and they are particularly likely to be found as a mode of metropolitan service in the larger urban areas (Figure 7-2).

Metropolitan special districts are popular. First, they generally are responsible for one program area, such as transit, water supply, sewage lines and disposal, or air pollution control. The limited operation is perceived to be a technological solution that will not disrupt the favored values of any of the local units to be served. Benefits and costs are seen to be distributed relatively equally. Second, these districts are generally insulated from the need for direct public financing and from public control and scrutiny. They finance themselves partially from user charges—tolls, rents, fees, and revenue bonds. They operate very much as private businesses do. When they require public subsidies, these come from local governmental units and not from direct taxpayer payments. Directors are chosen by the local governments, or by the state government, but not by popular vote.

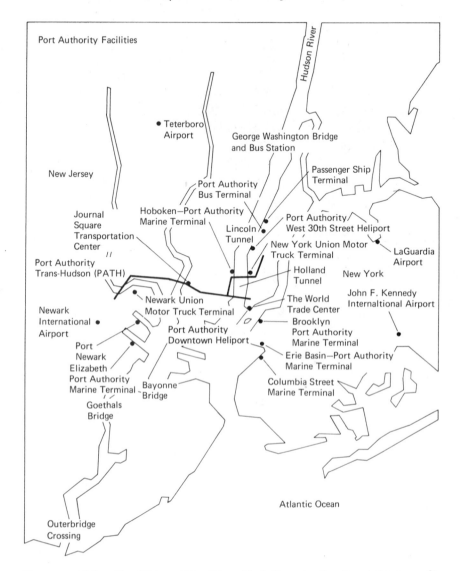

FIGURE 7-2. Facilities of the New York Port Authority: A Metropolitan Special District. (**SOURCE: Courtesy Port of New York and New Jersey Authority.**)

The largest 72 SMSA's utilize 155 special districts. The scope of district services can be quite extensive. For example, in addition to the Port of New York and New Jersey Authority and the Massachusetts Bay Transit Authority, bus and rapid transit systems are operated by the Chicago Transit Authority, the Bi-State Development Agency (St.

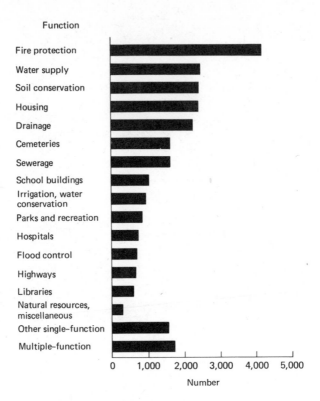

FIGURE 7-3. How Special Districts Are Used. (SOURCE: *1977 Census of Governments.*)

Louis) BART (San Francisco), and METRO (Washington, D.C.). Regional parks are provided by the Cleveland Metropolitan Park District, the Huron-Clinton Metropolitan Authority (Detroit) and the East Bay Regional Park District (San Francisco). Sewage facilities are operated by the Metropolitan Sanitary District of Greater Chicago, the Metropolitan St. Louis Sewer District, and the Municipality of Metropolitan Seattle. The Metropolitan Water District of Southern California brings water hundreds of miles from the Colorado River and then sells it in six southern California counties.

Interlocal Cooperation. Interlocal cooperation is another step beyond the autonomous local unit. Municipalities enter into agreements with other municipalities or with county governments to buy one service from the other or to share the costs or personnel in the administration of a service. Shared operations include airports, building inspection, civil defense, construction of buildings, correctional facilities, election day activities, fire departments (especially stand-by agreements to come to assistance in special emergencies), flood control, public health programs, and hospital services. Interlocal cooperation extends to libraries, personnel services, purchasing, tax assessment and collection, and to the centralized aspects of law enforcement, such as communications and identification. Sharing data processing is common.

Most agreements are contractual on a relatively small scale. The normal distribution of power and values of the many autonomous local units are not interrupted, and cheaper prices can often be offered to taxpayers. Most such contracts do not involve any voter approval, although they may require authorization by the state legislature. Analysis of interlocal cooperation in the Philadelphia area brought forth intriguing findings.[5] Cooperation is greatest on the periphery of things that matter—police radio bands for example. Cooperation is least on services that touch most intimately on life-styles—shared school systems and shared sewerage facilities. Among 534 contiguous pairs of municipalities in the Philadelphia metropolitan region, as the communities were *closer* in social rank (similar in terms of socioeconomic status), their propensity to cooperate increased.[6] The opposite was also true. As social distance increased, the probabilities of interlocal cooperation decreased.

Contracting Urban County.   The contracting urban county represents another form of incremental change in governmental structure in metropolitan areas. Sometimes the term refers to when a county provides services such as police protection to unincorporated areas within its boundaries (as St. Louis County does). Sometimes it refers to a situation in which a function is carried out for an entire urban area by the county government (such as registration of births and deaths, for example).

The archetypal contracting urban county is Los Angeles County. Under a system known as the Lakewood Plan (after a community which was among the first to use the county's services after it incorporated in 1954), Los Angeles County sells individual services and packages of services to all of the 77 communities within its boundaries. The county package of services includes 58 separate items. In all, the

---

[5] See Oliver P. Williams, Harold Herman, Charles S. Liebman, and Thomas R. Dye, *Suburban Differences and Metropolitan Policies* (Philadelphia: University of Pennsylvania Press, 1965).

[6] See Thomas R. Dye, Charles S. Liebman, Oliver P. Williams, and Harold Herman, "Differentiation and Cooperation in a Metropolitan Area," *Midwest Journal of Political Science*, 7:2 (May 1963), 145–155.

county has about 1,600 contracts and furnishes as many as 45 to one town and as few as seven to another. The most widely used county services are election administration, corrections, enforcement of state health laws and city health ordinances, and tax assessment. In addition, animal control, emergency ambulance, prosecution of local ordinances, inspections of mobile homes and trailer parks, libraries, building inspection, engineering, industrial waste regulation, weed abatement, rodent control, and law enforcement and fire protection are widely sold. The number expands as urban technology expands; radar equipment maintenance and helicopter police patrols are now available.

This system allows newer communities to avoid forming expensive governmental departments; it is simply easier and cheaper to buy the service from the county. Older cities also find parts of the package attractive, especially maintenance services. But whatever the services purchased, the political point is that they are *optional*, and they actually facilitate metropolitan autonomy. Even communities without the money to mount a major service on their own can still have that service and keep their political autonomy. The contracting urban county provides a means for functional consolidation without paying the price of political merger.

Councils of Governments.   A final incremental form of metropolitan organization are the councils of governments (COGs).[7] These are organizations whose members are units of local government, generally cities and counties, although sometimes special districts or school boards. Structurally, the councils have a legislative-type body, sometimes called the assembly, and an executive committee that does most of the work. Voting power is sometimes apportioned on the basis of the size of the constituent units and sometimes on a one unit, one vote system.

The councils of governments have had an interesting history. They were originally started in the 1950s as an offshoot of the metropolitan reform movement. Much like the Council of Europe and other supranational institutions in international relations, their goal was to foster understanding and communication on areawide prob-

[7] See Charles W. Harris, "Regional Responses to Metro-Urban Problems: Councils of Governments." Paper presented at the 1972 annual meeting of the American Political Science Association, Washington, D.C., September 5–9, 1972; James F. Horan and G. Thomas Taylor, *Experiments in Metropolitan Government* (New York: Praeger Publishers, 1977); and John J. Harrigan and William C. Johnson, *Governing the Twin Cities Region: The Metropolitan Council in Comparative Perspective* (Minneapolis: University of Minnesota Press, 1978).

lems. National associations of local officials gave great praise to the concept, but as late as 1965 only nine such councils were in operation, the foremost being in Washington, Atlanta, San Francisco, and Seattle.

Today, the number of councils has grown to more than 100, for an interesting reason. In a classic demonstration of the power of the federal government, new provisions for federal grant-giving stimulated the formation of new metropolitan councils. The federal government required that federal grant and loan applications for many programs, including public works and mass transit, be reviewed by some areawide agency. The agency had to perform a metropolitan or regional planning function. COGs were not the only organizations that could apply the seal of approval that released the federal largesse, but they were easy-to-establish and familiar mechanisms. They blossomed once they had a task.

The COGs do a great deal of planning on regional problems and physical facilities, including land use and transportation. They also do training programs for local officials and some lobbying. But approving grants is their major role. They turn few grants down in their clearing-house capacity. Their internal political processes resemble logrolling in the Congress, where the attitude is, "You vote for my program and I'll vote for yours." The federal bureaucracy uses some COGs to help raise standards and select areas of special need for the disbursal of federal funds. The incentive to use this form of metropolitan coordination has been cold cash provided by a higher level of government.

II. Moderate Change: Two Formats

County reorganization and metropolitan federation are two governmental forms that are more radical. Change of this kind alters the balance of power among governments and officials. It affects many people directly. Such plans usually require voter approval.

County Reorganization. County reorganization means assigning functions to a broadened county authority, but generally leaving some other purely local services in the hands of municipalities, which retain their identity. Since 1952, plans of this kind have been proposed for Lucas County (Toledo), for Cleveland, Dayton, Houston, Pittsburgh, St. Louis, and Miami. Only Miami voters approved.

In Miami, where a scheme for city-county consolidation lost in 1953, a plan for Metropolitan Dade County finally won in 1957 by the bare margin of 44,404 to 42,620, with a low voter turnout of 26 per cent and high support in the city of Miami.[8] The new county government continues the existing 26 municipalities. But it takes responsibility for a wide range of services: expressways, traffic, mass transit and terminals, central records, training and communication for fire and police protection, hospitals and health and welfare programs, housing and urban renewal, flood and beach erosion control, air pollution control, drainage, public utility regulation, and centralized planning for metropolitan development, along with control over zoning and other technical codes for the whole territory, and over uniform service standards for all services still provided by the municipalities. The form of government for the county changed to a nonpartisan ballot with a county manager. Many elective offices were eliminated. Despite lingering political attacks from opponents of the plan and also financial problems, the METRO survives and, according to its proponents, achieves a solid record.

Metropolitan Federation.   In metropolitan federation, a scheme closely related to county reorganization, a federated two-tier system operates. The areawide authority is not the existing county government, but either an expanded version of the city government or a completely new governmental authority. The areawide authority performs certain functions for the whole metropolitan area, but subunits retain some identity and some control over a few functions. A famous METRO was formed in Toronto in 1953, but by an Act of the Ontario (Canada) Provincial Legislature, not by any referendum vote.[9] The METRO government, called the Municipality of Metropolitan Toronto, controlled water supply, sewage, housing, arterial highways, metropolitan parks, and planning, and the 13 individual cities of the area (Toronto proper and 12 suburbs) kept police, fire, health, library, and welfare services. In 1957, METRO took over police, and, in 1965, welfare and education. In 1965, the legislature reduced the number of subunits to six. The METRO plan represented a political compromise between the total annexation desired by leaders in the city of Toronto and no action preferred at the time by suburban residents.

---

[8] See Edward Sofen, *The Miami Metropolitan Experiment*, 2nd ed. (New York: Doubleday, Anchor, 1966). For a review, see Aileen Lotz, "Metropolitan Dade County," in Advisory Commission on Intergovernmental Relations, *Regional Governance: Promise and Performance* (Washington, D.C.: U.S. Government Printing Office, 1973), pp. 6–16.

[9] See John Grumm, *Metropolitan Area Government: The Toronto Experience* (University of Kansas Publications, Governmental Research Series No. 19, Lawrence, Kansas, 1959); Frank Smallwood, *Metro Toronto: A Decade Later* (Toronto: Bureau of Municipal Research, 1963); and Albert Rose, *Governing Metropolitan Toronto* (Berkeley: University of California Press, 1972).

Toronto's METRO has had a number of highly publicized achievements, especially in the realm of public works projects. Several studies also suggest difficulties, especially over representation on the 32-member metropolitan council (on the basis of units, not people) and over social and welfare services.

DRASTIC CHANGE: ANNEXATION AND CONSOLIDATION

Two other forms of metropolitan integration are decidedly stronger medicine: *annexation* and *consolidation.*

Annexation. In the greatest era of central city growth, the nineteenth century, the primary means of integration was annexation. Some scholars argue that without annexation during this period, the central cities would never have achieved their size.[10] From 1900 to 1945, municipal expansion through annexation declined. Only Detroit, its growth and power fueled by the development of the automobile industry, and Los Angeles, the archetypal city of urban sprawl and with little sense of a central city, expanded much through annexation. After World War II, annexation followed several different patterns. A large number of very small annexations involve less than one square mile of territory. Older central cities annexed very little territory. A few cities, however, made very large use of annexation. Oklahoma City extended itself from about 50 square miles 30 years ago to more than 650 square miles today. It had the largest territory in the United States until 1967 when Jacksonville, Florida and surrounding Duval County consolidated. In terms of territory, annexation has made Houston, San Diego, and Kansas City bigger than the most populous city, New York, and also made Dallas bigger than Chicago. All of the annexing communities are the newer cities of the South and Southwest. They operate in a favorable environment of state legislative or state court support and have the backing of their city councils and their own citizens. The key is that in these areas there is little of the socioeconomic distance between the central cities and suburbs that exists in the Northeast. Finally, there remains a great deal of unsettled land in these regions, the fastest growing in the country in the last 30 years.

Consolidations. Consolidation is similar to annexation. In the cases of consolidation, the areas involved are more fully developed. Frequently, the absorption of such settled areas into a new identity or into the identity of the largest city requires popular approval. The impact is the same: a single government serves a larger, often

[10] John C. Bollens and Henry J. Schmandt, *The Metropolis* (New York: Harper & Row, 1970), p. 281.

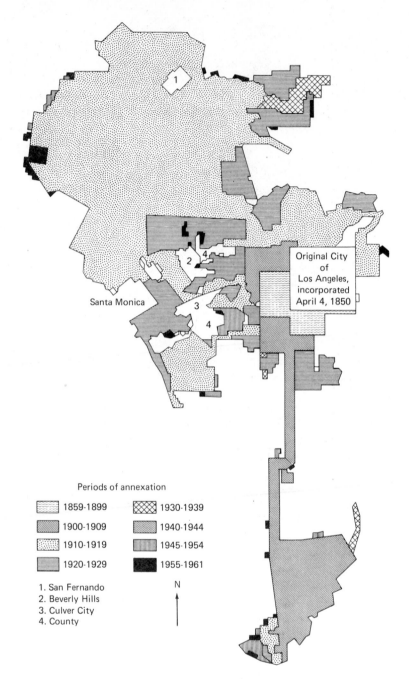

Periods of annexation

1859-1899	1930-1939
1900-1909	1940-1944
1910-1919	1945-1954
1920-1929	1955-1961

1. San Fernando
2. Beverly Hills
3. Culver City
4. County

N

Santa Monica

Original City
of
Los Angeles,
incorporated
April 4, 1850

FIGURE 7-4. Annexations by the City of Los Angeles, 1859–1963. Source: Winston W. Crouch and Beatrice Dinerman, *Southern Metropolis* (Berkeley and Los Angeles: University of California Press, 1963), p. 161. Reprinted by permission.

areawide belt of population. The consolidation method has had mixed support from voters. Albuquerque, Durham, Knoxville, Macon, Richmond (Va.), Columbus (Georgia), Memphis, St. Louis, Chattanooga, and Tampa defeated plans. Plans have been approved, however, merging Baton Rouge, Louisiana, and East Baton Rouge Parish; merging Nashville, Tennessee, and Davidson County; and combining Jacksonville, Florida, and Duval County. The Indiana legislature on its own consolidated Indianapolis and surrounding Marian County, a jurisdiction of 402 square miles and more than 800,000 people. No popular vote was taken in creating this "Uni-Government."

The successful consolidations, excluding the Indianapolis case, share some common characteristics.[11] The Baton Rouge, Nashville, and Jacksonville cases all included one county and one city, all occurred in the South, and all involved areas with few existing local governments. In each instance, a few municipalities within the consolidated boundaries were excluded. Each of these cities and also Indianapolis created two service systems within the new unit. That is, some services were provided areawide, such as roads, transportation, public works, and parks. Other services remained, at least temporarily, within the control of the former subunits. In Nashville, for example, the "urban services district" for the whole area manages the schools, the parks, and roads, along with sewers, branch libraries, and police.

Consolidations are the most politically difficult changes to bring about. In Nashville, a consolidation plan was defeated in 1958. The suburbs voted against the plan. Between then and 1962, Nashville annexed outright 82,000 suburbanites without the latter's approval. When the 1962 plan passed, it was opposed by city residents and overwhelmingly supported by the suburbs. One effect was that consolidation diluted the power of city-dwelling blacks just when that power was about to become a reality. The same charge is often made against the Indianapolis consolidation.

A RECAPITULATION: WHY IS MORE "RADICAL" METROPOLITAN CHANGE POLITICALLY DIFFICULT?

Because such a high percentage of metropolitan reorganization plans lose at the polls, Thomas M. Scott has argued that

[11] Ibid., p. 303. For a study of Indianapolis' Unigov, see York Wilburn, "Unigov: Local Government Reorganization in Indianapolis," in *Regional Governance: Promise and Performance*, op. cit., pp. 47–74. For Jacksonville, see John M. DeGrove, "The City of Jacksonville: Consolidation in Action," in *Regional Governance: Promise and Performance*, op. cit., pp. 17–25; and Joan Carver, "Responsiveness and Consolidation: A Case Study," *Urban Affairs Quarterly*, 9:2 (December 1973), pp. 211–250.

defeat is the "normal" response. The occasional successes, he suggests, should be seen as "deviant" cases.[12] Interestingly, the push for a more integrated metropolitan governmental structure comes from some of the same sorts of people involved in the reform movement *within* city government. There is the same collection of "good government" groups, including such national organizations as the National Municipal League and the Committee for Economic Development and their local counterparts in the form of local chapters of the League, and local business and civic organizations. Women's groups such as the League of Women Voters often support reform. Metropolitan government has been a cause frequently endorsed by the big-city daily newspapers and their clients, the downtown merchants.

The proponents of metropolitan government do *not* usually include one segment of the "good government" coalition as it works in purely local politics, namely those middle-class people who back council-manager government but live in the suburbs. Suburbanites tend to oppose centralizing mechanisms such as federation and consolidation. So do suburban interest groups, from officeholders in suburban and county governments to the daily suburban newspapers to real estate developers. In addition, political parties, which might fuel a drive toward federation or consolidation, avoid the issue because their own interests in such situations are clouded and uncertain. Generally, with Republicans controlling the suburban governments and Democrats in power in central cities, both parties gain from the status quo.

In addition, clear-cut racial considerations surface in any federation or consolidation plan. For example, if a core city controlled by blacks merges with a white suburban ring, then the blacks will be in a minority once more. For suburban whites, then, the choice becomes whether they would rather be part of one community with blacks and have racial integration in schools and other institutions or would rather live separated, knowing that in the central city—still important in their economic lives—blacks were in charge. For big-city blacks the choice is whether they would prefer to be a minority in a metropolitan area under one government if this would open up suburban schools and

[12] Thomas C. Scott, op. cit., pp. 501–502. For case studies of the Nashville consolidation, including the first unsuccessful 1958 struggle, see David A. Booth, *Metropolitics: The Nashville Consolidation* (East Lansing, Mich., Institute for Community Development and Services, 1963); Daniel R. Grant, "A Comparison of Predictions and Experience with Nashville 'Metro'," *Urban Affairs Quarterly*, 1 (September 1965), pp. 34–54; Brett W. Hawkins, *Nashville Metro: The Politics of City-County Consolidation* (Nashville: Vanderbilt University Press, 1966); and Robert E. McArthur, "The Metropolitan Government of Nashville and Davidson County," in *Regional Governance: Promise and Performance*, op. cit., pp. 26–36.

other institutions for their children or would prefer to control a big-city racial enclave with all of its jobs and economic resources. For both racial groups, the choice could go either way. Suburban whites, faced with possible black control of the central city of their metropolitan area, sometimes choose continued power in an integrated government. Conversely, blacks often prefer control over an isolated enclave that is, nonetheless, theirs.

MODELS OF METROPOLITAN LIFE AND POLITICS

So far, this chapter has dealt with forms of settlement in metropolitan areas and with alternative governmental possibilities. Many theoretical questions remain. Why are arrangements as they are? Who benefits from the present situation? How are problems solved at that minimum level necessary to keep the metropolitan areas at least functioning? After all, there have been no total breakdowns yet. What kinds of political changes might take place in the future? And what is the likelihood of such changes? Responding to these questions, we analyze four models of metropolitan life and politics.

MODEL I. THE POLYCENTRIC MODEL

One important theory of metropolitan development holds that an arrangement of multiple independent governments is a system, a polycentric system.[13] Polycentricity is "a pattern of organization where many independent elements are capable of mutual adjustment for ordering their relationships with one another within a general system of rule."[14]

Polycentric theory comes from the familiar economic market model. Such systems allocate by the natural working of the market or by an "invisible hand." Competition provides choice and reasonable prices. Multiple producers and multiple consumers, each with independent power, prevent the domination of any one center of economic power. In classic market theory, there are built-in propensities toward stability, despite the potential chaos of multiple independent units. In

[13] The discussion of this model is drawn from the pioneering work of Professor Vincent Ostrom and his associates. See Vincent Ostrom, "Polycentricity." Paper presented at the 1972 annual meeting of the American Political Science Association, Washington, D.C., September 5–9, 1972; and Vincent Ostrom, Charles M. Tiebout, and Robert Warren, "The Organization of Government in Metropolitan Areas: A Theoretical Inquiry," *The American Political Science Review*, **55**:4 (December 1961), pp. 831–842. For an explication of the model and an excellent bibliography, see Robert L. Bish, *The Public Economy of Metropolitan Areas* (Chicago: Markham, 1971).

[14] Ostrom, "Polycentricity" op. cit., p. 21.

modified market theory, when the independent units do not solve conflicts through cooperation or bargaining, government steps in as a regulator. The most powerful argument for the market model of the economy is that it works. All of these arguments about the polycentric model can be applied to thinking about metropolitan politics. In a seminal article, three scholars—Vincent Ostrom, Charles M. Tiebout, and Robert Warren—extended the polycentric concept to public goods and, by extension, from public goods in general to metropolitan government in particular.[15]

Ostrom and his associates examine *how* multiple governments manage to get things done. The authors reply, explicitly, to critics of the pattern of many local governments, whose views will be examined under Model IV, The Reform Model.

Ostrom and colleagues define the "business" of government as "providing public goods and services."[16] Public goods have three characteristics. First, matters become public when there is a need to control the indirect consequences of some behavior, what economists call the *externalities,* or spillover. When factories pollute, when crime cannot be managed by private police or vigilantes, when water can no longer be supplied by private vendors—in these circumstances, demand arises for public services. In other words, those needs that individuals cannot fulfill for themselves or those behaviors that affect innocent third parties negatively lead to government efforts to satisfy the need or reduce the negative costs.

Second, unlike private goods, public goods are not easily produced as separate commodities bought and sold by individual citizens in a marketplace. A car can be bought and sold. It comes in a packageable unit of one. But most public goods are different. How can you package fire and police protection or air pollution abatement? And when you have a set of services, how can you sell them, economically, only to those individuals who want to pay? This is a common concept when you think about national defense. How can you package it for individual consumers? How can you assess a price for individuals or give them a choice about whether or not to buy?

Third, there is with public goods a modified system of packaging. The method is to view public goods as "the maintenance of preferred states of community affairs."[17] A preferred state is one in which those who use a service, such as a city beach, are the same as those who pay for it, the city taxpayers. For some services, a preferred state cannot be

---

[15] Ostrom and others, op. cit.

[16] Ibid., p. 832.

[17] Ibid., p. 833.

maintained. Residents from surrounding communities may invade the beach. Or, particularly for pollution and sewage controls, no local boundary can encompass the whole zone of use.

With public goods, the preferred state requires compromise. For example, there can never be absolute police protection. To achieve that, a community would have to station police on every corner around the clock. The costs, in loss of privacy for innocent citizens, and in taxes, would be prohibitive. The solution is a level of police services in which the benefits of protection outweigh costs. But the benefits are hard to measure. Communities differ in their social environments, their basic crime rates, and their tolerance for crime. In addition, communities differ in willingness and ability to pay taxes. In practice, a decision about police services becomes a political judgment that seeks roughly tolerable levels of enforcement balanced against what is bearable in the property tax rate.

How Polycentric Systems Operate. Proponents of polycentricity admit small communities cannot fit their boundaries to the user-population necessary to pay for some services. Thus, for functions such as airports, mass transit, harbors, sewers, or importing water from great distances, a single government of metropolitan scope does the job best. But for other sorts of functions, where the constituency may range from a few thousand in a neighborhood who want a park, to a few hundred on a block who want a traffic light to 30,000 in a small suburb who want a school system, a fit of constituents and users is often *easier* to achieve for the smaller governments of a polycentric system.

Smaller governments, it is maintained, are also more efficient. Smaller governments shop around among vendors for the best price. Because many small governments probe the marketplace for street cleaning contractors, engineering services firms, data processing companies, and even educational providers, the number of potential vendors increases. In a metropolitan region with many smaller governments, the competition among many vendors for the purchasing funds of these communities brings down the price and thus increases the efficiency from the perspective of the community. In this context, the local administrator becomes consumer-oriented, always seeking a better deal for the inhabitants of his community. His concerns do not become divided between the interests of the citizens and the interests of city employees, organized into large fire, sanitation, police, clerical, and educational bureaucracies.

Smaller communities enhance their efficiency by offering themselves to potential inhabitants as more desirable than a neighboring city. Thus, some cities in a metropolitan region compete to provide the best school system. When this happens, citizens may have a choice of six or seven suburbs with good schools, all always striving to become better. Or communities may compete to minimize tax rates and compete among themselves to keep property taxes down. They may achieve their low taxes by cutting services or by drawing industry from nearby areas by promises of tax concessions. Those seeking a home can then pick the cheapest place to live when keeping their own public costs (taxes) to a minimum is the main goal. Many families could move to suburbs only because some suburbs in every metropolitan region pursue conscious policies of having the lowest tax costs in the area.

Ostrom observes that local governments in a polycentric system stress representativeness. Communities are composed of people who are there because they share values. Incorporation proceedings almost always have to be initiated by local citizens and approved by the local electorate. Local boundaries cannot be altered without consent. Home rule implies autonomy on a range of local choices, including what issues will be stressed in a community, how officials will be chosen, and how officials will be held responsible. Finally, the range of different communities guarantees representativeness. Individuals can maximize their own values by picking a community that has what they want.

How Polycentric Systems Resolve Disputes.

A major criticism of polycentric metropolitan systems is that they encourage selfish behavior. Each community looks out for itself and its citizens and avoids cooperating in solving problems, such as pollution or traffic control, that cross boundaries. Communities displace unpleasant costs onto neighbors but protect their own boundaries. In an environment of municipal competition, how are disagreements ever solved?

Ostrom argues that there are strong incentives and long-established practices in polycentric systems to resolve disputes. If communities do not work out their conflicts on their own, then the disputes are carried up to a higher level of government. When such disputes are taken to a higher level of government—to the state legislature, to the Congress, to the national political parties—resolution is then out of local hands. Thus, there is a built-in incentive to work things out.

Local communities may resolve conflicts by reconstituting themselves. One device for absorbing different social groups or settling water or land disputes is always annexation which, under state laws, almost always has to be by mutual consent. In the new cities of the Southwest, this technique frequently absorbs the dislocations of rapid growth and the needs for new capital facilities such as water plants or schools. Another device is voluntary cooperation. Local communities cooperate, from *ad hoc* assistance to each other in police and fire emergencies, to the purchase of various services from an urban county, to formalized institutional cooperation in a regional council of government. Cooperation may involve solving a technical problem or re-solving out-and-out disputes. Regional councils may work out patterns of water allocation or produce agreed-upon rules for using federal housing or sewer funds.

A final technique is to appeal voluntarily to another level of government. That level is often the courts, which decide water, land, and zoning conflicts on a case-by-case, rather than a general rule, basis. Or it may be to a governmental organization that, because it has no formal legal authority, is regarded as "neutral." Ostrom gives the example of the southern section of the League of California Cities, which negotiated water policy for the Los Angeles area. Eventually, a new agency, a special district, was formed to operate the Colorado River aqueduct for the region, the Metropolitan Water District of Southern California. Or, to cite a similar case, the Massachusetts Bay Transit Authority has as its membership the city of Boston and 79 surrounding suburbs. It operates mass transit throughout the Boston region. Conflicts on transportation policy are resolved within the MBTA.

Model II. The Life-Style Values Model — Decentralization

Oliver P. Williams has developed a model of metropolitan decentralization based on the concept of life-style values.[18] The polycentric model, he argues, does not explain how multiple communities arose in the first place, or the numerous noneconomic motives that underly the real-life choices people make. He observes that "the family is not simply an economic unit," and "social values" contribute to homesite selection.[19]

People locate in cities in such a way as to maximize pleasant and minimize unpleasant messages, consistent with what they can afford. The content of the messages that influence people's choices varies over time and from place to place. Although economic message exchanges are important, they are not the only ones. For example, "middle-class families choose suburban locations with lots of grass,

---

[18] "Life-Style Values and Political Decentralization in Metropolitan Areas," in *Community Politics*, ed. by Charles M. Bonjean et al. (New York: Free Press, 1971), pp. 56–64. See also Williams' "Urban Politics as Political Ecology," in *Essays on the Study of Urban Politics*, ed. by Ken Young (Hamden, Conn.: Archon Books, 1975), pp. 106–132.

[19] "Life-Style Values," op. cit., p. 58.

but, more important, these are locations where the variety of home-related message exchanges are compatible with middle-class values. These are usually more social and educational than economic."[20] In addition, choices of location are made to minimize unrewarding messages. Thus, "a middle-class family chooses a suburb that will also reduce unpleasant message exchanges from lower-class persons in the form of muggings, fistfights, and uncouth syntax."[21]

Every unit in the metropolitan area occupies a distinct place in the area's physical space, and thus the social units of household, factories, stores, churches, clubs, and offices could also be called *sociospatial* units. Each sociospatial unit determines what messages it defines as positive and which as negative. For local businesses, nearness to a high-quality labor force may be a high-ranking value, higher or lower for each firm than an advantageous tax rate. Households may seek good schools, pleasant neighbors, nearby shopping, or an easy commute. Whatever the values, they can be labeled the unit's *lifestyle values,* and they are enhanced or limited by the physical location of the unit in the metropolitan area.

Life-style values that are dependent on location become the sources of metropolitan conflict. Those locations that are most advantageous to the unit's life-style values have to be safeguarded. As Williams notes, "the curse of urbanism is the instability of site advantages."[22] Many social institutions protect whatever values the community ranks high by slowing down the forces of change and spreading the acceptable ways of living, the life-style. Particularly in child rearing, in middle-class suburbs, for example, enormous organized and informal efforts are mobilized to make sure that children learn the "right" values. One device is to try to have contiguous areas of similar values, so that all the children in a neighborhood will complement the values of one's own family. The one way to guarantee compatible neighbors is to make sure that similar housing units are built and maintained through the neighborhood.

Citizens turn to local government for zoning protection or for housing code enforcement. Local governments control many of the most immediate physical and social characteristics of any given sociospatial unit. Local governments control highway access patterns, parks, the location of all physical facilities, and the quality of life-style support services such as schools and police protection.

Williams says there are standard strategies governments follow. They specialize into small communities. Complementary and homo-

[21] Ibid., p. 58.
[22] Ibid., p. 58.

geneous groupings are the norm for most city planning, for subdivisions, industrial parks, and shopping centers. In a decentralized setting "diverse groups need not constantly compete in the same political arena, a situation characteristic of heterogeneous units, such as the core city."[23]

Homogeneous life-style values do not lead to identical communities. Rather, each metropolitan area contains numerous differentiated little communities. Williams argues that these are best seen as packages of values. Some suburbs emphasize large-lot zoning, good schools, and the country squire life, or moderate taxes and parochial schools. Using the life-style model, we can also expect even more exotic specializations, communities that cater to industry only, or that are vice centers protected by selective police enforcement, or that are devoted entirely to dairy farms.

Sources of Conflict in Metropolitan Politics. Conflict arises because specialized local units are interdependent. Williams says, "If there is an industrial suburb, there must also be a residential one; if there is a rich man's suburb, there must also be one for the poor. The fact of interrelatedness is dramatized twice daily by glutted commuter arteries, leading not only to the core city, but criss-crossing in every direction, through any major metropolitan area."[24] The dynamics of the areas require creating integrating mechanisms that impinge on the life-style of smaller units and create conflict.

The major mechanisms are the communication/transportation system, the utility system, and the central facilities system. Not all of these cause conflict. Utility systems supply power, water, and waste disposal services to a large area on a multimunicipality basis. They do not have different effects on different parts of the metropolitan area and, except for an unwanted power or disposal plant, do not result in the kinds of costs or special benefits that can arouse conflict.

However, the communication/transportation system critically affects the locational values of a metropolitan area, advancing life-style values for one area and threatening another. A new highway alters the whole pattern of accessibility within the area. Areas that were too remote for convenient commuting now become feasible in terms of time-of-travel. Interchanges become valuable locations for shopping centers, office buildings, or industrial parks. These new units promote different social and economic values than those already existing in the community.

[23] Ibid., p. 59.
[24] Ibid., p. 59.

These systems, by their nature, have to be planned. You could not build a highway by leaving the choice up to each community whether or not it would build its part of the road. That means highway planning must be managed by some areawide political authority, usually the state government, but often the federal government. Highways or mass transit generate intense politics, because the life-style of some areas is always sacrificed to maintain the life-styles of other areas. Even communities that gain economically from roads often oppose them because their life-styles are threatened.

The Consequences of Life-style Specialization. The larger the metropolitan area, the greater the amount of specialization of life-styles. The larger metropolitan areas contain many gradations of residential suburbs, along with the greatest variety of industrial, commercial, and other forms of suburbs. The older the metropolitan area, the more specialized its municipal units will be. Place identities and values become more crystallized and visible with time and, thus, harder to change. Finally, the more permissive state incorporation and other laws are about self-determination, the more specialized the municipal units in a given area will be.

Williams sees the specialization and protection of life-styles as setting the pattern for the future. Yet, he has reservations about the social consequences of this format. Although needed areawide facilities get built, the actions of dozens of individual enclaves protecting their life-style values can sometime lead to a "twenty-year gap between need and construction of a given facility."[25] Equally important, no one knows what happens when whole generations grow up in encapsulated, homogeneous communities. British studies of working-class suburbs near London showed contentment and the absence of conflict, but also poor schools and discouragement of upward mobility. Will that happen in American working-class suburbs, as well?

In addition, the specialized communities work best for whites. In the specialized suburbs, "the whole power of law, police, and social institutions is likely to be arrayed on one side of the conflict, and this assures that the possibility for racial residential mobility will be narrowly circumscribed."[26] Further, Williams is not optimistic that everything works out in the end in a metropolitan area. In each metropolitan area "there are developing obsolete suburbs and satellite cities that are as dysfunctional, in terms of locational and physical requirements for contemporary urban life, as are the old prairie, wheat-belt service towns. As the suburbs spiral down, they have an accumulation of tax,

---

[25] Ibid., p. 63.
[26] Ibid., pp. 63–64.

service and leadership woes."[27] In a unified metropolitan area encompassing heterogeneous values, or in a large core city, if one part declines, resources may be tapped from a viable section. But in a declining suburb, the citizens simply move away and abandon it. No larger unit of government and no citizens can be held responsible. In other words, maximizing life-style values for some people excludes other people. In time of trouble, many communities may well be left without help.

MODEL III. THE DIPLOMATIC MODEL — INTERNATIONAL RELATIONS

A third model of metropolitan politics uses the analogy of international relations. The clearest exposition is by Professor Matthew Holden, Jr.[28] The basic argument is that "metropolitics and international politics are analogous in that each occurs not within *political communities* but within *diplomatic systems.*"[29] A political community has a set of shared values, a system of common political symbols, a deliberative process for arriving at common decisions, and an administrative process for assuring execution of decisions. In the metropolitan area, these characteristics of a political community are not present. Rather, numerous units—counties, school districts, special districts, cities, and school boards—pursue their own interests. They mobilize to their own ends, utilizing civic activists, local politicians, money, lawyers, publicity, and legislative and political action at higher levels.

But, at the same time, the various units of a metropolitan area are interdependent. The actions of one affect others. Thus, they are part of an "ecological community." Interrelations among the units are similar to those in a *diplomatic community*, where there is also autonomy and interdependence. Relations are carried on by the governments themselves. Private citizens do not negotiate across municipal borders on municipal problems, anymore than private citizens of one country negotiate with foreign governments. As in the international context, information and legal authority are concentrated in the hands of local government officials.

Holden thinks we should study in local politics what we study in international politics, beginning with interactions among governments. The major interrelationship involves the physical environment, especially the road system.

Studying local governmental power, as we compare the relative power of nation-states, yields insights into metropolitan politics. Does

[27] Ibid., p. 64.

[28] "The Governance of the Metropolis as a Problem in Diplomacy," *Journal of Politics*, **26**:3 (August 1964), pp. 627–647.

[29] Ibid., p. 627.

the most powerful single local community, often the core city, use its control over crucial resources to force other communities to follow its bidding? Milwaukee for many years made annexation the price of using its water system. But other central cities have been less aggressive and have let suburbanites hook into their water supplies. We need to know more about how power is used in metropolitan politics.

We can look at the history of relationships among metropolitan governments much like relationships among nations. Are there municipalities with a "special relationship" of long-time cooperation, as the United States and Britain have had such an international relationship? Are there communities with a history of enmity, as between Turkey and Russia? How do historical patterns among local governments influence their contemporary behavior?

We use the international relations analogy to look at the procedures of intergovernmental relations in metropolitan areas. What is the nature of "ultimate conflict" in metropolitan politics? One might say that there is no ultimate conflict because local communities do not engage in war against each other. But perhaps there are "functional equivalents" of war at the local level. Litigation, in which one local government wins and the other loses (as opposed to bargaining where each gives up and each gets something), may be a substitute for war. Under what conditions do local governments take each other to court, or threaten to do so?

Holden suggests that the accumulated knowledge of international politics produces propositions to predict what behavior would, for example, increase cooperation among local governmental units. For example, a metropolitan consultative body, such as a council of governments, must have real tasks to perform so that important local actors— individuals and governments—can expect real benefits from the work. Otherwise, the body will atrophy. Assigning trivial goals to a multigovernmental body guarantees that individual decision makers, such as mayors, will stay away from it. Important individuals work only on situations appropriate to their rank. Finally, local governments trust each other more when they agree on important problems such as roads or sharing of school facilities, than when they simply sign platitudinous statements about unity and cooperation.

The international relations model is consistent with either the polycentric model or the life-style value model. It takes the existence of numerous independent but interdependent units as a given.

MODEL IV. THE REFORM MODEL

The fourth model of metropolitan politics, the reform model, is more a normative than an empirical model. That is, proponents of this model more often argue for how metropolitan politics *should be* organized than they describe how it really works. The reform model is worth examining. Many influential persons subscribe to its ideas, which have had considerable influence. The ideas of the reform model, for example, fuel the frequent efforts to establish areawide metropolitan governments.

There is no one single source of reform model theory, so this perspective relies upon two spokesmen. One is the Committee for Economic Development, a prestigious group of reform- and development-oriented businessmen who take a continuing interest in the problems of government. The other is Dr. Robert C. Wood, a path-breaking scholar in the local politics field.

The Committee for Economic Development. The Committee for Economic Development sponsored three major studies, each with recommendations, in the metropolitan government area: *Modernizing Local Government*[30] (1966); *A Fiscal Program for a Balanced Federalism*[31] (1967); and *Reshaping Government in Metropolitan Areas*[32] (1970). The summary of the committee's position draws from this last publication.

The committee starts with the proposition that "metropolitan America is in trouble" and argues that "metropolitan areas must develop a system of government that is capable—administratively, fiscally, and politically—of translating substantive programs into action."[33] Two paragraphs best capture the basic tenets of the committee's thinking:

> The structure of government in metropolitan areas has a profound impact on the daily lives of metropolitan citizens. But, as this Committee has long recognized, the present arrangement of overlapping local units is not serving the people well. Citizens in metropolitan areas are confronted by a confusing maze of many—possibly a dozen—jurisdictions, each with its own bureaucratic labyrinth. This baffling array of local units has made it difficult for citizens—the disadvantaged particularly—to gain access to public services and to acquire a voice in decision making.
>
> Clearly, a fragmented system of government works better for some than for others. In gaining access to the system, citizens with

---

[30] (New York, 1966).
[31] (New York, 1967).
[32] (New York, 1970).
[33] *Reshaping Government in Metropolitan Areas*, op. cit., p. 9.

greater political influence and sophistication may succeed in by-passing bureaucratic governmental procedures. Moreover, the system generally works better for suburbanites than it does for residents of the central cities. The haphazard arrangement of local governments in metropolitan areas has created great inequalities between resources and needs. In the suburbs, the combination of superior fiscal strength and fewer problems usually yields a higher quality of public service. But it is not entirely by chance that such disparities have developed. One of the principal failings of a fragmented system of government is its inability to take an overview in matters of planning, transportation, and population dispersal. Zoning and other land-use control powers wielded by small suburban communities tend to exclude from the suburbs black citizens and other low-income minority groups.[34]

Originally, the committee supported single, areawide government as the best solution to fragmentation and problem-solving inefficiency. By the 1970s, the committee moved to a modified position, looking for a governmental system that could simultaneously solve areawide problems and still permit local autonomy. This shift recognized the intensity of local resistance to consolidation of governments and loss of autonomy. The committee recommended two-tier government as the reform program for metropolitan areas.

Within the two-tier system, some functions would fall to the areawide government and some to community districts that would exist within the larger system. Some powers would be shared. When a metropolitan area fell within one county, the county government would be the new areawide system. But if a metropolitan area over-lapped several counties, then a new political entity would be created. The committee notes that "it is important to underline the full signifi-cance of the changes advocated here. City boundaries would become less important than they now are. There would be a boundary sur-rounding each metropolitan area as well as boundaries surrounding community districts within each metropolitan area."[35] The committee believes that state and federal aid should encourage metropolitan re-organization along the two-tier guidelines.

The key political question is, What powers go to which tier of government? The committee places the major authority over planning and zoning, with power over life-styles and property values, in the hands of the areawide authority, leaving local communities to zone

[34] Ibid., p. 10.
[35] Ibid., p. 21.

only smaller subareas within their boundaries. The areawide government could veto any local district plans it believed did not serve the entire metropolitan area. Likewise, primary authority over transportation policy, including highways, would be assigned to the areawide government. Finally, water supply and sewage disposal would be primarily under the areawide government.

With certain other functions, the committee is either unclear or believes that sharing is possible. The committee's position is vague on education and housing. On public health, the committee leaves environmental sanitation, control of communicable disease, and vital statistics to the areawide government. Maternal and child health services, laboratories, and health education services remain as local community services. Some aspects of police services would be areawide—laboratories, communications, records, detectives, and inspection. But patrol services would be under local community control. Finally, rubbish and garbage collection would be primarily local.

The committee's two-tier government recognizes that a completely unitary government for metropolitan areas is politically impossible and perhaps even undesirable. Caught between past preferences for one government and the realities of suburban entrenchment, the committee's proposals are a compromise. Yet in its call for areawide control over land use and transportation, and its hope for federal policy in housing, the committee has clearly not compromised its goals. It remains committed to consolidation of governments, to planning, and to social equity in the metropolitan area. Its shift to a "practical" proposal acknowledges political currents and also the success of the two-tier metropolitan government in Toronto, Canada.[36]

Wood's Reform View. Robert C. Wood, in a classic study—*Suburbia, Its People and Their Politics*—written in 1958, predicted the spread and political ascendency of suburbs.[37] Yet on theoretical, almost moral grounds, certainly normative ones, he argued that a nation of suburbs was a bad choice. The individualism of the suburbs, the consumer model, camouflaged selfishness as "free choice." The clubbiness of the suburbs meant conformity, lack of privacy, and personalized government. He maintained that "the persistence of the image of the suburb as all-American small town is unfortunate in our times. It represents another symbolic protest against the great organi-

---

[36] The League of Women Voters now actively advocates two-tier systems. See League of Women Voters Education Fund, *Supercity/Hometown, U.S.A.: Prospects for Two-Tier Government* (New York: Praeger Publishers, 1974).

[37] (Boston: Houghton Mifflin, 1958).

zation and the large society, and this is the most disastrous consequence of all."[38]

Wood prefers the "gargantuan city," the large organizational form applied to the local government context. In such a situation Wood saw the chance for the rule of law, as opposed to individualized government. Conflict would exist openly rather than being shut out by artificial boundaries. Strong, organized groups would help to manage that conflict. Wood prefers "urbanity"—anonymity, freedom to achieve at the top of one's potential, the need for civility in the face of diversity, and the advantage of being able to support unique cultural and economic enterprises. In about as lucid a statement in favor of the reform model as has ever been written, Wood concludes:

> These conditions of urbanity are the basic reasons for supporting the ideal of a single metropolitan government, and they seem more logically persuasive than the customary arguments of efficiency and administrative tidiness. A single local government comprehending an entire metropolitan area is likely not only to be better managed in the professional sense but more democratically managed as well. . . . The handicaps the city operates under, the loss of its middle-class citizens, the poverty of public finances, the absence of space and of solid residential sections would be removed. . . . By making the metropolis a true metropolitan political entity, a different type of blending of urban and suburban becomes possible. It would be less comfortable, perhaps, but it would be less comfortable, perhaps, but it would be more defensible in terms of the values the nation has accepted.[39]

CONCLUSIONS ABOUT METROPOLITAN POLITICS

From the materials of this chapter, the following conclusions can be drawn:

1. Multiple governments co-exist in metropolitan areas.
2. There are different modes of governmental cooperation. As one moves closer to merger of localities by annexation or consolidation, resistance increases, as does the likelihood that voters will reject such steps if put before them on referenda.
3. Four models purport to explain the existing metropolitan patterns. In some ways these models are consistent.

[38] Ibid., p. 301.
[39] Ibid., p. 298.

a. The *polycentric model* argues that multiple independent communities maximize the choice for individual citizens and still manage to cooperate where necessary.

b. The *life-style values model* says that multiple units result from the need to protect the locational aspects of common values against external challenge.

c. The *diplomatic model* suggests interactions among these communities are analogous to those of nation-states in international relations. Localities are interdependent and share space in the same territory, but lack the characteristics of political communities.

d. Finally, the *reform model,* viewing metropolitan politics from a normative perspective, urges the adoption of federated governments for metropolitan areas.

8

PEOPLE IN LOCAL POLITICS

This chapter examines what people bring to local politics and the patterns of their activities in the local public arena. We start with attitudes people have, turn to local participation, and end with an analysis of local public officials.

CITIZEN ATTITUDES: CLASS CULTURES

Many social scientists believe that different socioeconomic groups bring different sets of attitudes to local life. They label these attitudes *class culture*. The concept of class culture is not flattering to many people and engenders controversy. Hence, words of caution are in order. Many of anyone's attitudes respond to the structure of the society, such as the presence or absence of discrimination, of the opportunities for work, for saving, for security, and for upward job mobility. These larger variables result from national attitudes, political forces, economic development, and social history.

The concept of class culture does not apply to any particular individual. It is what sociologists call an ideal type, an abstract model that purports to explain and predict the social world. Propositions about class culture remain, at this point, speculative.

With these caveats, let us look at four class cultures, or subcultures: (1) the working-class subculture, (2) the lower-class subculture, (3) the middle-class subculture, and (4) the upper-middle and upper-class subculture. In spelling out the characteristics of each subculture, this chapter draws on the work of Herbert J. Gans and Edward C. Banfield.[1]

THE WORKING-CLASS SUBCULTURE

The working-class subculture is the value system of the blue-collar worker, unskilled and skilled. It is a peer group society, with most social interactions within the same economic sector. Visiting and other social relations are with blood relatives, rather than with acquaintances and friends, as in the mobile professional upper-middle and upper classes. Social life is frequently segregated by sex. Men socialize with men, in the family setting or in outside church activities or sports clubs, and women socialize with women, again in the family setting or in club or church activities. Working-class culture accepts, if not prefers, high-density living conditions with street life and low privacy. The home is closed off to all except the family. Visiting with neighbors is done in public places—streets, stores, restaurants, bars, clubs.

Although much time is spent in the family circle in the working-class subculture, family life is substantially different from the middle-class pattern, in which the husband and wife are supposed to be partners. In working-class life, the sexual roles are quite distinct. Women are supposed to stay in the home, if economically possible, and take care of the children and the men. Men place a high premium on masculinity, which excludes helping with housework or children. In child rearing, the goal is not the development of the child, but order, cleanliness, and control of the child's behavior.

The working-class subculture contains elements of both stability and instability. Sources of stability include the family itself, and the routine-seeking life-style organized around that family. Shared values cement the ties: family, order, reciprocal kinship ties, viewing the world as "us" versus "them," with the "them" being organized society in almost all its forms, from the large company to government to the middle and upper classes.

Working-class pride provides another source of stability—the sense of having come from even humbler origins, of having worked hard and honestly in physically difficult jobs, of having earned what one has the hard way. For example, a 53-year-old Chicago policeman explained himself to interviewer Studs Terkel in these terms:

---

[1] See Herbert J. Gans, *The Urban Villagers* (New York: Free Press, 1962, 1965); Edward C. Banfield, *The Unheavenly City* (Boston: Little, Brown, 1970), and *The Unheavenly City Revisited* (Boston: Little, Brown, 1974). See also Oscar Lewis, *La Vida: A Puerto Rican Family in the Culture of Poverty* (New York: Random House, 1966).

I was born in Chicago, my father was born in Chicago, and my grandfather was born here. His father came to America to dig the Sag Canal. They were promised they could have farmland where they could grow anything. In the winter, they'd dig the canal. Unfortunately, it was all rocks. So they wound up with a rock farm.

There's something you gotta understand about the Irish Catholics in Chicago. Until recently, being a policeman was a wonderful thing. 'Cause he had a steady job and he knew he was gonna get a pension and they seemed to think it was better than being a truck driver, although a truck driver earns far more than a policeman today.

Someone had to be police, you know? They sacrificed anything. They just knew that so-and-so in the family would be. It was another step out of the mud. You figured at least you'd have some security. They felt they no longer worked with their hands. They weren't laborers any more.[2]

All class cultures are, Gans notes, *"responses* that people make to the *opportunities* and the *deprivations* they encounter."[3] To be exact:

each subculture is an organized set of related responses that has developed out of people's efforts to cope with the opportunities, incentives, and rewards, as well as the deprivations, prohibitions, and pressures which the natural environment and society—that complex of coexisting and competing subcultures—offer to them.[4]

Sources of working-class instability come from outside the group. A standard working-class value is fatalism about technology, unempolyment, or social change. Despite unions, relatively high wages, better working conditions, and various kinds of health and pension plans, blue-collar work contains many insecurities. Layoffs are always possible, and jobs evaporate because of changes in technology, firms moving, or foreign competition. Chronic American inflation hits hourly paid workers very hard.

Further, working-class neighborhoods are targets for demands from outside. Frequently, these neighborhoods, despite their moderately cohesive social structure and highly patterned behavior, *look* like slums, especially to middle-class persons who control planning

---

[2] Studs Terkel, *Division Street: America* (New York: Pantheon Books, 1968), p. 108. Quoted by permission of the publisher.

[3] Gans, op. cit., p. 249.

[4] Ibid., p. 249.

agencies. Although the insides of apartments are usually very well maintained, the outsides of tenements may be run-down or littered. Population density is high. The buildings are old. Working-class neighborhoods throughout the older cities of the Northeast and Midwest become easy targets for renewal or for highway construction. The land under them is close to downtown and a potentially more profitable usage.

Low rents make working-class neighborhoods attractive to migrants to the city. Historically, newcomers—blacks, Southern whites, and Hispanics coming to the central cities—move into the lowest-rent districts possible. Working-class families who remain in their old neighborhoods feel under siege. For those who move to close-in blue-collar suburbs, old patterns of social interactions break down. Those who stay behind are the oldest and the poorest of the working class. For them, moving is either economically impossible or their flat, bungalow, or duplex is their sole property in the world. Those who leave most eagerly are second- and third-generation children of the original immigrants.

The Political Consequences of Working-Class Values.   Although nothing lasts forever, considering working-class values as relatively constant, it is possible to list their consequences for local politics. The political consequences for central cities follow. A large remaining working-class segment regards the changes of the post-World War II era—urban renewal, the civil rights movements for blacks—with defensiveness, fear, and hostility. This group seeks protection of its children from the unsettling influence of school exposure to other class children, and, perhaps above all, order in the streets from a get-tough police force.

In addition, feeling highly distrustful, working-class citizens are sensitive to symbolic rewards and slights in local politics. What is the class and ethnic origin of the mayor? The police chief? Who gets what patronage jobs? In whose neighborhoods do public improvements get built? When services are improved, who gets the benefits? Working-class citizens distrust liberal politicians, despite historic ties to the Democratic party. Thus, they may vote for Republicans. Working-class citizens may view all politics and politicians with cynicism, but they seek to fulfill distinct political demands through a personalized view of politics. They focus on individuals, personalities, and concrete, visible results, not abstract programs.

Working-class values run head on against other forces in the central city. The most obvious source of conflict, at the point where neighborhoods and school districts and shopping streets merge, is with lower-class blacks. When the urban population consists almost wholly of working-class whites alongside working- and lower-class blacks, the entire politics of that community can turn into a form of race competition or even race war.

What are the consequences of working-class life-style values for suburbs? Under the twin force of the demolition of working-class neighborhoods and the migration of new groups into those neighborhoods in the central cities, the more affluent working-class people move. Around every central city a thick network of primarily blue-collar suburbs forms. The residents of these suburbs often live close to the limits of their means, once they have purchased their homes. Thus, the heavy drive to keep property taxes down. Schools feel pressure to use conservative curricula and to emphasize discipline and order along the lines of family-oriented values.

Working-class suburbs transport the sense of being under siege from the central cities. The same sources of both stability and instability are present. With financial precariousness, the in-migration of other groups, including blacks and low-income whites, takes on particularly serious dimensions. Translated into suburban politics, the response resists school busing, federal- or state-sponsored public or low-income housing, any programs that threaten the hard-won social stability. In other words, working-class suburban politics is bound to be essentially defensive: an effort in the local public arena to protect hard-won and cherished private cultural values and financial resources.

THE LOWER-CLASS SUBCULTURE

Here is how sociologist Gans describes lower-class culture:

The *lower-class subculture* is distinguished by the female-based family and the marginal male. Although a family circle may also exist, it includes only female relatives. The male, whether husband or lover, is physically present only part of the time, and is recognized neither as a stable nor dominant member of the household. He is sexual partner, and he is asked to provide economic support. But he participates only minimally in the exchange of affection and emotional support, and has little to do with the rearing of children . . . the women use him as an example of what a man should not be. . . . the woman is much closer to working-class culture, at least in her aspirations, although she is not often successful in achieving them.

For lower-class men, life is almost totally unpredictable. If they have sought stability at all, it has slipped from their grasp so quickly, often, and consistently that they no longer pursue it. From childhood on, their only real gratifications come from action-seeking, but even these are few and short-lived. . . . Usually, the lower-class individual gravitates from one job to another, with little hope or interest of keeping a job for any length of time. His hostility to the outside world therefore is quite intense, and its attempts to interfere with the episodic quality of his life are fought. Education is rejected by the male, for all of its aims are diametrically opposed to action-seeking.[5]

The lower-class culture involves living from moment to moment. The future is seen as beyond the individual's control, and "impulse governs his behavior, either because he cannot discipline himself to sacrifice a present for a future satisfaction or because he has no sense of the future."[6] The lower-class person seeks action and immediate gratification. His work skills are minimal and he does not have the discipline to keep a steady job.

In this formulation, the lower-class male has a truncated sense of self-esteem, feels inadequate, and is frequently apathetic and dejected, and at other times very hostile, suspicious, and aggressive. He does not have stable relationships with any other people. He has female paramours and men companions, but not friends. He is resentful of all authority, especially the police, social workers, teachers, landlords, and employers with whom his life-style brings him into contact. He views himself as a victim.

Children in the female-centered, lower-class families are frequently neglected once past babyhood, or raised with an alternating pattern of permissiveness and harshness. At an early age, they fall into street life, where the lower-class stress on action, fighting, smartness, and risk-taking is quickly learned. Lower-class life is "extraordinarily violent."[7] It is ghetto life, whether it be for blacks, white migrants to northern cities from Appalachia, or Spanish-speaking people in the Southwest and in New York.

CHOICE OR ADAPTATION

Do lower-class people live as they do because they *choose* to or because they *have* to? Those who believe in the power of the individual to choose and shape his or her own destiny think it is a matter of

[5] Ibid., pp. 245–246.
[6] Banfield, op. cit., p. 53.
[7] Ibid., p. 63.

choice. In contrast, there is testimony that agrees with the description of lower-class life, but disagrees strongly about the causes. Many individuals who leave the lower-class life-style say it is not a life led by choice. They portray the life instead as a response to circumstances beyond the individual's control: poverty, discrimination, little opportunity.

Thus, in Claude Brown's *Manchild in the Promised Land,* the author-hero grows up amidst violence, drugs, crime, and sex in Harlem. He hits the street young, goes to reform school, comes back, decides to go to college, and works his way through Columbia University. His memories of his environment are bittersweet:

> I remember when I ran away from shelters, places that they sent me to, here in the city. I never ran away with the thought in mind of coming home. I always ran away to get back to the streets. I always thought of Harlem as home, but I never thought of Harlem as being in the house. To me, home was the streets. . . .
>
> You might see somebody get cut or killed. I could go in the street for an afternoon, and I would see so much that, when I came in the house, I'd be talking and talking for what seemed like hours. Dad would say, "Boy, why don't you stop that lyin'? You know you didn't see all that. You know you didn't see anybody do that." But I knew I had.[8]

Piri Thomas' *Down These Mean Streets,*[9] and also Malcolm X's *Autobiography,*[10] contain similar descriptions and tales of self-conversion and exit. Malcolm X argued powerfully that white discrimination forced the self-image of blacks into a self-destructive mode. Considering the suppressing aspects of the society confronting the lower-class person and the dismal prospects that lie before him, from some perspectives his behavior is adaptive and rational. Something of this view emerges from Elliot Liebow's study of black street-corner men, *Tally's Corner.*[11] Because there is no chance of steady work with possibilities for improvement and advancement, Tally's life pattern of not getting involved with work makes sense. Further, because the part-time jobs are without security, a pattern of transient personal relationships may be very rational. That is all Tally can afford, especially where women are concerned.

[8] Claude Brown, *Manchild in the Promised Land* (New York: Macmillan, 1965), pp. 428–429. Quoted by permission of the publisher.

[9] (New York: New American Library, 1968).

[10] (New York: Grove Press, 1966).

[11] (Boston: Little, Brown, 1967).

Being part of this unskilled, menial work force affects whites as well as blacks. For example, many of the white southern migrants in Chicago, whose lives are recounted in Todd Gitlin and Nanci Hollander's study, *Uptown: Poor Whites in Chicago*,[12] move in and out of temporary, hourly paid jobs. The Chicago whites are moved in and out of these jobs by private employment agencies who are imputed to have special arrangements with the employers. Economists call unskilled jobs for lower-class people the secondary job market. Some economists believe private and public agencies deliberately structure this market to keep certain kinds of labor quickly available at low cost.[13]

Another aspect of lower-class life can also be seen from two perspectives. From one angle, the female-centered family appears unstable, disorganized, and lacking in its ability to provide regular income or healthy male role models for sons. It comes to be viewed as a "pathological" form of family organization. From another perspective, however, the female-headed family appears as a rational adaptation to a tough world. In an economic situation in which regular work for men is unlikely, but where a steady (although small) income, provided by welfare, is guaranteed for the family unit if the man is out of the house, then the female headed household takes on a kind of rationality. Some stability is provided and role models of perseverance are provided, at least for girls.

Causes of Lower-Class Life-style: A Choice or a Response to Life Opportunities? The interpretation of lower-class life has important consequences for local and national politics. For example, Professor Banfield believes that urban lower-class life, including rioting by lower-class people, is based on choice, symbolized by the total focus of the lower-class person on immediate gratification. He regards this lower-class pattern as a long-term historical pattern. He says:

> In every sizable city there were transient laborers—and in the seaports, sailors, and in inland cities like Cincinnati and St. Louis, boatmen, wagoners, and drifters, who, like Huckleberry Finn's father, lived from hand to mouth, worked only when they had to, drank and fought prodigiously, felt no tie to the community, and left their women and children behind to fend for themselves or to be looked after at public expense once they had moved on. In every city there also were unassimilated immigrants from

[12] (New York: Harper Colophon Books, 1971).
[13] See Michael J. Piore, "Jobs and Training," in *The State and the Poor*, ed. by Samuel H. Beer and Richard E. Barringer (Cambridge: Winthrop Publishers, 1970), pp. 53–83.

countries—Catholic ones—whose cultures tended to be relatively present-oriented. It is safe to say, however, that transients and Catholic immigrants did not comprise the whole of the working- and lower-class population. In Boston, for example, which in 1817 had only about four hundred Catholics, old stock American residents must have patronized the city's two thousand prostitutes (one for every six males above the age of sixteen), hundreds of liquor shops, and the gambling houses open night and day.[14]

Banfield believes that historically many lower-class persons simply died off, and others accepted a future-oriented, middle-class set of values. What does it matter what one professor's interpretation is? Well, if lower-class life is largely by choice and if, in the end, lower-class families die out, and, further, if the relative proportion of lower-class people has declined since the nineteenth century, then the political morals to be drawn are quite clear. Extensive social programs aimed at uplifting the lower classes will fail. Efforts to impose middle-class values on lower-class people through social work or community organization will fail because lower-class people do not want to adopt the self-sacrificing, future-oriented outlook of the middle class. The proper strategy is to keep cool. A rising economy gives those who do choose to rise the opportunity; a violent life-style diminishes the number of those who do not.

Such counsel stands in stark contrast to public social policy since the 1930s. That perspective views lower-class life as a response to life opportunities. In the presence of discrimination, limited economic choices, and limited personal skills, lower-class people channel into a transient, action-seeking life. The lower-class life-style recognizes that no other avenues are open, and then adapts. From this logic, if society chooses to reduce the number of lower-class people, it will have to eliminate racial discrimination, provide more jobs for unskilled persons, and make the educational system more effective for low-income people. Seeing lower-class life as a response to life opportunities, strategy recommends a heavy dose of social programs and an effort to break down barriers that restrict life chances on the basis of race or ethnic background.

Government intervention results. Direct services for lower-class persons range from welfare payments to provide income, to food stamp programs to improve diets, to Medicaid and neighborhood health clinics to upgrade health. Other programs intend to upgrade other

---

[14] Banfield, op. cit., p. 64.

aspects of lower-class life. Manpower training programs are to improve work skills. Various educational programs—from Head Start to special aid to high schools—seek to upgrade reading skills, motivation, and educational attainment. Civil rights acts prohibiting discrimination in public accommodations, housing, employment, and voting aim to break down the structural barriers to a better life.

All of the major national political institutions—the Supreme Court, the Congress, the President, the political parties—participated in the vast flood of decisions and social legislation impacting on lower-class life. Many of those who supported the programs most enthusiastically believed funding was never at an adequate level and programs never given a full chance to work. Most Democratic officials and activists, reflecting their national constituencies and also their ideological beliefs, were more optimistic about improvements than their Republican counterparts.

The Political Consequences of Lower-Class Values: The View from Outside the Lower Class. There are two perspectives on the political consequences of lower-class values. The nonlower-class view regards persons with lower-class values as a source of numerous political problems. Lower-class persons cost money because they use local services in excess of their proportionate numbers. They require heavy welfare and social and educational services. Because the lower class are excessively the victims of criminals or the perpetrators of crime, their neighborhoods incur heavy police costs. Their neighborhoods are also dangerous and explosive. Sanitation crews cannot or do not pick up the trash. Housing, a continuous problem, is the worst in the area. They pay little taxes. Illicit, untaxed commerce pervades these areas, although gambling enterprises, especially numbers, and drugs provide employment and revenue for a few entrepreneurs.

To the degree that lower-class people participate in politics, it is in the framework of machine politics. They vote in return for favors from ward ethnic or race politicians. Their presence stimulates middle- and working-class persons to move out of the central city. Millions fled to the suburbs. Large numbers of lower-class people, with their high visibility, spread a sense of foreboding and fear over the central city.

Outlining the consequences of lower-class values for suburban politics is difficult. Few lower-class persons live in suburbia at this time, with the exception of a few completely lower-class areas. Where there are pockets of lower-class people in suburban communities, they present the usual claims on the public purse for special services. Mostly, however, lower-class values act on suburban consciousness by their presence in the nearby central city and in the resultant hostility to programs that might bring them into closer contact.

The Political Consequences of Lower-Class Values: The View from Within the Lower Class.   Most accounts indicate local governments look much different when viewed from within the lower-class subcultures. Governments are seen as providing services that do not meet needs. Police forces are seen as armies of occupation, schools as insensitive and as failing to help children. Cynicism reigns, with government portrayed in individual accounts and in survey reports as corrupt and unresponsive. Thus, political participation in the traditional forms, such as voting, is seen as hopeless, except under unusual circumstances. Such exceptional circumstances would include candidates from the same background, race, or class as the persons in the subculture.

Political participation occurs in demonstrations and neighborhood organizations. Much activity aims at preventing urban renewal and highway destruction of neighborhoods, or at forcing better services in clinics or schools. There is little optimism about success. General feelings of futility about the "system" apply to local politics.

From the lower-class subculture, the suburbs are viewed as part of the system that works against them. Well-to-do whites have achieved community control in their protected enclaves. The existence of the suburbs is a reminder and a taunt about the distribution of power in metropolitan America.

THE MIDDLE-CLASS SUBCULTURE

In numerical terms, middle-class values are most widespread. One hundred years ago, the urban population was predominantly working class, but today it is heavily middle class, and grows most rapidly in the upper-middle class. The primary characteristic of middle-class culture is the nuclear family, sticking together and trying to get ahead in the world. Middle-class persons derive most of their social and emotional gratifications from the nuclear family itself. The extended family of the working class is absent, and relatives play a subordinate role. Outside social life is with friends or work associates.

Work is very important, and the middle-class person expects a career, not just a job. Work leads to satisfactions, status, and advancement, as well as income. The rewards of work feed back into family life. Education leads to the desired job, status, and life-style. In Banfield's terms, the middle-class person is more future-oriented than the working-class person. He or she is interested in self-improvement and advancement. A primary goal is to send children to college. Middle-class culture respects the rights of others and abhors violence.

The Political Consequences of Middle-Class Values for Central Cities.   Being relatively affluent and not tied to particular neighborhoods, the middle-class person moves if his/her values are not satisfied by local political systems. All central city officials now know that millions of essentially middle-class families moved to the suburbs after World War II. Middle-class persons who remain want the protection of their life-style values *within* a heterogeneous central city environment. To be protected are the life values themselves—getting ahead, safe living, and good schools. Good public schools are absolutely essential. Amenities such as parks, sports facilities, playgrounds, libraries, and museums rate high.

The problem for central city governments is how to meet middle-class concerns. Suppose a central city government tries to protect middle-class values in certain neighborhoods. To the degree that this protection takes the form of better schools, better parks, better police services, there will be howls from other sections of the city. To the degree that this protection involves tacit acceptance of all-white schools, refusal to put public housing in the neighborhood, and a tolerant attitude toward private discrimination in housing, the city government is subject to complaints, demonstrations, and lawsuits. In other words, where the middle class is still present in central cities, efforts to preserve and protect it may, ironically, fuel more conflict.

How will central city officials resolve this dilemma? They can choose to ignore the remaining middle-class persons, on the grounds that the struggle is already lost. Or, they can move behind the scenes and hope that quiet support for a few schools and a few neighborhoods will at least maintain stability. This last might be considered a middle-range option. Still another alternative is to make a conscious effort to hold middle-class people or even lure them back by encouraging middle- and upper-income housing and by emphasizing various special features of central city life, such as convenient shopping and cultural facilities. The lure-them-back strategy amounts to using scarce and contested resources to cater to what now may be, in many central cities, a distinct minority.

The Political Consequences of Middle-class Values for the Suburbs.   The suburbs are not homogeneous. Nonetheless, as Robert C. Wood indicates, their dominant cultural theme recreates in the suburbs a sense of the homogeneous small-town community.[15] The suburbs become means to the end of protecting a life-style, and suburban political structures are eyed with that protectionist (or promotional) aim.

The main value to be protected and promoted is the school. Parents' intense commitment to school quality turns all educational issues into political issues. Thus, curriculum, teaching methods, and costs become important questions. The possibility of new students, either as residents in different kinds of housing (such as federally sponsored, multifamily low-income buildings) or as transients (by busing from another school district), arouses severe anxieties.

The second value is preserving the established life-style against outside threats, real or imagined. If land use is a crucial problem, then the politics of zoning are important. The standards and location of residential housing, single-family versus multifamily homes, commercial and industrial as opposed to residential uses—all make the suburban zoning board a tense body. One particularly common conflict pits economic development against preservation of the community.

The mix of services also reflects middle-class expectations. Good parks and recreation facilities (perhaps with supervised summer programs for children), honest and polite police, and frequent garbage collection are highly regarded. Further, middle-class suburban parents seek opportunities for service in different kinds of school and community organizations.

THE UPPER-MIDDLE AND UPPER-CLASS SUBCULTURE

The upper-middle/upper-class culture also centers on the nuclear family, but its prime values are individualism and self-expression. The goal is individual development, through work and through service. Incomes, status, and job responsibility are usually present, and the aim is to make these values both satisfying and useful to the individual and to the community. Women share these values, and women in this class are heavily involved in their own careers as well as in community activity. Gans suggests the family is not child-centered so much as it is adult-directed.[16] Members want educational credentials, all the way through professional and graduate school.

Persons in the upper middle/upper class also have an understanding of and a certain control over the outside world. Their high status and economic resources plus their self-confidence and interpersonal skills cause them to view the world as manageable. Accustomed to

[15] *Suburbia: Its People and Their Politics* (Boston: Houghton Mifflin, 1958).
[16] Gans, op. cit., p. 248.

responsibility for the lives of others, they view social phenomena in a partially abstract and generalized way.

In Banfield's view, people in the upper middle/upper class are most future-oriented. They expect a long life for themselves and are concerned about their family for several generations forward. They also are concerned about their community, the nation, even mankind, and are interested in doing "good." They feel a responsibility to serve and also, because of their view toward the long-run future, they have a stake in whatever happens.

People in this class raise their children with the idea of "development," and tolerate, even encourage, individual eccentricities. They do not become upset by children taking a long time to "find themselves." The upper-middle/upper-class person is open-minded toward unconventional activity in private behavior, art, and politics. He or she likes issues settled rationally "on the merits," sympathizes with minorities, and dislikes violence.

The Political Consequences of Upper-Middle/Upper-Class Culture for Central Cities.

People with upper-middle/upper-class values are the least numerous part of the central city. Yet, one does not have to believe in a power elite model to see how they might influence city politics out of proportion to their number. As individuals, people with these values are anxious, even self-compelled, to participate in service activities, from the boards of cultural and social welfare institutions to being public spokesmen for the causes of different minorities. Some, such as Banfield, consider their impulse to "do good" meddlesome, but others consider it useful.

By virtue of their status and resources, these persons get noticed and command attention. By their prominence in crucial institutions in the city—newspapers, banks, commercial and industrial firms—they have the ability to back up their goals. When they operate in an organized way on an issue, they are difficult to ignore. At the same time, their small numbers weaken their position, as do several other factors. The social elite does not hold political office. Many individuals in this class live in the suburbs, even if their work or social concerns are still in the central city.

The Political Consequences of Upper-Middle and Upper-Class Culture for the Suburbs.

The impact of this cultural set upon suburban politics is hard to identify. Once again there would be the drive for doing good and a sympathy for minorities. Yet, there is no evidence that predominantly upper-middle/upper-class suburbs open their doors or their schools to lower-income housing or to busing any more rapidly than do working-class suburbs. As in the middle-class culture, there is a heavy emphasis on the quality of schools, with added interest in educational experimentation. Members of this class have the option of using private schools. This class created the idea of "reformed," nonpartisan, honest manager-council government. Logically, there should be high support for such amenities as parks, playgrounds, libraries, and aesthetic, beautification, or restoration projects.

PARTICIPATING IN LOCAL POLITICS

We now analyze several aspects of individual and group participation in local politics. Political scientists describe the expression of citizen demands, concerns, and feelings of support or disapproval for officials or policies as *interest articulation*. They differentiate *manifest interest articulation* from *latent interest articulation*. In manifest interest articulation, it is clear who sends a message, what that message is about, and to whom it is directed. In latent interest articulation, the focus of message blurs. What is articulated is emotion, or mood. To whom it is directed is hard to fathom, as is the expected response.

THREE MODES OF MANIFEST INTEREST ARTICULATION

We find three modes of manifest interest articulation: (1) voting for officials in local systems of representative government; (2) voting on issues in systems of direct democracy; and (3) involvement in organized group activity.

Voting for Officials in Local Systems. In almost all populous, democratic political systems, selection of officials is a common mode of participation. (The alternative, town democracy, or decision making by all the citizens assembled in one place, lingers in some smaller New England communities, but is not widely utilized.) In democratic theory, high turnout indicates citizen interest and responsibility in choosing officials.

American voting turnout is lower in local elections than in national elections, and even in local elections, the turnout varies. The median turnout in partisan elections is 50 per cent, and in nonpartisan cities it is 30 per cent.[17] The reform movement achieved its goal: greater insulation of decision makers from the public. Without parties to organize electoral conflict and mobilize voters, turnout declines.

---

[17] Robert R. Alford and Eugene C. Lee, "Voting Turnout in American Cities," *The American Political Science Review*, 62 (September 1968), pp. 796–813.

Turnout is also higher in mayor-council than in council-manager cities. Working-class cities have greater turnout. Holding local elections concurrently with state and national elections adds to turnout.

All of the ambiguities that shroud the meaning of voting in national elections, including its linkage to public policy, are also present in local elections. Voting data cannot explain how turnout connects to policy decisions. Nor does high turnout necessarily indicate any link to future local governmental policies (any more than a high presidential turnout tells one what the president will *do* in the next four years). Low turnout may signify any one of several conditions, from consensus at one polar extreme to feelings of hopelessness at the other.

Voting on Issues in Direct Democracy Systems. Unlike the national government, state and local governments make frequent use of one form of direct democracy, referenda. Referenda are votes on specific policies. Local referenda have included every subject from property tax ceilings to fluoridation of water supplies, from ordinances prohibiting discrimination in the sale or rental of housing to the more customary yearly votes on school bonds or property tax rates. Referenda link citizens and policies directly.[18] There are some 3,500 local referenda in odd-numbered years and some 15,000 in even-numbered years. In one year there were 1,846 referenda in Ohio alone, all but a few of them local.

The turnout in referenda, as in the election of local officials, tends to be low. In Toledo, for example, only 22 per cent came out to vote on an open housing referendum. The sporadic nature of the appearance of referenda and the absence of partisan cues reduce knowledge. Many referenda pit "establishment" local notables against strong "anti" forces, whether on school tax rates or on fluoridation. Scholars analyzed 1,181 local communities where fluoridation decisions had been made. Where the issue came to a vote, it lost two out of three times, often despite support from public health officers.[19] The most successful route was through the support of a mayor or a manager, by administrative action, not popular vote.

Organized Group Involvement. Citizens also participate in local life through groups. Political parties combine voting and group identification. The local reform movement diluted the importance of par-

---

[18] See Howard D. Hamilton, "Direct Legislation: Some Implications of Open Housing Referenda," *The American Political Science Review*, **64:** (March 1970), pp. 124–137.

[19] See Robert L. Crain and others, *The Politics of Community Conflict: The Fluoridation Decision* (Indianapolis: Bobbs-Merrill Company, 1969).

ties, but they survive. Behind the scenes, they organize support in nonpartisan elections. Machines, or partial machines, still exist, primarily in the largest cities. Voting in state and national elections on a party basis indirectly affects local politics.

The big cities remain the bastion of the national Democratic party. The suburbs are not uniformly Republican, but Republicans do better in suburbs and in small and medium-sized cities than do Democrats. These territorial patterns reflect underlying ethnic, educational, racial, and other demographic variables and, ultimately, of the historical impact of elections. Thus, nothing about living in inner Philadelphia makes one a Democrat. The first machines in that city around the time of the Civil War were, in fact, Republican. And nothing about living in a suburb makes one a Republican. As the Democratic party develops a white middle-class base, or some of its formerly lower- or working-class supporters move to the suburbs, then outlying regions can be expected to give the Democrats a good vote. Conversely, if the Republicans ever become the new majority party nationally, one element in their new coalition will be working-class voters who formerly lived in central cities and voted Democratic. National forces shape local loyalties to the national parties.

Other Forms of Group Involvement: Ethnicity and Race. The most important bases for urban group solidarity and organization seem to have been *ethnicity* and *race*. Ethnicity refers to Americans—the roughly 70 million Irish, Italians, Poles, Slavs, Czechs, and Jews—who are not descended from Anglo-Saxon settlers. When the ethnics came, they were thrown inward upon each other for solace and survival, and they fought to gain control of what was new or what other Americans did not want—heavy construction, organized crime, entertainment. They often also turned to politics as a channel for upward mobility. The newest ethnics are the 10 million Spanish-speaking Americans, the Hispanics: Chicanos, Puerto Ricans, Cubans, and South Americans.

Ethnic identity persists, taking various forms. One form is the capture of a trade, occupation, or city bureaucracy by one group. New York is the archetypal model, where Jews are teachers and control the teacher's union, Irish are policemen and control the policemen's union, Italians are sanitation men and control that union, and Puerto Ricans man the hospitals and control that union. Ethnicity continues as a factor in voting. Members of one ethnic group vote disproportionately for members of their own group. Robert E. Lane observes that "in a real sense, the seat of ethnic politics is the local community."[20]

---

[20] *Political Life* (New York: Free Press, 1959), p. 239.

Two theories explain the continuance of ethnic behavior.[21] One, the *persistence theory*, holds that ethnic ties, forged in the face of adversity, linger on into subsequent generations. The other, the *mobilization theory*, holds that politicians deliberately bring forth and mobilize ethnic loyalties in their search for a simple, direct way of winning votes. Convincing evidence shows that mobilization of ethnic loyalties, through the deliberate use of symbols, patronage, and appeals to pride, prolongs urban ethnic solidarity. But at a social level, another factor operates, as witness the rebirth of ethnic pride among groups that were supposed to be assimilated. Ethnicity proves cultural identity in a formless, impersonal society.

Race operates the same way as ethnicity in local politics—as a point of solidarity for a group forced in upon its own resources and as a target for mobilization by political leaders. There are black majorities in many major cities, with black mayors and increasing numbers of black officials. Blacks, as much as the original ethnics, have been trapped by poverty and the difficulties of an internal immigration from the South.

LATENT INTEREST ARTICULATION: URBAN RIOTS

One mode of political participation qualifies as latent interest articulation, namely urban rioting. An "urban crisis" came to widespread public attention because of urban riots involving blacks during the 1960s, beginning with Watts (Los Angeles) in 1965 and continuing through similar conflagrations in large cities such as Newark, Detroit, and Washington, and smaller ones such as in Omaha and Rochester. In all, the President's Commission on Civil Disorders counted 164 disorders in 128 cities. This commission categorized the disorders as major (many fires, intensive looting, reports of sniping, violence lasting more than two days, sizable crowds, and use of National Guard or federal forces as well as local police); serious (lesser amounts of the same symptoms); and minor. Five per cent of the total were major; 20 per cent, serious; and 75 per cent, minor.[22] Another source, surveying 1963–1968, estimated the number of participants at more than 200,000, with more than 8,000 casualties and almost 50,000 arrests.

The President's Commission on Civil Disorders explained the disorders as a result of racial discrimination against black people. The commission saw riots as the black response to grievances against the larger society and also against local governments. A social science

---

[21] See Raymond E. Wolfinger, *The Politics of Progress* (Englewood Cliffs, N.J.: Prentice-Hall, 1974), for a summary of various theories and data. See also Michael Novak, *The Rise of the Unmelted Ethnics* (New York: Macmillan, 1973).

[22] National Advisory Commission on Civil Disorders, *Report* (New York: Bantam Books, 1968), p. 113.

explanation found the causes to be structural factors plus the expectations of the people who riot. This theory of relative deprivation suggests that riots occur at a point when people's expectations have been raised. In contrast, Edward C. Banfield, in a chapter entitled, "Rioting Mainly for Fun and Profit," suggests lower-class culture causes riots which have no political content.[23]

ORGANIZATIONS IN LOCAL POLITICS

Organizational activity provides visibility, permanence, mobilization, status, pooled resources. At the same time, organization incurs costs in time, money, and the compromising of individual views to arrive at one position. In the United States, only 31 per cent of all adults belong to an organization that takes a stand on any political issue, and within organizations, the number of persons who are very active is usually small, perhaps 20 per cent of the total membership at most. Not all organizations involve themselves in all local issues, nor do all organizations participate with the same intensity.

THE ROLE OF BUSINESS

Businesses, individually and considered collectively, command important resources: jobs, investment, taxes, political contributions, status. Business participation takes many forms. Individual firms are sometimes powerful, especially when the local economy is dominated by one industry or one company. In more economically diverse settings, businesses often organize by sectors, operating through trade associations in real estate, retail trade, banking, housing construction, or hotel, restaurant, and tourist attractions. Businesses in these fields care most about downtown development, any action that might affect real estate values, the distribution of taxes, and the general business image of the community. They are often joined by the local newspaper, which has not only a civic concern, but also an economic self-interest in what happens in the community.

Every city has a local Chamber of Commerce, whose members are all local businesses.[24] The Chambers operate on a continuing basis. *Ad hoc* groups of businessmen respond to particular problems. Thus, cities see business groups committed to downtown development, to

---

[23] Op. cit., pp. 211–233.

[24] For case studies of businessmen in Dallas politics, see Carol E. Thometz, *The Decision-Makers: The Power Structure of Dallas* (Dallas: Southern Methodist University Press, 1963); for St. Louis, see Richard T. Edgar, *Urban Power and Social Welfare: Corporate Influence in an American City* (Los Angeles: Sage Publications, 1970).

provide jobs for ghetto blacks and thus "cool" the possibilities of riots, and to promote convention facilities and tourist business.

Business interests attend to specific governmental decisions. Businesses care not only about highways in general, but where each road will go, who will build it, and what the impact will be on their own workers and customers. For small businesses, in particular, city government contracts remain lucrative—for construction, for office supplies, for legal fees. Businessmen, because of their high status in the community, deal with political leaders directly as individuals as well as through organizations.

Most observers of business in local life differentiate between the activism of locally owned firms and the more restrained role of national companies with local plants or stores. The national companies are concerned primarily with maintaining a low profile and a good image. Yet, when their direct interests are affected, through pollution code enforcement or through tax rates, these firms can become quite active. Further, wherever large-scale development is undertaken by national firms, in constructing downtown office buildings, or shopping centers or housing tracts in the suburbs, the companies become involved. Wherever governmental authority or activities touch upon business, business expresses its interests in the local system.

LOCAL LABOR IN POLITICS

The most active labor groups in local politics are those whose work situation and livelihoods depend upon local governmental decisions. Thus, building and craft trades know that housing construction, all building codes, and wage rates are influenced by what governments decide. The most powerful local unions represent city employees in the police, fire, and school departments. International unions participate less in local affairs, unless they have such a numerous membership that they constitute a sizable block of the total population, such as the United Auto Workers in Detroit.

Nonpartisan electoral systems mute the political participation of unions, give an advantage to high-status business interests, and make political action more difficult for workers. Nonpartisanship limits political parties, a traditional channel for organized labor. In partisan systems, local leaders of organized labor band together in a central labor federation. Labor leaders speak for sizable voting blocks in most big cities, and the numbers behind them generate influence. Political officials know voting turnout is higher among unionists than among nonmembers. Labor leaders enjoy direct access to mayors, managers, and local councilmen.

OTHER GROUPS IN LOCAL POLITICS

Many other groups intervene regularly in areas of concern to them. Black groups, from local branches of the National Association for the Advancement of Colored People and the Urban League to purely local organizations, try to influence antipoverty, school, housing, and police policy decisions. In suburbia, some groups focus on the schools on a continuing basis, and others monitor taxes. Professionals in the social work and health fields try to influence issues in their realm of expertise.

In all modern governments, much policy initiation comes from within. Programs are proposed by those who have day-to-day policy concerns in particular fields, and then the leaders and members (or unions) of these agencies lobby for what they want. The drive to initiate programs from within, or defensively to fight to preserve them is heightened by the loyalty of workers in modern bureaucracies to their agency, their department, their bureau. Hence, we talk about *bureaucratic groups*.

The result is predictable. In particular controversies involving city hospitals, the city health department will, through its top officials, have a position and attempt to see that position prevail. Should there be more staff? Should the form of city medical care be neighborhood centers instead of a hospital? Should the community get out of health care entirely and turn its citizens over to the county? And in which health plans may city employees enroll? On all of these issues, as well as what the health department's budget should be each year, the department will have a position.

The interests of city bureaucracies often put them in conflict with other elements of the government or the citizenry. Should the school budget and hence property taxes be increased? The teachers' union may say "yes," various citizens' groups "no," and the mayor and the city council (or the school board) be left to decide. Or maybe the issue will not be solved through politics at all, or at least not directly. Where city employees are unionized, they are ultimately able to force a decision by striking. We have seen city teachers, policemen, sanitation men, and others go the "job action" route frequently in the last 10 years. As white-collar municipal unionism expands, more participation by city employees lies ahead.

PUBLIC OFFICIALS IN LOCAL POLITICS

In all local politics, public officials play a central role. We now will discuss some characteristics of public officials and their views of their role in policy making.

City Managers and City Council Members

Let us first look at manager-council systems, beginning with the managers. The data for the entire United States show managers are young (45 years of age on the average), well-educated (64 per cent with college degrees), and with backgrounds in the social sciences. The old engineering bias for managers still shows up but is not as prevalent. Managers' background profiles would not be different from those of middle-level executives in many businesses. Managers come, clearly, from a narrower recruitment base than do elected mayors, whose range of prior experience and education is more diverse.[25]

At the level of what they think they are supposed to do in their jobs, however, managers move away from the older image, which held that managers administered the policies set by the elected councils. This style still prevails, but is strongest in the smallest cities. As cities increase in size, the managers adopt a more aggressive view of their role in making policy.[26] They view their job as political, as making judgments, and taking responsibilities. In Table 8-1, the first column indicates how managers accept a political view of their own responsibilities. Various factors account for this digression from the original administrative model of the council-manager system. As cities become larger and more diverse, and thus contain more internal divisions and conflict, mediating conflict and working out policy solutions become unavoidable for survival. Managers of larger cities fit the more cosmopolitan, professionally trained mold of those sensitive to the national standards of the International City Managers Association.[27] The tensions of the job surface in the statistic that in the 50 largest council-manager cities in the United States, the average tenure is two years.[28]

City managers' views create potential conflict with councils (Table 8-1). Only 22 per cent of the managers agree that policy matters should be left to the council; 88 per cent believe that a manager should assume leadership in shaping municipal policies; only 53 per cent believe that the manager should be neutral on controversial issues that divide the community; 44 per cent sanction intervention in recruiting for council seats; and barely 30 per cent think it proper to consult with the council before preparing the city's budget (where all sorts of

[25] See Joan E. Tighe, "Patterns of Urban Leadership: A Comparison of Mayors and City Managers." Unpublished honors thesis, Wheaton College, Norton, Mass., 1970.

[26] Ronald O. Loveridge, *City Managers in Legislative Politics* (Indianapolis: Bobbs-Merrill, 1971), p. 69.

[27] See Gladys Kammerer and others, *City Managers in Politics* (Gainesville: University of Florida Press, 1962).

[28] Tighe, op. cit., p. 49.

TABLE 8-1. Manager and Council Members: Conflicts in Policy Role Views

Items	City Managers Percentage Agree	(Difference)	City Council Members Percentage Agree
1. Policy Administrator "A city manager should act as an administrator and leave policy matters to the council."	22	(66)	88
2. Policy Innovator "A city manager should assume leadership in shaping municipal policies."	88	(46)	42
3. Political Leader "A city manager should work through the most powerful members of the community to achieve policy goals."	53	(41)	12
4. Policy Neutral "A city manager should maintain a neutral stand on any issues on which the community is divided."	24	(40)	64
5. Political Recruiter "A city manager should encourage people whom he respects to run for city council."	44	(21)	23
6. Budget Consultant "A city manager should consult with the council before drafting his own budget."	31	(18)	49

From *City Managers in Legislative Politics*, p. 96, by Ronald O. Loveridge, copyright © 1971, by the Bobbs-Merrill Company, Inc., reprinted by permission of the publisher.

crucial initial decisions are made). The data in Table 8-1 come only from the San Francisco Bay area. If they are not atypical, conflict between managers and councils occur regularly in the council-manager system.

As for the council members, in the largest study of their backgrounds, again conducted in the Bay area, they are a middle-class group, usually male, more educated, with higher income than the populations of their communities. This pattern of elected officials having elite characteristics is also typical of the United States Congress and, to a lesser degree, of state legislatures.[29] Council members were originally recruited from a network of elite voluntary activities, and they view their work as an extension of that voluntary civic participation.

Council members show little political ambition. Many retire voluntarily from office. Almost one quarter arrive in council office by being appointed to fill vacancies. The virtually nonpolitical role that Bay area council members adopt frees them to act in behalf of whatever they perceive the best interests of the community to be. They can tax the resources of the community for public purposes, although they are highly conscious of a low tax ethos in the public. At the same time, the council members do not seem very "accountable," because of their lack of ambition or concern for elections. In combination, what data we possess on city managers and council members fit what we already know about this council-manager government. Public officials fit a middle-class and upper-middle-class mold and desire insulation from political conflict.

MAYORS AND COUNCIL MEMBERS

Most elected mayors, particularly in the largest cities, operate under *strong-mayor systems* that give them, at the local level, the panoply of ceremonial and appointive powers that presidents and governors have at their levels. A few elected mayors, however, most notably in Los Angeles, operate under *weak-mayor systems*. With control over many vital functions and municipal jobs in the hands of the city council, the county council, or independent boards, the mayor becomes a kind of public relations figure. In Los Angeles, the structural weakness is accentuated by the nonpartisanship. Consider the testimony given by former Los Angeles Mayor Samuel Yorty before a United States Senate subcommittee:

SENATOR RIBICOFF: As I listened to your testimony, Mayor Yorty, I have made some notes. This morning you have really waived authority and responsibility in the following areas: schools, welfare, transportation, employment, health, and housing, which

[29] See Kenneth Prewitt, *The Recruitment of Political Leaders: A Study of Citizen-Politicians* (Indianapolis: Bobbs-Merrill, 1970), pp. 86–101. For similar findings on the background characteristics of councilmen in Ohio, see John S. Latcham and Howard D. Hamilton, "Purposive Roles of City Councilmen," paper presented at the 1974 American Political Science Association convention, Chicago, August 29–September 2, 1974.

leaves you as the head of the city basically with a ceremonial function, police, and recreation.

MAYOR YORTY: That is right, and fire.

SENATOR RIBICOFF: And fire.

MAYOR YORTY: Yes.

SENATOR RIBICOFF: Collecting sewage?

MAYOR YORTY: Sanitation; that is right.

SENATOR RIBICOFF: In other words, basically you lack jurisdiction, authority, responsibility for what makes a city move?

MAYOR YORTY: That is exactly it.[30]

Strong mayors, however, have control over the usual panoply of
executive prerogatives: appointments, lower patronage, ceremonial
functions. They derive real political power, as does a president, from
the combination of their formal and informal powers. They occupy the
center of the communications network for the city. In partisan cities,
they possess the power that comes from being party chieftan as well.

We know surprisingly little about the backgrounds and attitudes
of mayors. There are a great number of case studies of individual
mayors, but very little comparative data. As for recruitment, we do
have the evidence of one longitudinal study of Chicago that shows a
shifting set of background requirements. Originally, the mayors came
from the commercial elite. Since 1930, they have all been Catholic and,
until 1979, all rose to power as administrators within the political party
apparatus after long years of service in the lower echelons of the party.
Mrs. Jane Bryne shattered the traditional Chicago pattern by winning
nomination against the organization's candidate in 1979. After election
as mayor, she quickly moved to solidify her relations with the party.
Although Mrs. Bryne began her career as a protege of the late Mayor
Richard J. Daley, she shattered the traditional Chicago route to the
top. In other cities, a more flowing process already was the norm. In
San Francisco and St. Louis, local businessmen with extroverted personalities and a taste for political rough-and-tumble win the office.
Thus, personal charisma provides one alternative to the organizational
route of the party ladder.

As to the techniques of mayors and their role conceptions, despite
a wide range of case studies, little systematic data exist. Some mayors,
we know, operate as brokers among the many organized interests of
the city, waiting for ideas to be initiated by such interests or by
bureaucrats, waiting to see who lines up behind what, and then, at the

---

[30] "Hearings," Subcommittee on Executive Reorganization, *Federal Role in
Urban Affairs*, Part 3, August 23, 1966, reprinted in Leonard I. Ruchelman, ed., *Big City
Mayors: The Crisis in Urban Politics* (Bloomington: Indiana University Press, 1969), p.
314.

last possible moment, making their own positions known. In this pattern of behavior the mayor does not initiate and does not mobilize. On the other hand, other mayors take the initiative for extensive particular projects and some try to generate broad public support for change.

One fact is certain about mayors: they do not stay in office very long. One study suggested that for cities of more than 29,000 population, the turnover rate (combining defeat with voluntary retirement) is close to 50 per cent.[31] Another, analyzing 61 cities with population of more than 100,000, found that only 34 per cent of the cities had the same mayor as the 1970s began as they had in 1965.[32] The mayor's post does not lead very far either. Very few mayors rise to higher political posts, reflecting the high wear and tear of executive politics generally and of local executive politics in particular. The route to the Senate or the White House is not through City Hall.

Council members in mayor-council systems are generally portrayed as dominated by the mayor. When the council members are elected on a partisan district basis, they also respond to the ethnic, class, or racial interests of their geographical constituencies. In the tradition of recognition, they are from the majority ethnic, religious, or racial group in the district. The council members respond to demands from local block associations, from neighborhood businessmen, and others. They mediate between constituents and the city government agencies and also between them and the mayor. Council persons are congressmen writ small.

Council persons in mayor-council cities who are elected at-large on a nonpartisan basis are more likely to be blue-ribbon types. Endorsement by local media and civic groups becomes important because, in the absence of any territorial base, simple exposure counts. Ethnicity may also help some individuals, but the at-large basis reduces the representation that minorities would have if there were districts. No studies indicate how at-large nonpartisan council persons behave in office. They might adopt the overall volunteerism, amateurism, and nonpartisan stance of the council-manager system but with the sensitivity to group and block interests of mayor-council communities.

CONCLUSIONS

This chapter covers diverse material on people in local life. Following are some conclusions.

[31] Eugene C. Lee, "City Elections: A Statistical Profile," in *The Municipal Year-book*, 1963 (Chicago: International City Managers Association), pp. 74–84.

[32] See Wolfinger, *The Politics of Progress*, op. cit.

1. Scholars believe that there are widely held sets of attitudes called class culture, which are different, often competing, and which determine many aspects of the local environment and its politics. These class cultures are working-class, lower-class, middle-class, and upper-middle/upper class. The existence of these cultures and their consequences are controversial, particularly in the lower-class culture.

2. As in national politics, there are different modes or channels for participation in local politics. People participate as individuals in voting, demonstrations, riots, lobbying, running for and holding public office. Out of the configuration of social, economic, racial, and ethnic patterns of an area, group organization emerges as a widespread mode of political action. One particularly important form is the bureaucratic group, producing the activism in local politics of unionized teachers, firemen, and police.

3. We know something of the characteristics of people who hold public office in different types of local government systems and about the attitudes of managers and council members in council-manager systems. We also know about the career patterns of such officials, including, for example, that being mayor of a large city is a terminal post. Much more research in this area is needed.

9
PUBLIC POLICY AND POLITICS IN LOCAL LIFE

This chapter reports on three substantive issues in American local life—transportation, crime, and education. In addition, we look at an issue of governmental form—the many efforts to decentralize local government into still smaller units.

Transportation policy affects the distribution of people, homes, real estate values, and the quality and convenience of local life. Transportation politics involves alternate modes of travel, multiple levels of government, private interest groups, and citizens. Police and crime control touch on civil order as well as on the desirability of neighborhoods and communities. Schools take the largest single share of the local budget. Education reaches every value of local life, from the opportunity and life chances of individual children to the property values of a particular suburb.

TRANSPORTATION: HOW PEOPLE TRAVEL IN METROPOLITAN AREAS

The entire world has undergone an automotive revolution and has traffic jams.[1] Americans are not alone with their urban problems and the automobile. But the United States' life-style particularly depends

---

[1] See Wilfred Owen, *The Accessible City* (Washington, D.C.: Brookings Institution, 1972); and *The Metropolitan Transportation Problem* (Washington, D.C.: Brookings Institution, 1956). See also Martin Wohl, *Urban Transportation in Perspective* (Cambridge, Mass.: Ballinger Publishing, 1974).

on autos. Suburban life especially relies on automobiles. Suburbanization began when land on the urban fringe was opened up by horse trolleys, then electric railways, in the nineteenth century. A great burst of settlement accompanied widespread ownership of private cars in the 1920s.

After World War II, as auto registrations surged from 40 million in 1950 to 114 million in 1978, and as 18 million families owned at least two cars, suburbanization bloomed. Eighty per cent of all work trips are made by car, and among suburban businesses that figure reaches more than 94 per cent. For home-to-work commuting, the car carries between 70 and 75 per cent of all persons.

Mass transit offers a number of modes of moving people—buses, subways, commuter trains, and even the cable cars that still operate in San Francisco. The American mass transit industry, however, lost the competition with the auto. Although the urban population increased by more than 100 million between 1925 and 1980, urban mass transit patronage in 1980 was less than half of what it was in 1925. Between 1950 and 1980, mass transit lost more than 10 billion riders. Ridership declined as people took to cars and moved to areas farther from the traditional transit lines; as ridership declined, the systems fell into debt, and to cover their financial situation, they raised prices, decreased service, or both; as prices went up and service worsened, ridership declined again. One mark of the declining fortunes of mass transit systems is that they are publicly owned in 15 of the 21 metropolitan areas of more than a million population. But in the nineteenth and early twentieth centuries, private entrepreneurs eagerly sought franchises for transit routes. For the last 30 years, the franchises have been economic losers, passed on to public agencies, where they typically run deficits.

THE VICTORY OF THE AUTOMOBILE

There are a number of reasons why cars displace mass transit in metropolitan areas. The auto provides personalized transport. It leaves when the driver wants to go and takes the driver from point to point. There are some paradoxes in the economics of automobile ownership that explain widespread usage. Although the total costs of car operation are high, the cost of any additional trip by car is low. Variable costs of gasoline, while increasing, are still small which means that short trips cost virtually nothing. Most city and suburban trips are very short, with more than half of them under one mile. Two out of every three trips are nonwork trips, and about 85 per cent of these, for shopping and recreation, are made by private car. In the metropolitan area, daily automobile travel per urban resident is 7 miles per day.[2] Under such circumstances, with such a life-style, car trips are a good buy, despite high fixed costs.

Public policy highly favors the automobile. At the federal level, a sophisticated coalition of auto manufacturers, oil companies, asphalt and concrete makers, and highway contractors, lobbies successfully for federal dollars.[3] The result is a program that has constantly expanded since its inception in 1915. The crowning element is the federal Interstate System, close to 28,000 miles of freeway, one fourth of which has been or will be constructed within urban areas. The expense of freeway construction in urban areas, with high land purchase and clearance costs, is astronomical: ten miles of Los Angeles-Hollywood Freeway for $50 million; eight miles of Chicago's Congress Street Expressway for $50 million; and the estimated cost of the proposed Lower Manhattan Expressway for New York is $100 million per mile.[4] In total, the federal government alone spent more than $25 billion on transportation in 1978, and more than 80 per cent of that was on roads and streets for cars and trucks. The Highway Trust Funds, so called because they consist of fees raised from the users of gasoline and autos, are earmarked for roads. The Trust Fund raises in excess of $5 billion a year.

Among American consumers, transportation is the fourth most important item in the family budget, amounting to almost 13 cents out of every household dollar. And of this family spending on transportation, more than 90 per cent goes for cars. About half of all low-income families are not able to afford cars (but, somehow, half of all low-income families do have cars) and thus many poor persons depend on public transit.

WILL THE AUTO'S VICTORY LAST?

America now examines auto transit in the light of fuel shortages and rising fuel costs. Many predicted before the energy crisis that the automobile civilization had reached its limits. The symptoms of impending trouble were seen in the increasing amount of land used for

---

[2] Charles Luna, *The UTU Handbook of Transportation in America* (New York: Popular Library, 1971), p. 21.

[3] See David Hapgood, "The Highwaymen," in Charles Peters and Timothy J. Adams, eds., *Inside the System: A Washington Monthly Reader* (New York: Praeger, 1970), pp. 138–157; Helen Leavitt, *Superhighway-Superhoax* (New York: Doubleday, 1970); and Ronald A. Buel, *Dead End: The Automobile in Mass Transportation* (Englewood Cliffs, N.J.: Prentice-Hall, 1972).

[4] Luna, op. cit., pp. 25–26.

roads and car-supporting services (85 per cent of downtown Los Angeles, for example), the choking pollution, and the hopeless rush-hour traffic jams. But the energy crisis, escalating the price of gasoline and raising the long-term possibility of short supplies, forces a hard look at alternative forms of transportation. When people look at urban mass transit, they find the surviving shells of potentially useful systems, ideas for alternative systems, and many built-in difficulties.

MODES OF MASS TRANSIT: THE SITUATION

Figure 9-1 illustrates the recent history of mass transit patronage. Mass transit lost millions of riders during the 1950s and 1960s, stabilized in the 1970s, and recently has shown steady gains as gasoline prices have increased. Busses now carry more than 70 per cent of all mass transit passengers. All the mass transit modes have the potential to move more people through the same space in the same time as do private cars. Capacity is the greatest advantage of mass transit.[5] For example, a lane of highway with cars moving at an average speed of 60 miles an hour can accommodate only 1,200 cars. Even if every car holds five passengers, which is more than twice the average load, the number of people that moves over one lane in an hour is only 6,000. Mass transit, on the other hand, transports as many as eight times that many persons in the same time span. One hundred twenty 50-seat

[5] Ibid., pp. 29–30.

FIGURE 9-1. Passengers Carried by Public Transporation, 1960–1977. (SOURCE: *1979 Statistical Abstract of the United States.*)

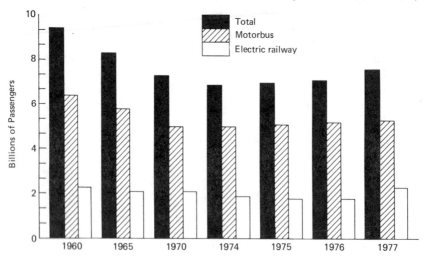

buses can carry 6,720 riders one way in an hour. In the same hour, 60 3-car streetcars could carry 14,400 passengers. Forty rapid transit cars can hold as many as 48,000 people for the same distance in the same time.

Mass transit systems developed during the period of greatest density, when residences and businesses were much more closely clustered. This historical connection of mass transit to urban spatial density is still evident in the problems facing any rejuvenation of such systems. More than half of all mass transit movement occurs in the cities of more than a half million population. The principal time of usage is for round-trip commuter travel between home and work. Systems are clogged for two hours in the morning and two hours in the late afternoon and are underutilized the rest of the time. Mass transit systems have high labor costs because they have to maintain and operate rolling stock that meets a capacity demand only twice a day. During these periods of peak demand, mass transit serves substantial proportions of the working population of the larger cities, ranging from 50 to 75 per cent in Chicago, New York, Philadelphia, Boston, and Cleveland.

Each mode of transit has some advantages and disadvantages. Rapid transit subways (or elevated lines) are fast travel on unimpeded rights of way, and carry large numbers of passengers. Such systems require great initial capital construction funds, especially subways, with their costly excavation and underground work. There are about 1,300 miles of rapid transit subway and elevated lines in American cities. This mode now appears to be in a resurgence. Although only 16 new miles were built between 1945 and 1970, 160 new miles will be built between 1970 and 1990. When completed, the Washington, D.C., METRO will connect the capital and surrounding suburbs in a 98-mile linkup of underground subways and surface high-speed trains. The San Francisco BART system (Bay Area Rapid Transit) will connect stations in Almeda, Contra Costa, and San Francisco counties (Figure 9-2). When the first bond issue for BART was approved in 1962, it represented the first commitment for a new mass transit system in the United States since 1907.

There have been other impressive efforts in the rapid mass transit field. Cleveland built a new rail link between the city and its airport. A successful new commuter rail line, the Lindenwood Line, connects a number of New Jersey communities and Philadelphia. In Chicago, a rail line has been successfully built along the median strip of the Dan Ryan Expressway. Extensions and modernization of existing systems are planned in New York, Boston, Chicago, Cleveland, Philadelphia, and New Jersey.

FIGURE 9-2. Cars on San Francisco's BART system. (SOURCE: Courtesy of the Bay Area Rapid Transit Authority.)

Many mass transit supporters believe buses should be emphasized. Buses operate over some 112,000 miles of routes. They have flexibility on their routes that other, fixed right-of-way, rapid transit systems do not. At the same time, buses carry more people at lower per mile costs than do private cars. Yet, to maximize their utility, buses must operate somewhat differently from cars. If buses share the streets and expressway with autos, although they can move more people, they are disproportionately slowed by the traffic. Especially in downtown cross streets, where they make frequent stops, buses move very slowly. The competitive position of buses could be improved. One strategy would give right-of-way advantages to buses on downtown streets and expressways.[6] On downtown streets, autos can be prohibited during certain peak hours or granted limited access by toll or surveillance systems. These changes would give buses an access advantage and allow them to move faster.

---

[6] John F. Kain, "How to Improve Urban Transportation at Practically No Cost," *Public Policy*, 20:3 (Summer 1972), p. 350. For the classic study, see J. R. Meyer, J. F. Kain, and M. Wohl, *The Urban Transportation Problem* (Cambridge, Mass.: Harvard University Press, 1965).

THE POLITICS OF TRANSPORTATION

Transportation policy involves the federal government, the state governments, various special authorities with metropolitan jurisdiction that operate transit services, and local government units.[7] The federal role dates from the passage of the Urban Mass Transportation Act of 1964. That act made relatively small amounts of federal funds available for capital improvements (new buses, subway cars) for urban transit operations. The federal government paid two thirds of the costs. These funds were helpful to some systems, but there were two problems. Compared to the capital needs of individual systems (often estimated at more than a billion dollars for New York or Boston alone), the less than $200 million a year allocated for the whole nation did not make much of a dent in the problem. Second, federal funds were not available for the huge operating deficits or for any operating expenses.

The Urban Mass Transportation Act of 1970 committed Washington to provide $10 billion over 12 years to aid mass public transit in the cities. The Secretary of the Department of Transportation obligated monies for improving and extending rapid transit systems, modernizing rail commuter lines, and purchasing new buses.

The political coalition behind federal support for mass transit has been largely one of liberal Democrats with some liberal Republicans. Pressure has come from the urban interest network, especially the United States Conference of Mayors. But, at the federal level, the mass transit interest never duplicated the political success of auto, highway, and truck interests or, for that matter, of the airlines. Until the energy crisis, mass transit systems seemed to be modes of travel that people did not want to use and that could not compete with autos in local communities. Public officials are reluctant to sponsor unpopular or uninteresting causes. Perhaps most important, the public mass transit interests were for years unable to crack the huge $5 billion a year Highway Trust Fund, the most easily accessible source of new transportation funds. Thus, mass transit is caught in a series of paradoxes. The systems are local and compete against modes of transport, particularly autos, that are more popular, and whose usability is underwritten by a constant flow of federal dollars for roads.

The companies that manufacture buses are also the same companies that make cars, and they earn much more money from cars. The

[7] See Allan Lupo, Frank Colcord, and Edmund P. Fowler, *Rites of Way: The Politics of Transportation in Boston and the U.S. City* (Boston: Little, Brown, 1971), pp. 171–236. See also William J. Murin, *The Politics of Mass Transportation* (Cambridge, Mass.: Ballinger Publishing, 1974).

companies that engineer rail systems and make rail cars have an obvious interest in mass transit, but they do not possess the same resources as private interests in the highway lobby. Some minor openings in the Highway Trust Fund have been voted, but without releasing large amounts of the Trust monies. We will see in the next 10 years how shortages and higher prices for gasoline affect federal transit policy.

MASS TRANSIT POLITICS IN METROPOLITAN AREAS

Frank Colcord reported on mass transit systems of operation, governance, and politics in seven metropolitan areas: Boston, Baltimore, St. Louis, Kansas City, Houston, San Francisco, and Seattle. In addition, Colcord drew on a separate project in Los Angeles and studies of New York City.[8] A close examination makes clear the divergent patterns involved in metropolitan mass transit.

Only four states—New York, Pennsylvania, Massachusetts, and Rhode Island—provide significant monies for urban transit. Only a few states have agencies with some responsibilities in the urban transit field. Of these, the most extensive state efforts are found in New York and New Jersey; there are agencies with more limited functions in California and Wisconsin. The result is that the urban transit field is left to the planning, financing, and organizing capacities of the localities affected. Colcord observes that "with few exceptions, governors of urban states do not have any regular means of receiving advice on total urban transportation problems or on transit in particular."[9]

METROPOLITAN TRANSIT AUTHORITIES

An urban transit system typically organizes as a regional or subregional independent authority. Responsibilities, territory, systems, and format for political control vary a great deal. In Boston and St. Louis, the systems have regional jurisdiction, full operating duties and, in terms of governance, are essentially state boards whose directors are appointed by the governor. For other authorities, the commissioners or directors are chosen by a set of local communities. The transit authorities are the premier independent metropolitan special districts. Operating much as private businesses, they are not bound by traditional city civil service, purchasing, or contracting rules. They care about balancing budgets and labor relations.

---

[8] Michael N. Danielson, *Federal-Metropolitan Politics and the Commuter Crisis* (New York: Columbia University Press, 1965); and Jameson W. Doig, *Metropolitan Transportation Politics in the New York Region* (New York: Columbia University Press, 1966).

[9] Op. cit., p. 176.

Weaknesses of Transit Authorities. Transit authorities often have to accept technically unqualified, political appointees to keep peace with various political decision-making bodies. Their need to maintain a businesslike posture and to finance many operations in private money markets reinforces a conservative pattern of behavior. Transit authorities in most metropolitan areas work within a difficult decision-making mileu. There is, for example, no one transportation system or any one body responsible for or concerned with transportation problems. Rail commuter service, metropolitan transit (subways, buses, trolleys, ferries), and highway development compete with each other for funds and users. All the impediments to metropolitan cooperation come together in the politics of transit development.

CRIME AND THE POLICE AS LOCAL ISSUES

Crime affects individuals, property, and attitudes about the quality of life. A good way to conceptualize the crime problem is to consider three types of crime: street crime, organized crime, and white-collar crime.

Street Crimes What most people think about when they mention crime are the street crimes of personal attacks on individuals or their property: homicide, muggings, rape, armed robbery, breaking and entering, and burglary. Those who commit street crimes may or may not be professionals, but they usually operate apart from any systematic organization.

The amount of street crime is a matter of uncertainty. The basic source of crime data is the FBI Uniform Crime Reports, which rely on local police reports. The accuracy of these local reports varies widely. In addition, people who are the victims of crimes often do not report them to the police. Although all murders get reported, the police are informed of only about two thirds of all robberies and perhaps as few as one half of all assaults. Rape is an especially unreported crime. Many persons who are the victims of crimes believe that the police will not be able to help and are too embarrassed to report.

It is difficult to analyze whether there is more crime in America than there used to be or what the chief causal factors are.[10] Certainly, crime is more publicized and the public is sensitized to it. Crime

---

[10] For a basic introduction to this issue, see The President's Commission on Law Enforcement and the Administration of Justice, *The Challenge of Crime in a Free Society* (Washington, D.C.: U.S. Government Printing Office, 1967).

increases with industrialization and with urbanization, and rates are highest in the urban centers. Yet, among cities, there is still wide variation in the overall crime rates and, especially, in the rates of violent crime. Table 9-1 indicates the rather stunning differences in the rates of crime for different metropolitan areas. Criminal activity is highest among young males, and the proportion of young men in the American population increased from 1945 until 1980. But, on the other hand, the rate of increase of young men was not as great as the increase in violent crime.

Some summary data on street crime can be presented with certainty. In 1960, there were 2,015,000 reported major crimes; by 1977, the number grew to over 10 million. The annual rate increase remained at close to 14 percent a year from the early 1960s until the late 1970s. At that point, the rates actually began to show a slight decline nationwide. There are fewer murders per 100,000 population today than there were in the 1930s or the exceptionally bloody period that followed the Civil War. There are fewer armed robberies today per 100,000 population than there were in the 1930s. The risk of burglary,

TABLE 9-1. Crime Rates per 100,000 Population for Different Metropolitan Areas (Includes Cities and Suburbs)

Metropolitan Area (SMSA)	Total Crime Index° (rate per 100,000)	Violent Crime†	Property Crime‡
Abilene, Tex.	3,742	174	3,568
Akron, Ohio	5,489	457	5,031
Atlanta, Ga.	5,673	590	5,083
Baltimore, Md.	6,433	971	5,461
Boston, Mass.	5,708	515	5,192
Detroit, Mich.	6,673	825	5,848
Fargo, N.D.	3,934	116	3,817
Houston, Tex.	6,026	468	5,557
Knoxville, Tenn.	3,934	300	3,633
Los Angeles, Calif.	7,013	1,004	6,009
Manchester, N.H.	3,869	108	3,760
New York, N.Y.	7,442	1,339	6,103
St. Louis, Mo.	5,806	663	5,142
San Francisco, Calif.	7,939	768	7,170
Seattle, Wash.	6,387	478	5,908

* The total crime index = violent crimes + property crimes.
† Violent crimes = murder, forcible rape, robbery, and aggravated assault.
‡ Property crime = burglary, larceny of $50 and over, and auto theft.
SOURCE: Federal Bureau of Investigation, *Uniform Crime Reports*, 1977 (Washington, D.C.: U.S. Government Printing Office, 1978).

however, is substantially greater, and more people have the kinds of possessions—color televisions, radios, etereos—that can be stolen and resold on black markets.

Different segments of the urban population bear different risks. Police maps divide cities and metropolitan areas into subunits, which indicate clearly that some areas are more crime-prone than others. In general, the most likely victims of violent crimes are poor blacks and poor whites living in the central cities. The risk of violent crime in central cities is five times as great as in small communities, and the risk of burglary is twice as great. Although the suburbs are safer, suburban crime rates have been rising rapidly.

Individual citizens are very conscious of the potential danger of street crime, even when the actual risk of physical assault is slight, as it is in higher-priced suburban communities. The well-to-do respond with private home protection systems, alarm systems, and even, in some areas, walled subdivisions with private police. Lacking the money for such protection, citizens in central cities organize their personal lives to reduce the risk. In two large cities, 43 per cent of the citizens in high crime areas said they stayed off the streets at night because of fear; 35 per cent would not speak to strangers; and 21 per cent used cars and cabs at night instead of walking, because they were afraid.

It is easy to understand the intense fear of crime. People feel forces beyond their control are at work and that the criminal justice system cannot help. There is some real justification for the feeling of helplessness. Figure 9-3 indicates the relationship of law enforcement efforts to crime. Of known offenses, less than 20 per cent led to arrest, and only 2 per cent lead to someone being jailed. Because actual crime may be as much as two and a half times the amount of reported crime, the percentage of persons jailed represents less than 1 per cent of all crimes.

Organized Crime. Street crime is what most people talk about and what most people fear. Yet, in dollar terms, organized crime is more extensive. Such crime consists of systematically organized conspirators, some of whom operate for brief periods and others that have 70-year continuous histories. Organized into gangs of families, and perhaps even loosely linked on a national basis, these criminals break laws in clear ways. Primarily, they provide illegal services to other Americans who want to buy them. The person who is robbed does not seek a relationship with a criminal. A person who places an illegal bet, patronizes a call girl, borrows money from a loan shark, enters into an

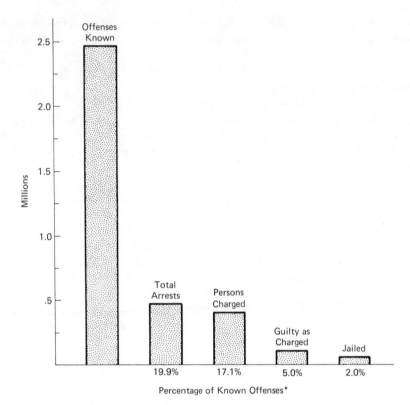

FIGURE 9-3. Law Enforcement Success Against Crime. (SOURCE: *1970 Statistical Abstract of the United States.*)

elaborate financial fraud, or buys illegal drugs wants to do what he is doing.

Organized crime has some particularly local consequences. Most gangs, syndicates, and families began as purveyors of illegal services to a neighborhood ethnic market, and then branched out to cover parts of cities or whole cities. Operating in this territorial fashion, organized criminals have typically come from whatever ethnic groups are at the bottom of the American socioeconomic ladder and are most discriminated against: the Irish in the nineteenth century; the Jews at the turn of the century until the 1940s; the Italians beginning in the 1920s and continuing to the present; and since the 1960s, blacks and Spanish-speaking persons. Organized crime is very lucrative and creates an illicit channel for social mobility.

Organized criminals are businessmen who organize black markets. Unable to use the legal system to enforce their agreements, they rely on their own armed violence or threat of violence. The sources of their revenue have shifted somewhat over the decades. At the turn of the century, prostitution was the main source of gang income; during Prohibition, it was liquor (and Prohibition ironically capitalized organized criminals into big businessmen); during the 1940s and 1950s, it was gambling. Today, gambling, loan sharking, systematic financial fraud, and the drug trade are the main sources of funds. Many organized crime families have heavy investments in legitimate businesses, including nightclubs, restaurants, hotels and motels, linen and towel services, garbage removal, and trucking.

Some paradoxes about organized crime peculiarly affect local law enforcement. There could be no organized crime if society did not enact into law moral preferences that some people hold strongly but others reject. There could be no organized crime without political corruption, which has to be at the local level where the illegal services are distributed. Some of the corruption takes the form of funds for political campaigns. An estimated 15 per cent of all state and local campaign funds come from the underworld.[11]

The part of the corruption that most concerns us here, however, has to do with the police. Periodically, scandals rock the police departments of large cities and there are lurid disclosures of policemen on "the pad," receiving regular payoffs from crime interests in return for ignoring illegal operations in their territories.[12] Police procedures, historically, were designed to insulate the police from such temptations; one such precaution is civil service exams, as opposed to appointment by political sponsorship. Yet, the scandals continue to occur. New York State appointed a special prosecutor to monitor the activities of the New York City criminal justice system and to uproot systematic corruption. Chicago is periodically wracked by exposures of high-ranking officers receiving systematic payoffs.

White-Collar Crime. Various tax scandals, the Watergate affair, and revelations of corporate bribery made the American public aware

[11] See Alexander Heard, *The Costs of Democracy* (Garden City, N.Y.: Doubleday, Anchor Books, 1962), p. 142.

[12] See Arthur Maas, *Serpico* (New York: Bantam Books, 1973) for the story of a major New York scandal. See John Gardiner, *The Politics of Corruption* (New York: Russell Sage Foundation, 1970) for the description of organized crime in an unnamed Pennsylvania community.

of white-collar crime committed by respectable individuals.[13] There almost seems to be a class structure to American crime: street crime for (and against) the lower classes, organized crime for the aspiring middle class, and white-collar crime at the upper-class level. White-collar crime includes corporate price-fixing, fraud, illegal campaign contributions, individual and corporate tax evasion, as well as outright bribery and perjury. White-collar crime also includes governmental crime, the illegal use of public authority and resources for personal and political ends.

THE POLICE FUNCTION: AN OVERVIEW

The criminal justice system consists of courts, correctional institutions, correctional officers, and police. The police work where crime is most acute, on the street. Police spend much time in various routines, patrolling areas of the community on foot or in cars, conversing with residents as part of an effort to develop intelligence information, appearing in court on pending cases, writing reports, providing information to citizens, handling medical emergencies, or responding to domestic disputes.[14]

Few local police forces deal very effectively with organized crime or white-collar crime. Individual urban police forces that are successful against these forms of crime use special units within their general forces. Against street crime, police have mixed success. They arrest someone in 59 per cent of cases involving violence, often because they obtain identification of the criminal from the victim.[15] But apprehension of offenders for property crimes is low—only 22 per cent of those reported. The law enforcement burden of the police is enormous.

Police Organization. For police services, control is local. Only 50 of 40,000 separate law enforcement agencies are federal, 200 are state, and the remaining 39,750 are dispersed among counties, cities, towns, and villages, the units of local government. Of these, more than 3,000 are county forces; about 3,700, city forces; and the remainder are distributed among smaller local government units.

---

[13] See the classic *White Collar Crime* by Edwin H. Sutherland, first published in 1949 and republished with a foreword by Donald R. Cressy by Holt, Rinehart and Winston, 1961.

[14] See National Advisory Commission on Civil Disorders, *Supplemental Studies*, "Police in the Ghetto," (Washington, D.C.: U.S. Government Printing Office, 1968), pp. 106–107.

[15] The President's Commission on Law Enforcement and the Administration of Justice, *Task Force Report: The Police* (Washington, D.C.: U.S. Government Printing Office, 1967), p. 1.

The federal agencies enforce national laws—taxes, interstate theft, counterfeiting, and narcotics. Federal forces provide identification services and training programs at the FBI and underwrite the costs of advanced education for local policemen through the Law Enforcement Assistance Agency. But, overall, the federal government plays a minor direct role in local police operations. The major federal impact on local enforcement may be through Supreme Court decisions that define constitutionally acceptable police practice in the arrest, questioning, and detention of criminal suspects.

The state governments have the constitutional responsibility for maintaining law and order within their borders. They enact criminal codes and control the prosecutorial, judicial, and correctional aspects of criminal justice. But they delegate most police duties to local forces. State police enforce traffic laws, provide identification and communications systems, and work with state and county attorneys in investigations.

Thus, local autonomy and decentralization of police prevail. Within any given metropolitan area, there are numerous legally independent police forces, often one for each incorporated locality, and each with its own territorial jurisdiction.[16] Figure 9-4 illustrates this tradition for the Detroit metropolitan area. County police serve unincorporated areas within metropolitan population clusters. Urban counties, such as Los Angeles County, sell police services on a contract basis to smaller incorporated communities, under the "Lakewood Plan."

Internal Police Organization and Issues in Recruitment and Behavior. Most big-city police forces are hierarchically organized and take their model from business management. To these principles add military command, because police, as paramilitary forces, legally use violence. Yet, as Elinor Ostrom and others observe, the police may best be understood as large-scale bureaucracies.[17] Most forces are

---

[16] For many citizens, this fragmentation may correspond to quite good services. See Roger B. Parks, "Police Patrol in Metropolitan Areas—Implications for Restructuring the Police," in *The Delivery of Urban Services*, Elinor Ostrom, ed. (Beverly Hills: Sage Publications, 1976), pp. 261–284.

[17] See Elinor Ostrom, "Institutional Arrangements and the Measurement of Policy Consequences: Applications to Evaluating Police Performance," *Urban Affairs Quarterly*, 6:1 (June 1971), pp. 447–475; E. Terrence Jones, "Evaluating Everyday Policies: Police Activity and Crime Incidence," *Urban Affairs Quarterly*, 8:3 (March 1973), pp. 267–280; and Elinor Ostrom, Roger B. Parks, and Gordon Whitaker, *Patterns of Metropolitan Policing* (Cambridge, Mass.: Ballinger Publishing Co., 1978).

FIGURE 9-4.   Fragmentation of Urban Police. [SOURCE: President's Commission on Law Enforcement and Criminal Justice, *Task Force Report: The Police* (Washington, D.C.: U.S. Government Printing Office, 1967), p. 69.]

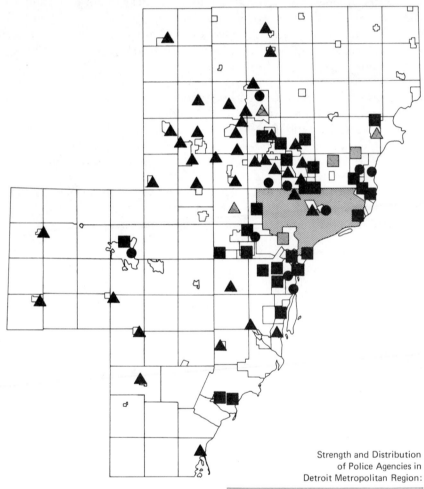

Strength and Distribution
of Police Agencies in
Detroit Metropolitan Region:

Number of Men	Departments	Code
0-20	40	▲
21-50	27	◼
51-100	10	●
101-150	5	△
151-200	2	▨
201-5000	1	▨

highly oriented to their own internal mores and procedures. They recruit, primarily from lower-middle-class backgrounds, persons who tend to be highly accepting of authority and are comfortable in the difficult and authoritarian world of police work.[18] Police forces promote to field command and central administration, as well as the more prestigious plainclothes jobs, almost entirely from within. There is little circulation of personnel from the nonpolice world into police work or among policemen from different cities. So most police forces, inbred by nature, view themselves as separate from civilian society.

The difficulty of police work accentuates this view.[19] Faced with very real dangers on the street, perceiving themselves as resented by some segments of the population, and held to a narrow line of legality by the courts, the police see the world as "us versus them." Table 9-2 contains the perceptions of more than 400 police of the satisfactions and dissatisfactions of the job. Most satisfying is working with other police officers and with police supervisors. Most troublesome is the lack of respect from citizens and the pay.

[18] See William K. Muir, Jr., "The Development of Policemen." Paper presented at the Sixty-Sixth Annual Meeting of the American Political Science Association, Los Angeles, September 8–12, 1970.

[19] See Jonathan Rubinstein, *City Police* (New York: Farrar, Straus & Giroux, 1973).

TABLE 9-2.   The Policeman's Satisfactions and Dissatisfactions with His Job

	Dissatisfied		Satisfied				No An-swer
	Very	Some-what	Very	Some-what	Don't Know	*100*	
	Per Cent	Per Cent	Per Cent	Per Cent	Per Cent		
The respect you get from citizens	22	32	10	33	1	(434)	3
Pay	28	26	9	36	0	(435)	2
Physical danger you often face	17	32	11	28	11	(431)	1
Resources and facilities for your job	22	27	19	31	0	(436)	1
Working conditions	13	34	11	42	0	(436)	1
Flexibility in doing your job	15	22	24	38	1	(435)	—
Other policemen with whom you work	2	12	52	33	1	(436)	1
Your supervisor	3	10	51	33	1	(432)	2

SOURCE: National Advisory Commission on Civil Disorders, *Supplemental Studies* (Washington, D.C.: U.S. Government Printing Office, 1968), p. 106.

Citizen Views of the Police.   Overall, citizens approve of the police, with approximately 70 per cent thinking that the police do a good job of enforcing the laws and the same percentage showing a "great deal" of respect for the police.[20] Further, these data showed a marked increase in supportive attitudes over similar studies conducted in the 1940s. Local studies substantiate these nationwide data. For example, a study of three precincts in Washington, D.C., showed that 60 per cent of the people thought the police had a high reputation in their neighborhood, 85 per cent thought that the police deserved more thanks than they got, 68 per cent thought the police should get more pay, and 78 per cent thought that only a few policemen were responsible for bad publicity. Similar studies of San Diego and Philadelphia found that white community leaders thought police-community relations were good, with some dissent, and similar findings emerged from a 16-jurisdiction Michigan state study.[21]

Citizens' attitudes toward the police depend on the life circumstances of the people questioned, on the likelihood of their having any contact with the police, and on the form these contacts take. Thus, the more upper or middle class the community (and the less crime there is in the community), the more favorable attitudes toward the police are. Citizens in such communities come into contact with police in friendly, nonconfrontational situations, where police are at their most polite and helpful. On the other hand, from a wide range of national surveys, respondents in minority communities hold a very different view of police.

Police-Minority Relations.   Confrontations between police and members of minority groups are much more frequent. Various police practices, particularly in ghetto neighborhoods, arouse bitter resentment. Particularly resented are stop-and-search procedures that police often use in high crime, poverty neighborhoods, and the lack of respect that black people especially believe police have toward them. For example, in a 15-city study, 43 per cent of all black men and 38 per cent of all black women believed that the police did not show respect for people in their neighborhood and used insulting language. More than 40 per cent thought that people were stopped and searched without good reason, and about the same percentage thought that police rough people up unnecessarily when they are arresting them, or afterwards. Yet, the minority view of the police is not limited to poor blacks.

---

[20] President's Commission on Law Enforcement and the Administration of Justice, *Task Force Report: The Police,* op. cit., p. 145.

[21] Ibid., p. 146.

In fact, blacks with higher education report more insults, searches without cause, and stopping of their cars without cause.

Just as race is a pre-eminent problem of American urban life, it is also a major factor in any consideration of police practices. Efforts have been undertaken to improve relationships. Most police departments have community relations departments and special officers, but these attempts are viewed as simply public relations gimmicks. Police are being sent to college classes and to sensitivity courses in record numbers to try to raise the level of awareness of minority views and problems. Some critics think that improvement is unlikely until more members of minority groups are recruited into the forces. Others hope that the election of black mayors will lead to the improvement of minority-police relations.

The Police in Local Politics. Throughout the history of American cities the police have been an important factor in local politics. In the late 1800s, as modern forces were developed, police jobs and promotions were often part of the patronage of local ward and party leaders. These leaders often had a stake in lax vice law enforcement. Throughout the twentieth century, most big-city forces have been centralized and bureaucratized, and thus the connections between politics and police have become less direct and more complicated. In recent years, former policemen won mayoralty posts in Los Angeles, Philadelphia, and Minneapolis, and held high elective office in New York City. How successful police can be as an interest group varies from city to city. The key variable seems to be how centralized or decentralized power is in the community to begin with, especially how strong the mayor is. Ruchelman found a standoff in New York, rather complete policy cooptation (and eventual election of the mayor) in Philadelphia, and the mayor in charge in Chicago.[22]

EDUCATION

Education is always a crucial local issue. Local governments share control over education with state governments to a great degree and with the federal government to a lesser, though still important, degree. Although local communities maintain some universities and numerous two-year community colleges, our concern will be with publicly

---

[22] "Police Politics: A Comparison of Three Cities," Paper presented at the 1971 Annual Meeting of the American Political Science Association, Chicago, Illinois, September 7–11, 1971; and *Police Politics: A Comparative Study of Three Cities* (Cambridge: Ballinger Publishing, 1974).

supported elementary and secondary education. Forty-six million students attend these publicly funded schools. In addition, 5 million students enroll in private schools, primarily Catholic-supported schools.

These millions of students are educated in some 88,000 schools under the jurisdiction of about 20,000 school districts. Public elementary and secondary education, viewed collectively, is one of the largest enterprises in the nation, spending more than $107 billion each year on operating expenses. More than two million school teachers are employed in the classrooms. Hundreds of thousands of administrative personnel work in public education—in the schools, in the school districts, in state education departments, in federal education administration units, in educational training programs in the state universities, and in private foundations.

Public schools have taken responsibility for inculcating public and group values since education first became mandatory for all children, beginning with Massachusetts in 1852 (and extending to all states when adopted by Mississippi in 1918). The initial goal of universal childhood free education was to provide educated citizens. Contemporary public schools, however, are asked to do far more than simply socialize students into citizenship. They are supposed to provide technical skills necessary for employment; to be a channel of upward mobility for racially disadvantaged groups; to promote an integrated society or, in the views of others, cultural awareness on the part of minorities; to help children adjust psychologically to each other and the world; to improve the health and nutrition of children through special programs; to teach children to appreciate the arts through exposure to music and fine arts; to make children aware of public values such as driving safely or avoiding drugs; and to keep America ahead of other nations in skilled and motivated scientists and engineers.

Less explicitly, schools are expected to keep students out of trouble and off the job market until a certain age. They are viewed by parents as protectors of the dominant life-style values of the neighborhood, the city, or the suburb involved. As such, what is taught, how it is taught, the tone, and the reputation of the school concern many different people. Certain basic controversies occur in every metropolitan area.

RACIAL INTEGRATION, EQUALITY, AND SCHOOL BUSING

In 1954, in *Brown* v. *Board of Education*, the Supreme Court found the Southern system of racially separated schools unconstitutional. The Court based its verdict on a finding that such segregated schools were inherently unequal in their impact upon children. This

1954 decision did not address the somewhat different Northern problem of *de facto* segregation, in which schools lacked racial integration
because of the accidents of residence and social class rather than any
malign and deliberate social policy. The legal situation today is that all
racial segregation by law is illegal. Any segregation of schools that
results from the drawing of neighborhood school lines in the past or
the present with *intent* to segregate is illegal and may be corrected by
court order throughout an entire school district. But segregation that is
a genuine accident of residence is outside the corrective powers of the
courts. Nor have the courts yet been allowed to combine independent
school districts in a metropolitan area to create integrated schools for
all.

According to the latest available data, nationwide approximately
37 per cent of all black students attended public schools with less than
half of the students black; the comparable figure for Spanish-speaking
students was 42 per cent in schools less than half Hispanic. These
figures represent large increases over 15 years ago, but leave a long
distance to travel.

THE ACADEMIC BENEFITS OF INTEGRATION

Early studies showed distinct benefits to minority children from
school integration. But subsequent studies cast doubt on those early
findings and uncover little consistent, positive academic gains. The
arguments and the findings about school integration may be sum-
marized as follows. First, those who favor desegregation argue that
black students obtain access to high-quality academic resources they
are otherwise denied, particularly science laboratories, smaller classes,
and experienced and better educated teachers. The reply is that in
dollar terms, integrated schools spend only slightly more than segregated schools. In some places, the expenditure may actually be less
(especially where "compensatory" programs increase the spending for
poor schools that are also likely to be racially segregated). Further, one
analysis indicates that neither overall school spending nor particular
kinds of school programs have any consistent improving effect upon
black students' performance on the standard achievement tests.[23]

A second argument of those who favor integration is that it puts
black students in contact with white classmates, and this experience
itself is highly beneficial. Data from the 1966 Coleman Report, *Equality of Educational Opportunity*,[24] bear on this issue. Its starting point

---

[23] Christopher Jencks et al., *Inequality: A Reassessment of the Effect of Family
and Schooling in America* (New York: Basic Books, 1972), p. 98.

[24] (Washington, D.C.: U.S. Government Printing Office, 1966).

was standard pupil achievement tests showing that minority students, with the exception of Oriental Americans, scored lower at every level than white students. The author, James S. Coleman, analyzed what factors might account for low minority achievement scores. He found that "variations in the facilities and curriculums of the schools account for relatively little variation in pupil achievement."[25] The quality of teachers showed a stronger relationship, especially for minority students in the higher grades. But, most important, he discovered that a "pupil's achievement is strongly related to the educational backgrounds and aspirations of the other students in the schools."[26] When minority students from one family background were put into schools with students of a different background, they achieved at higher levels. Thus, the composition of student populations related strongly to the achievement of black and also other minority pupils.

Critics of this second argument about the benefits of desegregation make several points. One is that whether white schoolmates are useful for blacks depends on what happens in a particular school. If students are simply put under the same roof without being brought into the same educational and social community, little good may result. Or if blacks and whites become enemies or if social tensions increase in the community as a result of school integration controversies, education will not be advanced.

A third argument in favor of desegregation is that teachers in integrated schools may expect more of black students, who therefore will learn more than in black schools. There is little empirical evidence but a great deal of impressionistic writing that suggests little optimism about this point. The popular works of Jonathan Kozol and John Holt suggest strongly that there is often hostility, especially in big-city urban schools, among white teachers toward minority students and toward economically deprived children generally.[27]

A fourth argument is that desegregation as a symbolic gesture may persuade minority students that they have a chance to get ahead in the larger society. Christopher Jencks, who believes that the academic benefits of integration would narrow only a small portion of the achievement test differences between whites and blacks, offers a related argument. That is, "if we want a desegregated society, then we should have desegregated schools."[28] It becomes a matter of values.

[25] Ibid., p. 22.

[26] Ibid., p. 22.

[27] Jonathan Kozol, *Death at an Early Age: The Destruction of the Hearts and Minds of Negro Children in the Boston Public Schools* (Boston: Houghton, Mifflin, 1967); and John Holt, *The Underachieving School* (New York: Pitman, 1969).

[28] Jencks, op. cit., p. 106.

Critics of this perspective argue that the symbolism may not be worthwhile if teachers and students in white schools are hostile to blacks. In a different variation on this theme, many black educators feel that it is better for the personal development of black children to be educated in schools that feature "community control" by blacks and that teach racial pride and cultural awareness.

SCHOOL BUSING

One way to integrate schools even when neighborhoods are segregated is to transport children by bus so as to achieve racial balance. Busing causes enormous controversy where it is used as a tool of desegregation. As a matter of fact, children have been transported to school by bus, especially in rural areas, for at least 50 years, and the use of buses in sprawling suburban districts became common after World War II. All told, today slightly more than 40 per cent of all public school students are bused, of whom from 2 to 4 per cent are bused specifically for desegregation purposes.[29] Busing accounts for 3.6 per cent of total public school costs.

Busing has been used for desegregation only within individual cities or counties. Various federal courts considered consolidating independent school districts as a way of overcoming the barrier that white suburbs present to blacks, but no such plan has been put into effect yet. The United States Supreme Court has been cautious in confronting busing, as well as northern *de facto* segregation overall. The Court ruled busing legal, as one tool of desegregation, but held that busing should not be used if the time or distance involved endangered the child's health or education.

Busing has been ordered in a variety of both southern and northern cities. Among cities affected have been Pontiac, Pasadena, Detroit, Denver, Harrisburg, Charlotte, Rochester, Chicago, Evanston, Berkeley, Hartford, Boston, and Los Angeles. There has also been experimentation with small-scale, voluntary programs of busing black children to white suburban schools. The opposition to busing among the overall American public is strong, and busing plans are put into effect only after federal or state court orders. In one national poll, 70 per cent of the public opposed busing, despite the fact that in the same poll 67 per cent said they favored school integration.[30]

[29] See United States Commission on Civil Rights, *Your Child and Busing*, Clearinghouse Publication No. 36 (Washington, D.C.: U.S. Government Printing Office, 1972), p. 7.
[30] United States Commission on Civil Rights, "Public Knowledge and Busing Opposition" (Washington, D.C.: Mimeo, March 1973), Appendix I, p. 1.

The effects of busing are hotly disputed. James S. Coleman, whose work in the 1960s stirred hopes for integrated schools, argued in the 1970s that busing actually impeded integration, by encouraging frightened whites to move out of big cities or to put their children in private schools.[31] He maintained that busing plans accelerated the "white flight" to the suburbs, especially in larger districts with a high proportion of minorities and surrounded by accessible nonminority suburbs. Others disputed his "white flight" thesis.[32] In sum, busing remains a controversial public policy, affecting the lives of hundreds of thousands of children and parents. David J. Armor comments that "school desegregation has such an incredible ideological momentum that objective and rational assessment of its true effects often seems unattainable."[33]

PUBLIC SCHOOL FINANCING

Most school monies are raised from the property tax. The federal government provides about 9 per cent, and state governments, an average of 40 per cent. Costs have risen consistently in response to the successful negotiating efforts of organized teachers to improve their salaries. Cost increases must be added to property taxes, which are frequently either collected separately or clearly allocated on the property owner's bill to go toward schools. Voters with regularity defeat referenda to raise tax rates to pay for school costs. Many local districts, particularly in the suburbs, burdened themselves with enormous capital costs to accommodate the post-World War II baby boom and expanded their school facilities. For many, the costs remain, even now as school populations, reflecting the changing age structure of the country, decline.

A basic issue is the allocation of costs among the three levels of government. The federal share has remained stationary since the 1960s and seems unlikely to increase. The size of the state share varies. Wealthier states and more urbanized states spend more per pupil than do poorer and more rural states. However, the proportionate share of total costs borne by the poorer state governments may be the same, and the effort to support schools may be greater than that of the richer states considering available resources. Four states have adopted total state financing of local education costs.

Costs are bound up with other issues. One is who controls what

[31] See James S. Coleman, "Population Stability and Equal Rights," *Society*, 14:4 (May-June 1977), pp. 34–36.

[32] See Christine Rossell, "The Effect of School Desegregation in White Flight," *Political Science Quarterly*, 90 (Winter 1975), pp. 675–695.

[33] "The Dangers of Forced Integration," *Society*, 14:4 (May-June, 1977), p. 44.

goes on the schools—how much teachers will be paid, who will be hired with what qualifications, what the physical facilities will be, what will be taught as part of the curriculum, what the size of classes will be, how much emphasis will be placed on sports and other extracurricular activities, and how much will be spent on special programs of various kinds. The issue of equality is also bound up with the problem of cost. We have been examining equality from the perspective of equality of *results* for different segments of the population. Another perspective is equality of expenditures on pupils in different school districts.

The current expenditures controversy is over the amounts spent on pupils in different school districts within individual states. The total resources available to any individual school district vary according to the values of the homes and businesses it can tax. Wealthier districts spend more to educate pupils than poorer districts do. Wealthier districts with a lower tax *rate* can actually spend more on students than can poorer districts because the former have greater potential resources upon which to draw. Many poor districts have higher tax rates on property than do wealthier ones. The effect is to translate wealth into public school benefits for children who live in more prosperous communities. Formulas for state aid to districts, called "foundation" programs or "equalization" programs, aim at leveling off these disparities, but their impact has been small.

The United States Supreme Court rejected school financing equality as a constitutional requirement, leaving the problem for the states. Several state courts ordered greater efforts at equalization. City school leaders are often ambiguous in their responses. Many urban schools already spend more, especially with compensatory programs for deprived children, than other districts. Equalization might actually drain money from their programs. In the suburbs, the fear is that, as one possibility, a ceiling could be put on the money spent on education, a direct challenge to the suburban effort to preserve life-style values. Or, as another alternative, money might be drained from wealthier suburbs to pay for education in poorer suburbs or in rural areas.

THE POLITICS OF EDUCATION: RESPONSIBILITIES OF DIFFERENT LEVELS OF GOVERNMENT

The Federal Role. The federal government pays less than 10 per cent of the public education bill. The main federal legislative act, the Elementary and Secondary Education Act of 1965, provides aid to districts with concentrations of children from low-income families, for libraries and materials, and for supplementary services of various kinds. The major federal impact comes through the Supreme Court and the federal district courts. The Supreme Court defines what constitutes integration and equal opportunity. The district courts approve or disapprove specific plans for busing in individual cities and counties. Generally, the courts have been far ahead of public opinion. Those branches closer to the electoral process have been reluctant to risk the pressures and conflicts. Having established their role in educational decision making, the courts are not likely to retreat now.

The State Role.   State control over public education has increased steadily over the last 30 years. State law indicates how tax money can be raised and often sets limits on rates and total amounts, as well as ceilings on borrowing for capital expenditures. State education departments fix the number of days a school must hold classes to qualify for state aid, set the standards for the training of teachers, manage the certification program, require certain tests and courses in the curriculum, and monitor school performance.

Local school boards, teachers, and administrators develop ties with state officials. Dubbed "the schoolmen" by Robert H. Salisbury, they include those in the state education department along with statewide associations of administrators and teachers.[34] These officials and group leaders sometimes take different positions on the amounts of money to be allocated to different policies. But they unite on one perspective, namely, in promoting education as a field in which the most important decisions should be made by experts. They support each other at the state and local levels against various other claimants—civil rights groups, business, labor, and agricultural interests, as well as elected political leaders.

The Local Role.   Localities retain primary control. For example, local decisions determine the curriculum, the number and location of school buildings, the size of classes, the selection and termination of personnel, and the total amount of money to be spent. With decisions of that magnitude, competition is intense among various groups and factions.

A typical listing of participants includes the following:

1. *Professional administrators*—superintendents, their assistants, and principals—are activists in setting local policy. They claim professional expertise and urge the elected school board and the public to follow their advice. The specific views of these professionals vary from setting to setting, but their claim to expertise, to "keeping the

---

[34] "State Politics and Education," in *Politics and the American States*, ed. by Herbert Jacob and Kenneth N. Vines, 2nd ed. (Boston: Little Brown, 1971), pp. 388–432.

schools out of politics," is a frequent defense against efforts by others to be involved in setting school policy.

2.   *Teachers* in American public education are highly organized. Nationwide, the largest organization is the National Education Association (NEA). In the largest cities, the American Federation of Teachers (AFT), affiliated with the national AFL-CIO and conceiving of itself in traditional trade union terms, is often the legal bargaining agent for teaching personnel. The NEA for years spurned strikes, but, spurred by the success of AFT locals, it too now resorts to job actions. Fall strikes are commonplace in numerous cities. Teachers' contract concerns are not only wages and benefits, but also the terms for the hiring and firing of personnel, the size of classes, and working conditions in schools. Well-organized, politically conscious, and sophisticated, the teachers exert a powerful force in school politics.

3.   *Local citizens* participate in school decisions. Many spending decisions require approval on referenda. Most important, almost all public schools are still governed by ordinary citizens—the school board. In some communities, the mayor still appoints school board members but, in most, they are elected independently and in a nominally nonpartisan manner. School boards often possess independent taxing powers.

The board makes all of the decisions—hiring, spending, subject matter, capital plant. School board elections can become very intense. There is little empirical evidence about the kinds of people who become members of school boards, about what motivates people to take on these unpaid, time-consuming, and often tension-ridden positions. Nor is there any systematic evidence about the kinds of conditions under which boards act independently of the professional schoolmen, particularly the superintendent, and under which they accede to the desires of the professionals. Probably the socioeconomic and life-style characteristics of the particular community have a great deal to do with school board styles. In the big cities, where disagreement exists about the goals of the schools, school boards are probably more divided, or at least more inured to conflict, than in upper-middle-class suburbs, where there is a greater consensus. School boards have become more professionalized. Their need to negotiate with teacher's organizations leads them into national organizations of their own.

Citizens engage in group lobbying over educational policy. Many organizations focus on school issues as a regular part of their participation in local politics. Such groups appear most frequently in the big cities, with their heterogeneous interests. In addition, *ad hoc* groups form around particular issues, related to programs, to personnel, and to the form of governance of the school system itself. For example, in several large cities citizens urged decentralization of the school system into semiautonomous, smaller districts, each with "community control" over aspects of school operation.

Suburban citizen participation in schools seems to be less structured than in the larger cities, perhaps because communities are more homogenous and group interests less organized. But *ad hoc* citizen groups form with regularity, and passions can become aroused over educational policy. School prestige and quality become synonymous with preservation of the life-style values of the entire community.

4. *Elected political leaders* stand in an ambiguous relationship to the schools. In most cities elected public officials have had very little official say in school policy for many years. Yet, if schools are the most important single expenditure item in the municipal budget, the case could be made that the most visible and accountable public officials should be involved.[35] Where school boards report to mayors, the boards obtain the political backing they need within their own communities and with state legislatures. The precedents for "keeping the schools out of politics" are strong, but more elected officials are likely to become involved in the future.

DECENTRALIZATION OF LOCAL GOVERNMENTS AS A POLICY GOAL

Public services are not the only policy goals of citizens. The structure of local government, as Chapter Five recounted, has long been a major source of public controversy. One structural goal of many citizens seeks to split local governments into smaller units, within either central cities or within the larger suburbs. These subgovernments could manage one service or a set of services, or simply be administrative outposts of the larger government. Such subunits bear the catchy political labels of "decentralization," "neighborhood democracy," or "community control."[36]

Douglas Yates identifies three alternative modes of decentralization.[37] *Political decentralization* emphasizes citizen participation in advisory boards or elected councils, but without control over government administrators or employees. *Administrative decentralization* puts more government administrators on duty at the neighborhood level to increase their flexibility, authority, and accountabil-

[35] See Robert H. Salisbury, "Schools and Politics in the Big City," *Harvard Educational Review*, 37:3 (Summer 1967), pp. 408–424.

[36] For a balanced view of all perspectives, see Joseph F. Zimmerman, *The Federated City: Community Control in Large Cities* (New York: St. Martin's Press, 1972).

[37] *Neighborhood Democracy* (Lexington, Mass.: Lexington Books, 1973), pp. 24–25.

ity. *Community control* gives neighborhood units policy making and administrative control of employees. The greatest controversy emerges from the last alternative, community control.[38]

ARGUMENTS FOR AND AGAINST COMMUNITY CONTROL

Arguments for Community Control. The main arguments for community control are that it gives residents control over the services that most affect their lives and allows them to make sure those services reflect their values. Independent suburbs maximize the values of middle-class whites. Why should not the same control over schools and police be extended to black or Spanish-speaking populations in central cities? In the bigger cities, the populations served would be larger than in many suburbs. Community control over schools in black or Hispanic neighborhoods, for example, would allow the hiring of minority personnel and a curriculum that would reflect group achievements. Having power over services would give residents a sense of self-worth and add to their willingness to help out and support public institutions. In other words, in this argument, the services would be better, the special clientele served would be better off, and the entire community would benefit.

There is some argument over what kinds of services should be decentralized into subgovernments in large central cities, even among those who favor the principle. The list usually includes schools, police patrols, health clinics, parks, and garbage collection. Financing, however, is expected to be done on an areawide basis, which means from the entire central city territory. Likewise, the central city would continue to provide for roads, transit systems, water, sewers, central police service, record keeping, operation of hospitals, universities, libraries, tax assessment, and tax collection.

Arguments Against Community Control. Critics of subgovernment argue that it maximizes group values to the exclusion of common public values. Specifically, they hold that it will intensify racial and economic segregation in the largest cities and prevent federal, state, and local efforts for school and police integration. Furthermore, in southern cities whites could use community control as a device to protect their neighborhoods, as could well-to-do whites in the northern cities. The end result portrays community control in big cities as the fragmentation of government into segregated neighborhood enclaves.

---

[38] See, for example, Milton Kotler, *Neighborhood Government: The Local Foundations of Political Life* (Indianapolis: Bobbs-Merrill, 1969); and Alan A. Altshuler, *Community Control: The Black Demand for Participation in Large American Cities* (New York: Pegasus, 1970).

Worse, perhaps, critics feel poorer neighborhoods would suffer in the following way. Under community control plans, financing is to be for the whole territory, and funds would be equally provided on the basis of population or some need-based formula. But in a city arranged into subdistricts, each with its own budget, people in each neighborhood could calculate whether they were net gainers or losers in terms of their tax money. Independent suburbs do not pay for each other's services. But in subdivided cities with a central tax collection, well-to-do neighborhoods would be expected to finance other neighborhoods. They do that now, in fact, but the money goes into a general treasury without an exact accounting. If the accounting were made, would people subsidize others, especially if total political control were vested in the subunit, rather than in a central political body in which all have representation? Many suspect that funds could not be raised and that subgovernment in big cities would worsen class and racial conflicts.

DECENTRALIZATION IN PRACTICE

At least nine forms of decentralization have been tried in American cities. Yates identifies (1) self-help organizations; (2) advisory boards; (3) neighborhood field offices and little city halls; (4) ombudsman structures (where special officials have the duty of investigating complaints against the government); (5) multiservice centers; (6) model cities programs; (7) community corporations; (8) neighborhood health corporations; and (9) community school boards.[39]

Yates' study of decentralization in New York and New Haven concluded that decentralization forms that dealt with concrete service problems had greater success than those with more broadly defined, less specific tasks.[40] A review of 250 case studies found the major outcomes of decentralization experiments were increased information between servers and served, along with an improvement in services.[41] Decentralization strengthened a neighborhood approach to local policy analysis, improved officials' understanding of neighborhood institutions with citizen participation, sustained human service delivery, and increased accountability of officials. But observers report declining interest in decentralization. Nonetheless, just as interest in local government reform has had its ups and downs for decades, at some point renewed interest may emerge in yet smaller units of local government.

[39] Op. cit., pp. 28–29.
[40] Ibid., p. 66.
[41] Robert K. Yin and Douglas Yates, *Street-Level Governments* (Lexington, Mass.: Lexington Books, 1975), p. 173.

LOCAL ISSUES: SOME CONCLUDING NOTES

This chapter examined the substance of three contemporary urban and suburban issues: transit, crime, and schools. The political response to them is interwoven among the different levels of government. Transit is a particularly metropolitan issue, because solutions involve crossing boundaries, and because planning is involved. As the main source of new money, the federal government is deeply involved in transit. With crime control, the main political response remains local. And with schools, state governments and local citizens and governing agencies are actively in the field. Not all issues in local life are directly substantive. Decentralization would split local governments into yet smaller forms. Discussing this structural innovation illustrates that local policy includes, as always, the form of governance itself.

10

URBAN FUTURES: SOME OPINIONS AND SOME ALTERNATE SCENARIOS

In this concluding chapter, we turn to normative and speculative evaluations of the future. In such an endeavor, judgments are necessarily made about which variables are most likely to be important, about which models most likely describe reality, and about the possibilities of different values being supported in the political process. Systematic speculations of this kind force us to think about the implications of what we know to extend our empirical knowledge. They also focus our own values. What do we *want* to happen?

How can urban futures be analyzed? A common technique identifies the main forces operating in the past and projects them forward into the future. A normative element enters in when the analyst indicates what *should* be done. We approach urban futures in two sections. First, we present the viewpoints of three eminent scholars. Second, we sketch out the author's original scenarios. The scenarios of this second section build on informed expert views.

EXPERT VIEW 1: NORTON LONG'S PROPOSAL FOR A HUMANE COOPERATIVE

In his book *The Unwalled City,* the distinguished urbanist Norton Long starts from a frankly normative perspective.[1] His main concern is

---

[1] Norton Long, *The Unwalled City: Reconstituting the Urban Community,* © 1972 by Basic Books, Inc., Publishers, New York. All quotations printed by permission. Long reiterated his position in "A Marshall Plan for Cities?" *The Public Interest,* **46** (Winter 1977), pp. 48–58.

the older central cities, but he notes that "turning our cities around is of the greatest moment not only to the cities, but to the nation as well."[2] Long discusses the causes of the condition of the modern central cities and proposes aids to cure the worst aspects.

To Long, the sense of community glues a city together. For the first medieval cities, the sense of community rested partially on the city's existence as a defense area, behind walls. But it also rested on a set of shared values that made the urban center different from the peasant countryside. Modern cities are without walls. They are not self-defense communities. Modern industrial cities gained appeal and viability from economic strength. As centers of transport, manufacturing, and commerce, the cities attracted population. The concerns of the older central cities at the height of their power and prosperity were "poverty and prosperity, class, religious, and racial accommodation."[3] The governments of the central cities were able to mobilize men, women, and resources. In contrast to central city governments stood the "toy governments" or "miniatures" of suburbia.

In our era, however, we find a declining set of central cities, many of them fatally ill. Among the damaging factors are changes in transportation, especially the decline of the need for a "hub" of rail and boat transport, and the rise of the car and truck; the aging and obsolete physical structures in the older cities; and a rise in crime and other undesirable social conditions. The major problem facing the central cities is economic rebirth. In fact, "the health of the city is the employment and the upgrading of the employment of its people."[4]

Long sees four areas in which local governments fail to assert their own interests. He criticizes big-city schools for ignoring the world of work in training their students. The interests of the students and the citizenry would be better served by placing young people directly into work situations, in work-study programs, and developing habits of regularity and reliability that would make them attractive to employers.

Long bitterly criticizes the way that city governments have capitulated to what he regards as the cannibalistic demands of municipal workers. Observing that most city employees do work that is either not subject to gains in individual productivity, or not measurable in any case, he points out that most of the rise in municipal expenditures is accounted for by large salary increases. These in turn are reflected in higher tax rates. Further, he cites studies which show that many mu-

---

[2] Ibid., p. xi.
[3] Ibid., p. 46.
[4] Ibid., p. xii.

nicipal services, such as garbage collection, cost more when provided by public employees than by private firms. Local employees' demands are limitless. Elected officials are birds of passage, unable to stand firm, and anxious not to rock the boat.

A third factor Long cites is the abandonment of a historical commitment of big-city governments to take special care to protect the "good" sections of the city. Large cities always possessed neighborhoods and schools of differing quality. The police and sanitation men took better care of the best neighborhoods and that is where the best schools with the best teachers were. The case can certainly be made that in the name of equality of treatment of citizens these practices were unfair, but the practical effect of enforcing equality through all neighborhoods and citywide school systems is to frighten away those who lived in the previously protected places. The result has been to heighten the exodus of middle-class people from the central cities, because these people demand good schools and personal security.

The fourth problem, as Long sees it, is the approach leaders take to their difficulties. They constantly turn to Washington for financial aid, turning the central cities into "reservations."[5] In a "reservation," the officials become caretakers and keepers. Their population is not economically viable. Citizens cannot support themselves. But the outside society wants them docile, and the keepers constantly emphasize this aspect in asking for funds. So the central city is maintained by funds from outside.

THE ELEMENTS OF THE HUMANE COOPERATIVE

Long states his goal for the future:

The unwalled city, open to all with none compelled to stay, must earn a loyalty it cannot require. Ideally, its citizens will be citizens of choice rather than compulsion; its walls will be the shared purposes its activities make possible. That is why the future of the city is as a humane cooperative directed to the improvement of the economic and social condition of its members.[6]

Who will want this city and what will be its appeal?

Its appeal will be to those who need it, need it because they are poor and must pool their scant resources of money and labor to

[5] See Long's article, "The City as Reservation," in *The Public Interest*, **25** (Fall 1971), pp. 22–38.

[6] Ibid., p. 159.

produce what they cannot purchase, because the productive possibilities of active citizenship are nowhere else so possible, and
because the rich diversity of the city offers far more potential for
creativity than the homogenized condition of the like circum-
stanced and like minded. The strength of the city is in its diversity, its varied appeal, capabilities, and activities; its decline has
been accompanied by the homogenization into the city of old industry, old people, the poor, the discriminated against and their
keepers.[7]

Long offers specific suggestions. First, he wants each city to do a
systematic inventory of its assets and liabilities, particularly the employed population. That would give some idea of what skills its people
have. The next step would be to measure the citizen's aptitudes and
capacity to receive training. Then the requirements of jobs in the present mix of industries should be assessed, along with some projection
of what types of skills will be required in the future.

The skills and jobs inventories should be the basis of a thorough-
going reform of big-city education. Long does not minimize the resistance to any such effort. But he feels that if education does not pay off
in jobs, it is useless. Any educational system fails that leaves 20 to 40
per cent of the youths it turns out unemployed or in the worst jobs.

Those who do not receive an education that makes them employ-
able end up in street crime. Long sees the young black male on the
streets contributing to a range of urban ills as well as to the demorali-
zation of the school system. Unemployment of young blacks "may be
one of the more important causes of whosesale losses in property values, the rise in dependency and illegitimacy, and the waste of massive
expenditures in education. . . ."[8] Whatever part of this problem improved, job-oriented education cannot solve, Long hopes better police
practices will. He urges that police develop early warning systems
and do more to prevent crime than to process juveniles "through a
hopelessly inefficient criminal justice system."[9] It is hard to know how
hardened police officials would react to Long's idea that:

one better way might be to use police knowledge of who are
criminals or likely to become criminals, not to try to catch them
and send them to reform schools that do not reform but to put them

---

[7] Ibid., p. 166.
[8] Ibid., p. 166.
[9] Ibid., p. 167.

in touch with those who could at least attempt to interest them in alternatives to criminal occupations.[10]

Above all, Long believes the central cities must reorient themselves to self-help, the encouragement of the profit motive, and the development of entrepreneurs. Small businessmen should be encouraged. City planning should turn to the economics of the city. City governments should learn how their policies affect potential economic development. Long knows the argument that the only hope for the city's poor is to move to the suburbs where much new job creation is. But he rejects such thinking because it is unlikely that the central city poor will be able to move in large numbers. And he does not accept giving up on the central city.

Instead, Long hopes that the poor will be given a sufficient stake in inner-city industries that once again these plants, stores, and offices will be safe. Safety in turn might lure more viable enterprises back. He is particularly hopeful for the development of the health industry, which could be utilized in several fruitful ways. Experience with hospital workers indicates that people who are unskilled or minimally skilled can have their skills upgraded on the job. In addition, in the cities' unused and underused facilities, especially apartments and large older buildings, there is the plant for nursing homes, geriatric care centers, and child care. All of these could hire the cities' poorer people as employees who would be supervised by medical professionals.

Long puts his greatest hopes in the vision that somehow the poor of the cities will pool what resources they do possess to improve themselves and their communities. His model is the success of the Black Muslim Church, which has shown the "capacity to turn criminals, drug addicts, prostitutes, dependents, and other unpromising material into people with self-respect who evince capacity for self-help. . . ."[11] But even if the urban poor are so transformed, he believes that it will take determined leadership and a strong effort to turn around the present direction of the urban bureaucracies. He would like the unions and public employees to see their stake in the city, but notes that there is now no incentive for them to act other than they do, which is to constantly try to bring their wages up to those in the private sector without increasing their productivity. He implies that, failing self-reform by municipal unions, strong leadership should try to bring them to heel. Long is not optimistic about whether his remedies will

[10] Ibid., p. 167.
[11] Ibid., p. 183.

be adopted or, apparently, even certain that they would work if they were. He writes from two traditions: the scholarly observer and also as the lover of the big city with its diversity, traditions, and culture. He ends his book:

> Of all those with power and a rational self-interest in the city's future none have more than the public employees whose own future and that of the city are hopelessly interlocked. Can they be made to see their interest in the city as their cooperative, a producer as well as a consumer cooperative that offers them in every rank a vocation with meaning, challenge, and reward? Can the incentive system of the city unite management, employees, and citizen consumer producers in a humane cooperative to improve the lives of the whole city? These questions will probably remain for the labor movement, the young doctors, the public-interest lawyers, the artists, middle class, the black leaders, who from widely divergent perspectives see a need for a future in the city.[12]

EXPERT VIEW 2: JAY W. FORRESTER'S URBAN DYNAMICS

Professor Jay W. Forrester of the Massachusetts Institute of Technology developed computer models to simulate the dynamics of industrial development. At the urging of former Boston Mayor John F. Collins, a professor at the Institute after he left office, Forrester undertook to apply the same techniques to urban development, and the assumptions of his modeling, the equations, and the results are reported in a book entitled *Urban Dynamics*.[13]

Modeling found many complex systems, such as cities, to be counterintuitive. That is, they give indications that suggest corrective action which often will be ineffective or even adverse in its results. The policies adopted for correcting a difficulty actually intensify it. This happens because of the fundamental difference between a complex system—a city, an economy, a corporation, a government—and simple systems. We are accustomed to situations in which there is only one major variable and in which cause and effect are closely related in time and space. For example, in obtaining warmth from a fire, the main variable is distance from the flame. Too close, and the hands are burned; too far away, and they stay cold.

But complex systems are different. Cause and effect are not usu-

---

12 Ibid., p. 189.
13 (Cambridge, Mass.: MIT Press, 1969).

ally closely connected in time or space. No one variable dominates the behavior. There are a large number of innerconnected relationships. A difficulty in a complex system may be distant in time from the apparent problem, or in a different and remote part of the system from where it appears to be. As a result, a commonsense response to an apparent problem often produces the opposite of the desired effect. The preceding discussion sets the basis for Forrester's controversial findings and recommendations about many traditional "solutions" to urban problems.

THE URBAN DYNAMICS MODEL

Forrester presents a cycle of urban growth and decay, a process he assumes applies to all cities. He assumes that cities start in a national environment with several characteristics. The environment affects the city, but the city has no significant effect upon the nation. In addition, each city within the national environment becomes more or less desirable to elements outside it, based on differences between it and surrounding areas. As it becomes more desirable, people and industry move into it. Or, as it becomes less desirable, people and industry leave.

Forrester's model analyzes interrelationships among three subsystems: business activity, housing, and the employment categories of the population. In the business activity subsystem, the model is concerned with the progression of enterprise units through stages. An enterprise unit is a standard land and building area with a set mix of types of employees, depending on its category—new enterprise units, mature enterprise units, or declining industries. To illustrate some relationships, a new enterprise unit employs four managers, 20 laborers, and ten underemployed workers, for a total of 34 employees. But a declining industry employs one manager, ten laborers, and five underemployed workers, for a total of only 16 workers.

The housing system represents the construction, aging, and demolition of urban housing. There are types of housing for each category of citizen, with premium housing for the managers, laborer housing for the laborers, and underemployed housing for the underemployed people. The housing gets passed down. Premium housing declines into the laborer housing category, and laborer housing declines into the underemployed housing category. The rate of obsolescence from laborer to underemployed housing depends on time and demand. A low-cost public housing program creates housing directly for the underemployed, but other underemployed housing is destroyed through the slum housing demolition and urban renewal programs.

The population is divided into three categories—managers, laborers, and underemployed. The laborers are skilled workers who participate fully in the local economy. The underemployed workers include the unemployed and unemployable, along with people in unskilled jobs, those in marginal livelihoods, and those normally out of the economy but who might work in times of high economic activity. Each category has its own internal birth rate. There is both upward mobility from one class to the next and downward mobility from laborers to underemployed. How these flows operate depends on the mix of categories in the population, available housing, and the jobs provided by enterprise. The population density in laborer housing is twice that of managerial premium housing, and the density in underemployed housing is twice that of laborer housing.

The dynamics of the Forrester model are what he calls the flow rates, the relationships between changes in the subsystems and time, expressed as a series of equations. An urban area goes through a cycle of 150 years. It starts with empty land, grows to full land use, quickly matures into an internal balance, and finally falls into an equilibrium. In the equilibrium phase, the main characteristic is stagnation, with unemployment, faltering industry, and increased taxes. This appears to be a natural cycle, given the characteristics of job creation, housing, industry mix, population mix, and the attractiveness of the area to industry and to people of different categories. In this natural cycle, the growth period ends at 100 years. At that point, new enterprise and premium housing have peaked. The managerial population, laborer population, and number of laborers are at a maximum. The laborer housing construction boom ends. The urban area is at the end of its buildup phase, with the land area almost fully utilized.

Past the 100-year phase, the area ages. The land is filled, and new construction cannot proceed. The businesses mature and decline, and so do the premium and laborer housing. At various points after the 100-year mark, the growth phases of the different positive forces peak. At year 140, for example, the aging and deterioration of mature business, which is bringing about a rise in the number of declining industries, reaches its height. Eventually, an equilibrium is reached. The flood of underemployed persons who came to the area at the peak of growth phase stops because of a general unattractiveness. Old buildings and declining business come to dominate the landscape, and the city now has a high proportion of unskilled and unemployed people. The entire cycle reaches a steady state of stagnation at the 200-year mark.

URBAN PROGRAMS AND THE URBAN LIFE CYCLE

Forrester recognizes that describing an urban life cycle by computer simulation does not deal with the impact of various social and political programs designed to help prevent decay or help older central cities. As another part of his analysis, he tests the impact of certain types of common programs: job training for the underemployed, tax expenditures for welfare and education, and a low-cost housing program for underemployed persons. He found that the introduction of a job training program for 10 per cent of the underemployed has only slight effects, and those operate unfavorably. The job training program does not change the commercial or industrial mix, but is done "by some artificial process such as transporting people to jobs elsewhere or creating public-service types of work."[14] At first, the program increases employment, but fairly quickly the gain dissipates with increased migration of underemployed persons to the area and a decline in housing conditions, with more overcrowding. The larger number of underemployed persons increases the tax requirements, which depresses the creation of new businesses.

Another alternative job program upgrades the underemployed into the laborer or skilled category. The effect is favorable, but the plus factor, however, does not entirely redound to the benefit to the city. A labor excess is created. The result is a flow through of skilled persons out of the area. Forrester concludes that although the program does not produce as many people with increased skills as a simple projection might indicate, it is nonetheless a service to society. But "as a service to the city, its value is far less clear. The area is more crowded, the land fraction occupied has risen slightly, housing conditions are more crowded, the total of underemployed has risen very slightly, and the ratio of labor to jobs is higher, indicating a higher degree of unemployment."[15]

Forrester sought to determine the impact of state and national aid, an external subsidy. There are slight increases in the numbers of underemployed persons, in underemployed housing, and in unemployment for underemployed people. The area becomes more attractive to migrants, but without appreciable increase in the level of business activity, so that the ratio of unemployed persons actually increases. Therefore, there is an increased need for internal taxes within the city. The greater number of unemployed increase welfare demand and the outside aid brings no measurable change in the assessed values of city property. The conclusion is very gloomy: "The changes discussed . . . suggest that financial support from the outside may do nothing to improve fundamental conditions within the city and may even worsen conditions in the long run by causing an unfavorable shift in the proportions of population, housing and business."[16]

[14] Ibid., p. 53.
[15] Ibid., p. 59.
[16] Ibid., p. 65.

In his modeling, Forrester considers the effect of low-cost housing programs. The program he tests is similar to federal public housing, a gift to the city from external sources and available only to the underemployed segment of the population. The goal is to build housing for 5 per cent of the underemployed each year. Because of land shortages and the problem of available labor, the program never reaches this goal and stabilizes in its fiftieth year of operation at housing for 3 per cent of the underemployed.

As the program gets under way, the housing available for the underemployed rises immediately. In turn, more underemployed are drawn to the city, and their number increases for the first 10 years. Meanwhile, however, the low-cost housing program exerts such pressure on the total stock of unfilled land that the atmosphere is less desirable for other types of construction. As a result, again, laborer housing, premium housing, new enterprise, and mature business all slowly lose ground. As this process occurs, in turn, the number of available jobs shrinks, and the economy declines. What seems to be a modest and beneficial program, increasing low-cost housing, actually has a detrimental effect on the city. The end result is that "a low-cost housing program is much more detrimental to the long-run conditions of the urban area than the job program, training program, or tax subsidy. . . ."[17]

THE EFFECTS OF ADDITIONAL URBAN PROGRAMS

The conclusion follows that traditional remedies for urban decay do not work. Forrester then tests other remedies: (1) constructing housing for the skilled workers, (2) constructing premium housing, (3) building new enterprises, (4) demolishing declining industry, (5) demolishing slum housing, (6) discouraging housing construction, and (7) encouraging industry. All of these are potentially usable urban policies.

Here the results are mixed. Some alternatives turn out not to help, whereas others show hopeful signs. Increasing worker housing does not help, because the additional land used reduces the amount of new enterprise construction, and thus creates housing for more people than can find work. In addition, the increase in housing units constructed under a deliberate program reduces normal construction of such units. In the end, building worker housing does not lead to urban improvement. Similarly, building more premium housing (a frequent result of urban renewal programs) has a small but detrimental effect. Forrester concludes:

[17] Ibid., p. 65.

Construction of housing in any price class through externally imposed programs seems detrimental to the stagnant city. The reason
is fairly clear if the fundamental problem of the city is too much
housing and too high a population, particularly in the lower economic groups. Additional housing fills land and makes new industry more difficult to initiate.[18]

Constructing new enterprise is not something most cities could do
by direct action, although most encourage such activity indirectly. The
results of such a program are favorable, although the result is not all
that might be expected. Planned construction depresses the number
normally produced by altering the total economic mix of the area.
Even the favorable change of constructing new enterprise is not
enough to overcome economic imbalance.

Forrester analyzes other programs that are more within the direct
political authority of city governments. Demolishing declining industries reduces the amount of such industry and opens up land for other
areas. New enterprise and mature business increase, and the total supply of housing and the population both decline. The combined effect
of these changes reduces the tax rate by 9 per cent. At the same time,
the number of underemployed in the city increases.

Demolishing slum housing, thereby clearing land for productive
economic uses, has favorable effects. Such a program removes 5 per
cent of the underemployed housing each year. Sensitive to the political fallout of such governmental activity, Forrester suggests implementation by changes in tax laws and land zoning. The program
makes more land available, leading to new industrial construction and
more jobs. A resulting natural upsurge in the construction of housing
for skilled workers supports a larger labor force. Although the economic
environment is more favorable, a larger number of underemployed persons are not attracted to the city because of a perceived unavailability
of housing. Blocking off such migration allows a net economic gain for
the city. Overall, new enterprise and mature business increase by 45
per cent, and declining businesses increase by only 9 per cent. Although underemployed housing goes down by 54 per cent, premium
housing and skilled worker housing go up by 30 and 34 per cent,
respectively. Taxes drop by one third.

Another surprising effect of this complex system occurs when a
slum demolition program and a restriction on worker housing are combined. Despite a conscious restriction in housing, the total amount
increases slightly, because of a large increase in the upward economic

[18] Ibid., p. 79.

mobility of the population. All the other variables react favorably as well: premium housing is up, underemployed housing is down, the taxes are down, the number of underemployed is down, and the number of new enterprises and mature businesses goes up. Forrester also models encouraging new industries. The effect is favorable, providing upward mobility into the skilled labor group.

SOME COMMENTS ON THE FORRESTER MODEL

We outline the Forrester computer simulation because it represents a different approach to urban problems from the customary ones of the sociologist or political scientist. It uses the most sophisticated modeling techniques to try to test the impact of variables in a complex system. Forrester's concept of urban growth and decay represents a model with assumptions. But for those looking at the rise and decline of many of the older cities over time, the assumptions appear reasonable.

There are shortcomings to the Forrester model. He posits the city in isolation without dealing explicitly with interaction in a metropolitan area. He expects that all units in the metropolitan area, with their different stages of growth and decay, confront the same problems. Effects within the metropolitan area are not treated in the model. He does recognize the central direction needed to stop stagnation. His route to prosperity is to cut down on the city as a residence center and to let economic forces utilize the land for productive ends. Forrester demonstrates that the process would not necessarily involve displacement of the poor who are already there. But what about the historic role of the central cities as a place to which the poor go? There seems to be little role or place for newcomers in this system. Forrester summarizes his views as follows:

> The city has been presented here as a living, self-regulating system which generates its own evolution through time. It is not a victim of outside circumstances but of its own internal practices. As long as present practices continue, infusion of outside money can produce only fleeting benefit, if any. If the city needs outside help, it may be legislative action to force on the city those practices that will lead to long-term revival. Such outside pressure may be necessary if internal short-term considerations make the reversal of present trends politically impossible. The revival of the city depends not on massive programs of external aid but on changed internal administration.[19]

[19] Ibid., p. 129.

EXPERT VIEW 3: GEORGE STERNLIEB'S PREDICTION: THE CITY AS SANDBOX

George Sternlieb, Professor of Urban and Regional Planning at Rutgers University, produced a number of widely noted studies of urban communities. He studied intensively the characteristics of individual communities and the attitudes of their citizens. Two of his works are classics. In *The Affluent Suburb: Princeton,* he describes the life-styles of people who have achieved success and want to keep things the way they are.[20] In *The Zone of Emergence,* he focuses on Plainfield, New Jersey, an older suburb where people moving out of the decaying inner city of Newark find some satisfactions for their aspirations.[21] In addition, Sternlieb is a foremost authority on urban housing and the author of a landmark study on urban housing economics, *The Tenement Landlord.*[22] In this latter work, he documents the declining profitability of slum real estate and the advantages to cities of having owner-occupants of such property.

In an essay in *The Public Interest,* Sternlieb responded to the question, Is the inner city doomed? His answer appears to be "yes."[23] He notes the argument, made by many city leaders, that the cities are intrinsically wealthy but mistreated by their suburban neighbors, who use central city facilities but do not return the city resources they soak up. He rejects this view, that the cities are colonies exploited by outside interests. The position of big cities would not be re-established if only there were equity, if only they attained adequate aid from outside. He argues that it is not exploitation but indifference and abandonment that endangers the old cities.[24]

The cities' crucial function in the past was as "a staging area for the floods of immigrants who came from Europe and elsewhere. Cities provided jobs, schools, and an infrastructure that helped earlier groups of immigrants move upward and outward. Although each of these groups left a residue of those who didn't make it, on the whole the city was an extremely successful processing center."[25] This reason for existence is no longer valid, however, because the floods of immigration are essentially over. The central cities are losing population. What immigration remains is no longer in their direction. In addition, earlier immigration was closely tied to the immigrants' need for jobs and

---

[20] (New Brunswick, N.J.: Transaction Books, 1971).
[21] (New Brunswick: Transaction Books, 1972).
[22] (New Brunswick: Rutgers University Press, 1966).
[23] "The City as Sandbox," *Public Interest,* 25 (Fall 1971), pp. 14–21.
[24] Ibid., p. 15.
[25] Ibid., p. 16.

willingness to work long hours at low wages. But American labor is no longer competitive at the bottom of the wage scale. Low-wage industries no longer locate in the central cities because revolutions in transport have made it cheaper to export these jobs to places such as Puerto Rico, Formosa, Hong Kong, or Singapore. The welfare system undercuts individual willingness to take sweatshop work. For example, a woman with three children on welfare receives between $400 and $500 a month, which however inadequate, is the equivalent of $9,000 a year for a working husband with a wife and three children.

Two main signs point to how the cities have lost their historic function. First, the primary remaining economy is the public economy, the jobs that go with the school system, paving the roads, controlling the CETA program. Sternlieb notes that property interests, especially in jobs, are important to individuals, and people struggle over them. In the absence of wide-scale private employment opportunities, the only game in town is public. This situation accounts for the bitterness and intensity of politics in the older central cities. There is, of course, a public policy content to municipal programs and an urge to promote the public interest. But the other reality of *who* will get the action becomes a desperate struggle when the private economic environment is so sterile. As the public sector grows in size and importance, the conflict intensifies.

The decline in the waves of immigrants removes two traditional ways people made economic successes of themselves, as tenement owners and as labor brokers. For many immigrants, capital accumulated through ownership of slum property, acquired one piece at a time, and rented to countrymen. For those who followed this route, acquiring more and more property and often better and better property, enough capital could be put together to expand into other businesses. But the economic underpinning of slum real estate has always been the presence of high demand. With that demand gone, the business is no longer viable. Sternlieb says that "slum tenement ownership has become a dead end, instead of an avenue to wealth—a fact symbolized by the abandoned slum dwelling."[26]

Some immigrants also got ahead as labor brokers. They mediated between their countrymen, who were willing to take unskilled jobs and who often did not speak English, and the outside world, which wanted certain economic tasks performed and often did not speak Italian or Yiddish. Thus, many Italian contractors began hiring non-English-speaking Italian immigrants to do the heavy work of digging ditches or paving sidewalks. Jewish garment manufacturers had non-

[26] Ibid., p. 16.

English-speaking countrymen working 15 hours a day doing need-lework for the garment trade and the emerging general department stores of the country. Irish businessmen handled the rough immigrants in gangs on the docks. The workers were exploited by their country-men, who became rich. But for the go-betweens with entrepreneurial talent, this route was a time-tested way upward. Now there are fewer immigrants to do this work, and less of this work to be done.

A FUNCTION FOR THE CITIES: SANDBOX

If the old role is gone, now what? Sternlieb says the present role for central cities is as a sandbox: "A sandbox is a place where adults park their children in order to converse, play, or work with a minimum of interference. The adults, having found a distraction for the children, can get on with the serious things of life."[27] The city has become the sandbox. Urban programs create a bureaucracy that is supposed to do something for the poor, but instead lives by the existence of the poor and the threat of their occasional uprisings. Little money filters down, and there is not much change in the problem. When programs do not work, they are repackaged or relabeled as new programs. According to Sternlieb, "this is the height of sandboxism."[28]

The programs do have some effects, but not the intended one of alleviating poverty. In addition to the sandbox effect of keeping the children quiet, some may generate some new indigenous leadership. More important, the programs are symbolic action, a kind of nonmedi-cal placebo. They persuade the children in the urban sandbox that someone cares and something is being done. The media may be satisfied and those who do care may be reassured that action is being taken. The failure of urban programs results from the inadequacy of social theory about what works. In a bitter critique, Sternlieb ob-serves:

> One simply took apparently salient parameters of the failed pro-gram and reversed them. The facade of intellectual rationalization was produced *post hoc*. Make classes smaller. If smaller classes don't work, what is left? Ah! Skin color, the teacher's doesn't match that of the student; change the skin color. That doesn't seem to be working as well as one would have anticipated? It must be the supervisor's color—paint principal black. Principal black doesn't seem to provide the answer? Paint the board of edu-cation an appropriate hue. And when this entire mountain of

[27] Ibid., p. 18.
[28] Ibid., p. 18.

strategems brings forth nothing but mice, bring the parents in. Parents don't want to come in? Pay them, we'll call them para-professionals. And so it has gone.[29]

Sternlieb feels there is no going back. The suburbs possess the bulk of retail trade. Small suburban shopping centers replace the neighborhood stores of the central city. Even cultural life moved to the suburbs as they achieved a critical mass of buying power and population to permit first-run theaters and other activities. New hospital construction and medical facilities are in the suburbs.

Although Sternlieb does not spell out how it might be done, he suggests that if we put aside the romanticized image of the glorious central city of the past and any hope for its resurgence, there may be some alternative future role. Such a role would be doing any productive work in contrast to the sandbox effect of present-day programs. But he is not hopeful:

> The plight of the inhabitants of our central cities, and the strategy we seem to be adopting to meet that plight, indicate that we are opting for the sandbox. What this will mean for our society in the future we do not fully know; but that the consequences are likely to be cruel and disagreeable has become only too clear.[30]

SOME OTHER SCENARIOS FOR THE FUTURE

Building from this book and thinking about the future, anyone can speculate about alternative urban Americas. One would select the most important national and local trends, weigh existing developments, and predict. One could assess the probability of each scenario actually coming to pass. It would be appropriate, as a normative judgment to suggest why any outcome appears desirable or undesirable. What follows are five such scenarios I have devised. They are arranged in a continuum, beginning with a scenario that relies upon the least governmental intervention from any level, and moving toward those requiring the most purposeful governmental activity.

Scenario 1. More of the Same: The Continuing Decentralization of American Urban Communities

The likeliest possibility is that the major trends of the last 100 years will continue. In spatial terms, decentralization of the population

[29] Ibid., p. 19.
[30] Ibid., p. 21.

will continue. Suburban areas will continue to spread. The occupied land area will be larger and larger, with a continuing drop in densities. Jobs will be created along the belt highways that link the suburbs, and retail trade will grow in large shopping centers. As the critical mass of people and money in the suburbs increases, major institutional facilities locate there: college and university campuses, hospitals, sports stadiums.

A continuation of the suburbanization of America presupposes certain conditions. One is no reversal by governmental action or by adverse changes in America's technological or economic position. It is hard to imagine a political coalition that would have any reason to try to reverse suburbanization. The population of the central cities is declining, absolutely and relatively. So is the total amount of business and industry. Further, as a "cause" aligning liberals, intellectuals, and central city officials, the "urban crisis" commands less and less support and intensity. Other problems preoccupy the country.

On the other hand, one cannot be completely certain about outside forces. Suburbs expanded as the central city lost its unique economic functions, based on the technology of steam power and rail transport. The suburbs developed because the automobile made individual mobility possible and because trucks made industrial and commercial mobility possible. Advances in communications reduced the need for people who interact at work to be physically proximate. America's system of roads, cars, and trucks depends upon national affluence and the availability of fuels to run the vehicles and to light and heat individual homes and huge shopping malls.

If fuels are in short supply, quite serious disruptions would occur for the present patterns of settlement. Limitations on gasoline and heating fuels would limit work and life-styles. At present for the suburbs, there is no alternative system to the automobile. Mass transit is difficult when people live over wide areas at low densities. Energy limitations would slow down and cripple suburbanization.

If the present suburbanization continues, however, we expect the many trends identified in this book to recur. Suburbs will be specialized, relatively homogeneous enclaves. We expect a suburban politics devoted to protecting life-styles, which means preserving real estate values and cultural homogeneity. Not all suburbs will succeed. The oldest suburbs will change as poorer residents from the central cities move in. These people improve their position as they move into such communities, and the previous settlers will move out. But the older suburbs then receive the problems commonly associated with central cities: a population with heavy demands for services, higher crime, and a declining tax base.

In this scenario, the fate of the older central cities is what Sternlieb called the "sandbox." Long's proposal that the older central cities revitalize themselves economically through a "humane cooperative" is difficult to see coming to pass. Although it is an appealing hope, the "humane cooperative" runs counter to historical experience. The economic vitality of the older cities in the past built unique locations and technological capabilities that are now obsolete. Those who developed the resources of the central city for economic ends were private operators organizing immigrant populations for heavy construction, labor-intensive sweatshop industries, and profiting from slum real estate. In none of this is there a precedent for successful cooperative, municipal-government-inspired mutual economic progress. Further, any government effort today occurs when markets are nationalized and where the expertise and capital rest in large corporations.

That is not to say that the central cities have no opportunities for economic progress. The Forrester urban dynamics model suggests some possibilities. But, in the absence of strong governmental intervention, the central cities will see more of what they have been seeing. Their economic position declines and the economically most able of their population exit. An interesting question is how these trends affect the newer cities of the South, Southwest, and West. Settlement in these communities developed differently from the older cities of the Northeast. It remains to be seen whether, in time, they will decay.

More of the same raises questions about two important subjects: racial integration and the quality of urban life. The central cities will be more and more populated by blacks and Spanish-speaking minorities, and political power will pass to them. Older suburbs in the zone of transition may be integrated at various times, but their population remains unsettled. And the great bulk of the suburbs will remain essentially white. Educational racial integration would require busing across community lines and could not be achieved by busing within cities. It is unlikely that there will be political support for such busing from the white suburban community, and there may very well be little support from central city residents.

Focusing on life in the suburban-dominated metropolitan area involves, as Scott Greer notes, recognizing these new patterns of settlement are here to stay. An urban *texture* replaces the earlier rigid urban form.[31] Accepting the decentralized city as inevitable means

---

[31] Scott Greer, *The Urban View: Life and Politics in Metropolitan America* (New York: Oxford University Press, 1972), pp. 326–327.

developing, planning, or guiding the texture so that all people have access to the necessities and desirables of life in the metropolitan area. Transportation and communication systems must connect the various subcenters to each other. Greer also believes that ways must be found for the many local governments to relate to each other. The time has come to accept suburbs as permanent.

For individuals in the suburban-dominated metropolis, the quality of life will vary, as it does now, depending on where one lives. Location reflects amenities, crime rate, school quality, even choice in shopping. Prime locations bring prime prices. In other words, in a metropolitan area that mirrors the market economy in diversity and quality, higher income means a higher quality of life. The future metropolis continues to be shaped by market forces.

Scenario 2. A Mixed Urban Mode: More of the Same but with Some Governmental Inputs

Scenario 2 posits what might happen if federal and state governments tried to shape urban futures. A mixed mode of urban futures might see the following. The central cities would not be abandoned completely, despite the continued erosion of their political and economic power. The federal government would spend as much as it does now, and perhaps more, and achieve better coordination of its programs. Thus, it would not build low-rent public housing for the poor at the same time it destroys lower-income housing by highway construction. Federal policy could be based on a concern for the "showcase" aspects of decayed cities for a great nation; a sense of social justice for the inhabitants of these cities; a sense of fear about the possibilities of civil disorder; the need to save energy; the urge to protect already established programs and employees.

Here are some programs for the central cities that might be forthcoming from Washington. Urban renewal, which has been cut back, might start again. The six- to nine-year completion time for an average project should not obscure the contributions these projects make to the commercial viability of central cities. Washington might provide special incentives to industries to locate in central cities by awarding them federal contracts. Further, federal grants to local governments for services in crime control, education, pollution control, or energy saving might provide increased funds for those whose personnel live within the cities where they work. Already ongoing federal mass transit programs, which work best for high-density populations, might make central city employment and living more attractive if fuels are short. Special fuel allotments might go to firms that operate near central city mass transit, or to builders who construct dwellings near such facilities.

In this mixed mode scenario, the emphasis is on economic, not social, programs. All of the foregoing suggestions are far from handouts to the "reservation" that Norton Long posed. Further, they are consistent with Forrester's natural cycle of urban land use. Federal operations would not depart greatly from the present system.

There might also be restrictions of the suburban orientation of federal programs. Federal home loan guarantees, which favor low-density suburban housing, might be limited. The endless federal subsidies of the automobile, especially in the form of more and better roads, seem silly in the light of gasoline shortages. The federal government would modify its supports and leave suburbs to their own natural appeals.

In the mixed mode scenario, the federal government would begin national settlement planning. Recommendations would only serve to call attention to choices in the years ahead and to stimulate debate on metropolitan, regional, and state planning.

State governments may also act in this mixed mode scenario. Many states are now moving toward comprehensive land use plans for all property within their boundaries. Land use plans restrict the zoning powers of municipalities by requiring higher-level approval for all land uses. One other possibility, under discussion in many states, is state financing of local education costs. Statewide financing would reduce the differentials between poorer and richer communities.

In this mixed mode scenario, suburbanization and the play of market forces still dominate. There is no move toward metropolitan government, for example, nor attempt to impose on local communities any "rational" system of organization. Urban policy remains only a medium concern of federal and state governments. Localities, for better or for worse, remain primarily on their own. The difference between this scenario and Scenario 1 is that some efforts are made at the higher levels of government. One cannot say the mixed mode scenario is 80 per cent likely to happen or 40 per cent likely to happen. But there is, in my opinion, a good chance that many of the programs suggested by this script will be undertaken.

SCENARIO 3. A NATIONAL OR STATE GOVERNMENT POLICY OF PLANNED URBAN DEVELOPMENT

A national or state government policy of planned urban development is a conceivable scenario. First, with extensive centralized planning, many allocative decisions now made by individuals or in the marketplace would be made by government planners. Second, to guarantee implementation, there would be coercive controls as limitations of what people are free to do. Third, there would continue to be the widespread incentives to bring individual behavior into line with the plans.

Centralized planning for urban development is not new. Many nations have plans for urban growth and rely on a variety of negative sanctions and positive incentives to obtain compliance. Lloyd Rodwin compares urban policies in five countries—Venezuela, Turkey, Great Britain, France, and the United States—in his *Nations and Cities: A Comparison of Strategies for Urban Growth.*[32] American policy making is at a beginning stage. Any planning requires reliable estimates. But, as Anthony Downs has demonstrated, there are widely divergent estimates about the extent of urban growth that will take place in this country between now and the year 2000.[33] The Census Series A estimates growth at more than 144 million persons; HUD estimates more than 96 million; the Census Series D estimate is more than 80 million; and Downs calculates an increase of 55 million.

In the early 1970s, federal policy was to aid private developers who built "new towns." Credit guarantees encouraged private investment in such communities.[34] Several widely publicized, privately developed new towns, especially Columbia, Maryland, and Reston, Virginia, were built. A few new towns were aesthetic and design successes. Columbia, at least, appears to be an economic success.

The few successful new communities are moderate in size, essentially middle- and upper-middle-class communities, with minimal provision for low-income persons.[35] Further, within the new towns, there are interesting questions of governance. Developers wield primary political power. Sharing by residents either occurs gradually over a period of years or residents play only an advisory role. Because of the difficulty of making these privately developed new towns profitable, they become, in political terms, modern variants of the old company towns.

By and large, the "new town" experiments of the federal government ended in failure by the late 1970s. The "new towns in town"

---

[32] (Boston: Houghton Mifflin, 1970).

[33] "Alternative Forms of Future Urban Growth in the United States," *Journal of the American Institute of Planners,* 36:1 (January 1970), pp. 3–11.

[34] See David R. Godschalk, "Reforming New Community Planning," *Journal of the American Institute of Planners,* 39:5 (September 1973), pp. 306–315.

[35] For an inclusive discussion, see the articles in *New Towns: Why and for Whom,* ed. by Harvey Perloff and Neil Sandberg (New York: Praeger, 1973).

program never got off the ground.[36] The new towns financed from scratch went under financially. Future federal efforts, building upon knowledge of past failures, will have to take a different track.[37]

The most likely centerpiece of this scenario is more extensive federal planning for the future, accompanied by more extensive federal standards and controls for the private market. The planning would project growth for metropolitan areas and, perhaps, even growth quotas. The standards would probably be indirectly enforced as conditions for loan guarantees or fuel allocations and might include rules on density, insulation of housing, even design of housing, and perhaps restrictions on the quantity and construction of commercial and industrial facilities. In addition, equal opportunity provisions for racial minorities and perhaps for income-class minorities might be imposed. The controls are difficult to visualize. It is a long jump from present practice to federal permits for housing construction, or submitting local subdivision and shopping center plans to federal authorities.

A constituency consisting of planners, many local, state, and federal governmental officials, and some elements of the public supports more governmental planning and management of local development. We already see some state government metropolitan planning and predict more for the future. Anthony Downs has suggested that the state governments might be the best vehicles for such planning.[38] They have the unquestioned legal authority to impose conditions on municipal governments. Several states already have statewide land use plans that require state approval for variances in usage or construction. Looking at this prospect realistically, some states are more likely to undertake land use planning than others, because of their historical traditions and political cultures. We expect such states as Minnesota, Wisconsin, and Michigan to experiment with planned metropolitan development.

SCENARIO 4. SOCIAL DISINTEGRATION AND MILITARY APARTHEID

None of the preceding scenarios assume what social scientists call a "worst case" possibility. Each overlooks the worst predictions made at the height of the 1960s urban crisis. Looking out upon the social disintegration of urban riots, the destruction of property, the fear and

[36] See Martha Derthick, *New Towns In-Town: Why a Federal Program Failed* (Washington, D.C.: The Urban Institute, 1973).

[37] See the avenues explored in Robert K. Yin, Karen A. Heald, and Mary E. Vogel, *Tinkering with the System* (Lexington, Mass.: Lexington Books 1977).

[38] "Alternative Forms . . . ," op. cit.

hostility of whites leaving the central cities and blacks trapped in them, the President's Commission on Civil Disorders[39] made dire predictions. We would become two nations—one white, one black—with civil order maintained in the older cities by force of arms. Several years after the initial report, the commission noted the heavy investment of city police forces in equipment (including, in a few cases, tanks) and the absence of improvement in housing, unemployment, crime, and uneven delivery of social services.[40]

What follows, then, is a "doomsday" scenario that assumes the worst. It overlooks the election of black officials to top offices in major cities, the absolute rise in black incomes, and the integration of many suburbs. It focuses instead on continuing high unemployment of blacks and Hispanics, especially minority youth, in relation to whites; the physical crumbling of whole sections of the central cities; and the social disorganization of high crime rates, general despair, and hostility. Further, this scenario presupposes a nation preoccupied with problems other than minorities. Suppose the country seeks to preserve middle-class living standards in an ever more pressured economy. The economy is not expanding at its prior rate, inflation increases, and the American middle-class life-style may actually be declining. Suppose further that there began to be new demands from the urban poor and riots or threats of riots. In this context, Scenario 4, Social Disintegration and Military Apartheid, becomes discussible.

What form would the system take? Politically, there would be a national decision not to tolerate any more "trouble" from the discontented central city dwellers. Police forces would receive authority to maintain order. They would infiltrate neighborhoods and groups with informers. They would conduct widespread searches to uncover weapons and materials and to disrupt social interaction or conspiratorial planning. They would instigate a policy of precautionary arrests or even imprisonment, which would require new legal authority or ignoring present restrictions. The effect of these policies would be increased tension, actual outbreaks and crimes, and police response with heavy use of legal violence. Restrictions on police use of firearms would be lifted, and robbers, muggers, rioters, and even bystanders could expect to be shot for any provocation. The other parts of the criminal justice system would also respond with harshness: heavy jail sentences, lessening of individual rights for the accused, and punitive prisons.

[39] *Report of the President's Commission on Civil Disorders* (New York: Bantam Books, 1968).

[40] *The State of the Cities: Report of the Commission on the 70's* (New York: Praeger, 1972).

The central city population would be regarded as something apart, to be treated differently from other Americans. As fear mounted, the "us-versus-them" mood would support other control measures. Free access into and out of affected zones might be restricted through military checkpoints. Such measures would reassure nervous suburbanites. To make sure that people are where they are supposed to be, all citizens might be required to have identity cards to be carried at all times and submitted for inspection upon demand of legal authorities. To make sure that "troublemakers" did not move into peaceful zones, a system of internal passports could be instituted. Any request for employment in certain areas or for residential moves would have to be screened and approved by the proper authorities. Individuals could be monitored and quickly checked on nationwide computer systems.

The economic life of the central cities would be very circumscribed. New industries would locate only where the highest security measures could be guaranteed for their plants. Banks, office buildings, and downtown stores would increase their own security measures, and there might be "cleared zones" with specially protected access for the downtown areas. The superhighways leading from the suburbs to such areas would be carefully monitored "sanitized corridors" with access based on need to use them, and with checkpoints. Although economic life might seem unpleasant and unlikely in such a situation, people can adapt to almost anything. Selective perception would mean that persons working in this environment would literally not see the repressive measures taken to protect them, or, indeed, might find their own insularity psychologically and symbolically reassuring.

Although the mind boggles at this scenario, it does not institute the worst, such as calorie rationing for the central city welfare population or chemical or drug controls. All the control measures outlined have been used before somewhere, from military checkpoints in occupied areas to identity cards, common at one time in Europe and in South Africa today, to the internal passports of the Soviet Union.

America under Scenario 4 would be a different country from what it has been in the past or is today. The social bonds would be severed. The commitment to social betterment through government would be abandoned for order at any cost. It would be a grim country. The scenario is highly unlikely.

SCENARIO 5. REVITALIZATION OF THE CENTRAL CITIES WITH SOCIAL JUSTICE

There is a last scenario, one that often appears as a goal, a hope, a kind of modern-day Utopia. That scenario projects the central cities somehow rebuilt with social justice for all citizens. Wealth will be reallocated. Racial tensions will decline. Civility will return to urban life. How might such a scenario come to pass?

Any such widespread change would be preceded by shifts in American attitudes. Any more equal distribution of existing wealth requires a willingness for most Americans to be taxed more. Long in his *Unwalled City* is so sure this change is not likely that he does not even discuss it as an economic strategy for the central city poor. Income redistribution fares badly in American political campaigns. Talk of equality of wealth was more common before the economy developed a high annual growth rate. Economically, a "rising tide lifts all the boats" and quiets the demands that occur when the size of the pie is fixed. But suppose American growth slows? Suppose the pie shrinks? Talk about redistribution for greater economic equality among individuals will surely surface. Redistribution could become the platform of a populist political party.

Even in the unlikely event that monies flow to the urban poor, the revitalization of the central cities will not follow automatically. Perhaps the poor, now no longer so poor as before, will choose the suburbs.[41] But federal power could reduce the appeal of the suburbs. By fuel rationing or the allocation of construction materials, federal authority might strengthen the present Councils of Government or provide bonuses to localities to merge. In an era of declining public school enrollments, local costs become especially burdensome. Washington might award special financial relief to districts that integrate with the no longer so poor children of the central cities.

In addition, natural economic forces might again build the central cities. If there is continuous energy rationing, rail transport will undergo a resurgence, for both freight and passengers, and central city locations will once again become desirable. Some of the incentives to investment that Forrester discusses might come into play, especially if city policies encourage productive expenditure. The suburban advantages in attractiveness will be reduced.[42] If the suburbs are less attractive, compared to the central cities, for industry, for residential living, for crime rates, for schools, or for taxes, then the elaborate political

[41] See Harold X. Connolly, "Black Movement into the Suburbs: Suburbs Doubling Their Black Population During the 1960's," *Urban Affairs Quarterly*, 9:1 (September 1973), pp. 91–112.

[42] One observer, T. D. Allman, suggests a process of central city revival and suburban decay has already begun. See his "The Urban Crisis Leaves Town," *Harper's*, 257 (December 1978), pp. 41–56.

structure designed to protect old advantages will crumble. Local government merger might come about voluntarily.

Overall, we rate scenario 5 as unlikely. It would be even more logical to predict under the same changed economic differences a completely different political scenario. Scarcity, changed technology, and a leveling of growth could lead to a lessened concern for the poor and the central cities. Concern for social justice peaked in the economic and social programs of the post-World War II era, the period of greatest affluence. And, as every analysis presented in this book indicates, the central cities attract investment only when sound reasons of personal necessity or gain so dictate. Sentiment alone leads to little.

AMERICAN POLITICS AND THE FUTURE OF LOCAL LIFE: SOME CONCLUDING THOUGHTS

The scenarios presented here are intended to help the student formulate his or her own thoughts about what local life in America will become. Local life will always be affected by changes in technology, by national trends in politics and economics, and by the values people hold. What happened before conditions what is possible or even likely in the future. We have presented an exercise in extrapolation, in thinking about what might lie ahead.

There is plenty of room for the student to make an original contribution. Despite centuries of effort, there is no such thing as a science of government. Systematic thinking about futures remains in an early stage. There is plenty of room for new knowledge, from the larger questions of patterns of settlement to why some individuals play more active roles in local politics than others. Improved social science and a concerned citizenry will add to our incomplete understanding.

INDEX